The
Winter Kitchen

Mrs. Appleyard's Winter Kitchen

LOUISE ANDREWS KENT
AND
ELIZABETH KENT GAY

DECORATIONS BY ROBERT MACLEAN

Keats Publishing, Inc. New Canaan, Connecticut

To
PATIENCE BARLOW
who stencils walls,
makes miniature furniture, cooks and
paints on velvet with Mrs. Appleyard
and who says she wonders
what will happen next

Acknowledgment

Sooner or later most of us repeat our conversation and those of us who enjoy cooking give away the receipts for our favorite dishes more than once. Mrs. Appleyard is no exception. One of the pleasantest opportunities she ever had to talk about cooking was in the pages of the *Ladies' Home Journal*. She and her daughter are grateful for being allowed to use, in *The Winter Kitchen*, some material that has appeared in the *Journal* in a different form and they thank the editors for inspiring them in the first place.

Appleyard Center is an imaginary place with real people, sometimes imported from a long distance, in it. Mrs. Appleyard only wishes that they were always there.

She says that any attempt to apply the geography of Kents' Corner to the Appleyard Center landscape will only make you dizzy.

Contents

I. *The Winter Kitchen*   I

           HOW FAR DOWN?   7
II. *October*   MUSICAL COOKS   16
           HARVEST SUPPER   26

           BRIDGE PARTY   39
           DEER SEASON   49
III. *November* THANKSGIVING   59
           OLD HOME DAY   74

           APARTMENT WARMING   93
IV. *December* CANDLELIGHT   104
           BRADSHAW CHRISTMAS   120

V. *December –*
  January   EPACT OF TURKEY   135

           INTERNATIONAL NEW YEAR   151
VI. *January*   FURRED AND FEATHERED FRIENDS   164
           SNOWBOUND   174

Contents

	JINGLE BELLS	185
VII. *February*	FAMILY FAVORITES	195
	SWING YOUR PARTNER	202
	SOUP'S ON .	215
VIII. *March*	QUIET PLEASE	232
	DEMOCRATIC PROGRESS	253
IX. *April*	VENTILATION TOUR	275
	WHAT AM I OFFERED?	293
X. *May*	THE RIGHT MIX	301
	INDEX	

NOTE

* *Indicates recipes printed in this book.*

† *Those found in* The Summer Kitchen.

The Winter Kitchen

Mrs. Appleyard has had a winter kitchen for years but it is only recently that she became a winter person. She realizes with humility that she will never be the genuine seasoned article: she didn't start soon enough. However, she can no longer be classified with City Folks or Summer People and be lightly dismissed from consideration.

There she is, a solid fact, in the costumes well known over the years in Woodbrook Green, Massachusetts. Appleyard Center is now becoming acquainted with her two fur coats, one long, one short. (They can both be mistaken for mink at quite a distance.) It recognizes easily that Burberry raglan, known as

Old Ironsides or the Family Disgrace, the hats, veterans of many a symphony concert, the violet suit, the velvet and fur boots. These exterior decorations are becoming as familiar to Appleyard Center as the orange snowplow or evening grosbeaks eating sunflower seeds or petunias in the store window.

Mrs. Appleyard was surprised and delighted to find that petunias that had been a white ruffled cascade all summer would blossom all winter too. They would not do it for everyone, but any plant Mary Angell puts in the store window always thrives. To have a green thumb and to be able also to run a cash register with speed and accuracy is a combination of abilities much admired by Mrs. Appleyard. She knows an author who has trained a poodle in manners suitable for the court of Louis XIV and who also inspires perfect cooking in her cook. This is harder than improvising something yourself, she says. She also has a relative, her daughter Sally as a matter of fact, who plays field hockey and lacrosse, teaches Greek, is capable of being the whole alto section in a cathedral choir, performs agreeably upon the flute and deals competently with sweetbreads and mushrooms. Who said this was an age of monotonous specialization?

The store window at Appleyard Center is a sort of club. Neighbors bring in geraniums or begonias that have been sulking at home and they cheer up instantly. People also leave copies of the *Saturday Review* and *The New Yorker* in the window in case someone hasn't seen them. Mrs. Appleyard may often be found among the petunias on a sunny morning waiting for the mail and working on a Double Crostic. If there were only a cracker barrel, she'd be a philosopher, she says.

Her own house has no central heating so she has shut it up for the winter. Like a sharp sword sheathed in ice, the cold hangs in the ten bedrooms, in the two kitchens and in the period bathrooms. The living room with the birds on the walls and the map room are full of porch furniture. Loaves of fruitcake soaked in brandy are mellowing for next summer in the pantry. The furniture of miniature rooms is packed away so that mice will have plenty of space to dance. Shutters are closed. They were green not long ago but rain, snow, and the white light of winter are turning them blue. No wonder, thinks Mrs. Appleyard, blowing on her fingers.

She was delighted when her daughter Cicely suggested that some rooms in her house near the store could be made into an apartment. There is nothing she likes so much as changing the sizes and shapes of buildings. The southwest corner of Cicely's house soon sprouted bay windows that catch every ray of sunshine. Shelves for china appeared in surprising places. An electric unit that could do everything but plan menus suddenly lurked in a strategic corner. Before anyone could say Pouilly Fuissé Château Latour 1939 (pronounced in Vermont Polly Fish) the stove had burned the bottom out of Mrs. Appleyard's new double boiler. The makers of the stove had prankishly marked the front burners "R." Cicely, a woman of decision, definitely not the type to tolerate the orders of misplaced robots, snatched off the handles and transferred them so that the front burners are now marked "F." It took a little while for Mrs. Appleyard to learn that they meant what they said. She still keeps posted a notice lettered in her early Chaucerian hand. It says:

Questions for Morons

Which burners do you think you turned on?
Which did you really turn on?
Do you think you turned them off?
Which?

Thus equipped she has gone into action. Every now and then something she has cooked turned out pretty well, as she might have said in Massachusetts, or not badly — as she has learned to say now that she is a Vermonter. In the *Winter Kitchen* she reports some of her less disastrous experiments.

Every now and then someone from effete tropical Massachusetts writes to Mrs. Appleyard and says: "So you live in Vermont, in the country all winter now. How wonderful!"

Yes, it's wonderful — that anyone survives it. If you yearn for clean air, clean snow, water that tastes like water, birch logs blazing in the fireplace, new-laid eggs and Vermont turkeys, it is well to realize that you have expensive tastes. Clean air is delicious but at twenty below zero it has to have the chill taken off it before you can breathe it comfortably. Snow has to be shoveled not only off the front steps and a bit of sidewalk, as in the city, but off roofs and porches. It has to be plowed with a tractor so the oil man and the gas man can make frequent visits to their tanks. It must be plowed away from the garage in time for the snowplow to thunder along sending plumes of snow towards the stars and plow you in again.

Water runs downhill — except in winter. This statement can be the basis for the conversation of seventeen people for a whole evening. Mrs. Appleyard will not report all the reasons and suggested remedies. As evidence that the problem is a real one she will simply quote a neatly written notice from the bulletin board in the store: "Since our water will not run till spring, we would like to arrange for baths and will be glad to pay for expense and trouble."

As to those blazing birch logs: city folk think that wood grows on trees. Well, so it does and it stays right there unless someone cuts the tree down, saws it into four-foot lengths, splits it, cuts it the length you want and piles it where it will dry. A year later you can carry it into your woodbox. It costs rather more than burning oil but the smell of the smoke and the look of the flames are worth it, especially if some other tree falls on the power line some zero night and your thermostat stops working.

New-laid eggs are delicious and every now and then some are laid in a Vermont henhouse in winter. In Appleyard Center local ones can be bought and they are the right color, a warm brown like some Vermonter who has been in Florida all winter. However, in other shops they are more likely to come from some Connecticut chicken hotel where the lights blaze all night long and the eggs are white. They pay extra for white eggs in New York, Mrs. Appleyard understands. She thinks this is splendid and hopes all white eggs will go there.

Vermont turkeys are wonderful, just as good as you think. When some of Mrs. Appleyard's favorite neighbors came to their summer house from Salt Lake City for Christmas, they immediately set out shopping for a turkey. Because of the size of the oven, the roasting pan and the family it had to be of special dimensions. It was an excellent bird and bore upon its broad breast the announcement that it was a Product of Utah. Few Vermonters have ever tasted a Vermont turkey. To meet one socially is like getting into an exclusive club. You put your name down on a list. July is a good time to start. It helps if you have a couple of sponsors whose ancestors came to Vermont over a blazed trail before 1800.

Until a few years ago you could pick your own wild cranberries from a bog near Cranberry Meadow Pond: if you got there first, that is. With industry, a flexible back and perfect eyesight you could collect perhaps two quarts. However, the beavers have now been at work and unless you are a talented skin diver you had better get your cranberries in a package from Massachusetts.

One pleasant thing about living in the country is to bring in your own Christmas tree and make wreaths with your own evergreen and cones and berries. Cicely Bradshaw bought a woodlot to be sure of getting these materials. The tree this year was handsome and cost, before trimming, about a hundred dollars, Cicely figures.

When she had spent her first winter in Vermont, Cicely started to collect material that would help other winter amateurs. She filed the information in an envelope labeled "How to live in the country and not make a fool of yourself." After ten years she gave up the idea of writing on this subject. It is not possible, she says.

Her mother knows Cicely is right. That is why she is writing so rapidly about winter before she knows too much about it.

October

How Far Down?

IF MRS. APPLEYARD believed the calendars she has received from affectionate insurance companies and plumbers, she would expect winter to begin in December. In Vermont this is nonsense. Even in September, Vermonters begin to say to each other in somber tones, "It won't be long now." Sometimes they add suspiciously, "But perhaps you like it."

Mrs. Appleyard hastily repels the suggestion. She says she likes snow in pictures and to look at while she is indoors with a good fire going. She adds that she does not wish to shovel it, walk in it or drive in it. This is the Party Line and is greeted with polite groans of approval. It is however timidly admitted that the storm in the first week of October was kind of pretty. Indeed it was.

In order to achieve this particular effect, you first arrange to have all the maples turn their most brilliant colors. This happy combination of crimson and plum color, peach and scarlet, gold and vermilion is not arrived at, as city folk are apt to think, by any casual night of frost. It is a process of ripening that takes place first on the sunny side of a tree as it does on the sunny cheek of a peach or an apple. It has been prepared for ever since spring by the correct amounts of sunshine and rain, delivered at the right time, and in autumn by warm days and cool nights. A light touch of frost helps, but a sharp frost scorches the leaves and makes them fall with either wind or rain.

This year everything had worked together for good. Elms were great golden wineglasses, maples had turned into rainbows without a leaf lost, birches and poplars were still delicately green just spangled with gold. Beeches were orange and bronze. Over them one night snow sifted quietly down. The next morning the hills were a sight not easily forgotten. The snow was not deep. On hayfields and lawns the grass underneath gave it a strange greenish tone as if northern lights were flickering over it.

Yesterday it would have seemed impossible for the leaves to be more brilliantly scarlet and yellow than ever. Yet they were. Officially it had stopped snowing when Mrs. Appleyard first looked out but the air was still quivering with tiny prismatic particles between her and the sun. She turned and looked down the valley. Stretching from one hill to the next, rising out of maples, descending into elms and firs was — not a rainbow — a snowbow, a complete arch of color.

It was sharper and clearer than any summer rainbow. As she watched, a second arch grew below it.

"This is too much," Mrs. Appleyard said to Cicely.

"Not for the foliage festival," her daughter said firmly. "If we could just keep it there for the photographers for a week — "

"No one would look at it," her mother said. "They'd just think it was a travel poster."

"Well, we needn't worry," Cicely said. "It's fading."

In a moment both bows were gone, but during the morning there was another change in the color pattern. Slowly, gently, leaves began to fall from the trees, making pools of color on the snow, like mirrors reflecting the crimson or gold above. It happened on every hill, changing the distant ring of mountains from blue violet to deep amethyst. Except on the highest hills the snow melted fast and the mirrors under the trees became neatly arranged Persian carpets.

By this time, Cicely and her mother were on the road, bound for the Dowsers' Convention. This is, Cicely considers, the high point of the Foliage Festival. There is the fascination of seeing the dowsers at work, a handsomely arranged landscape with the White Mountains shining in the distance and one of the best dinners served anywhere. Cicely is an expert on community meals and her mother was more than willing to accept her guidance.

When they arrived, the dowsers were already at work. They were walking across a bright green field, still with snow lying in the shadow of its southern stone wall. The dowsers' ages ranged from eight to eighty. Their dowsing rods were as varied. Mrs. Appleyard saw forked twigs of apple, of cherry, of willow. There was one of maple with crimson leaves still fluttering on it. There were rods of aluminum and of stainless steel. Their owners wore quilted jackets of scarlet silk, mackinaws with the tartans of Scottish clans, old football sweaters, caps of many colors, new dungarees as stiff as boards or old ones mellowed to the color of an ancient wheelbarrow.

Mrs. Appleyard noticed a pair of gray flannels and a tweed jacket with leather patches on the elbows. Have college professors taken up dowsing? — she wondered. There were also some flowered prints. These were showing under the coats of some rather large ladies. One was using a turkey wishbone for a rod. They were, Mrs. Appleyard noticed with regret, doing a good deal of giggling. Can her sex take nothing seriously?

Most of the men had that splendidly cleanshaven look of those who meet the razor once a week. There were, however, two who displayed thick prickly stubble, one a sable — or perhaps a fox — silvered, the other the color of a new horse chestnut. Mrs. Appleyard heard them agreeing that the stick worked its best if you had at least a week's beard. Happily adding this thought to her collection of reasons men give for not shaving, she admired their man-made fur and also the silky curly brown beard of a young dowser in sandals, Bermuda shorts and a Mexican poncho. His stick — dowsers, she learned, don't talk about rods — was of silver.

It seemed to work neither better nor worse than other sticks. As the men crossed the field their sticks seemed to turn at about the same point. Each marked the spot with a wooden tab on which was his number. He also handed the judge a card on which were his number, name and an estimate of how far down the water was and how many gallons a minute it would run.

Of course Mrs. Appleyard had her favorite candidate, a spry gnarled dowser with wonderful deep wrinkles. Seen in profile he seemed to have been carved out of an old chopping block but when he looked in her direction, she saw that he had gentle, faded blue eyes, the color of his dungarees and a smile as genial and toothless as a five months old baby's.

Mr. Stanford — that was his name — held his applewood stick lightly and not very high. It seemed to drop lightly rather than wrench itself over. Everything about him seemed easy and natural. Other men wrestled with their sticks, talking to them all the time. Most whispered or muttered but one could be heard across the field.

"Here? Is it here? To the left a foot? Yes! Yes! How far down? Ten? No. Eleven? No. Too far? — Oh, ten and a half? Good! How many gallons? You don't want to tell? Come on — two gallons? Three? Four? Too many? Three and a half? Good! *Good!*"

He mopped his forehead, sweating in spite of the cold breeze, and showed how the bark had twisted from the forked ends of the stick.

"It's nonsense, isn't it?" a man near Mrs. Appleyard said.

The one next to him answered, "No, not really. I don't have the power but I tried it once with a man who had. I was on my own place, close to where I knew there was an old well. I walked across it, holding the stick. Nothing happened. I said 'It's just about here, I know' and when the dowser put his hands on my shoulders, I felt something like an electric charge run through me. The stick seemed to fight to turn in my hands. When it dropped, the bark twisted off just like that one there and the palms of my hands were sore for a day. They'll start digging now, I guess."

In the background was a large machine rather like a dinosaur. It was painted a cheerful orange to harmonize with the blazing hills and it was called a backhoe digger. It began lumbering into position, for all the dowsers had had a turn. Even the lady with the turkey wishbone had teetered across the field on her pointed heels and her friends had clumped across in their plastic over-shoes.

"We'd better go to dinner," Cicely said. "It will be ages before they get the digging done."

Dinner was in the town hall across the green from the church. The food was served in cafeteria style and you paid for each item. Choosing among the delicacies offered was quite a strain on the nervous system.

The menu was written on a blackboard:

Black Bean Soup*

Baked Ham   Lobster Newburg   Roast Turkey

Potato Salad   Tossed Salad   Jellied Fruit Salad

Hot Rolls   Popovers*

Apple Pie   Cranberry Lattice Pie*

Coffee   Tea

Mrs. Appleyard does not know how all the items were made but she used her mental dowsing stick on the ones she chose and gives her diagnosis.

Black Bean Soup

1 pound black beans	¼ teaspoon thyme
2 quarts water	1 onion, sliced
hambone	1 stalk of celery, cut fine
½ teaspoon garlic powder	3 tablespoons butter
¼ teaspoon allspice	1½ tablespoons flour
4 whole cloves	6 tablespoons sherry
1 bay leaf	2 lemons

3 hard-boiled eggs

Soak the beans overnight with the water. In the morning put them on to cook with the hambone and the dry seasonings. Slice the onion and cut up the celery and sauté in a tablespoon and a half of the butter. Add them to the soup and simmer it four hours. Add hot water from time to time. When the beans are soft, strain off part of the liquid and set it aside, remove the hambone and the cloves, put the rest of the mixture through the blender and run it till it is smooth. Make a roux of the rest of the butter and the flour, add the liquid slowly, stirring well over very low heat. Cook it two minutes, add the bean purée. Some people add 2 tablespoons of tomato ketchup at this point. It gives it a good color, Mrs. Appleyard admits, but she prefers hers without. The soup is now ready but it may be kept in a double boiler until you are ready to serve it. Have the plates very hot. In each one put 1 tablespoon of sherry, two slices of lemon, three slices of hard-boiled egg. Pour the soup over. Serves six.

Popovers
(FOR 12 POPOVERS)

1½ cups milk	1 tablespoon butter — extra butter for pans
3 eggs	1½ cups flour, sifted three times
	½ teaspoon salt

Mrs. Appleyard knows that popovers can be made successfully by starting them in cold ungreased pans in a cold oven, only they are made by someone else. She has tried both the hot and cold methods and has better luck with the hot one. It's like dowsing: you have to follow your luck.

Use round iron pans or set ovenproof custard cups on a cooky sheet. Put half a teaspoon of melted butter in each cup. Light the oven: 450°. Set in the pan or sheet of cups. Now here is Mrs. Appleyard's contribution to popover lore. You are told to fill the pans half full and this is harder than it sounds. To get twelve pans all with the same amount in them is, in Mrs. Appleyard's experience, a most coincidental event. However, it is possible — if you have a measure. Mrs. Appleyard has one: it is a wooden tab intended as a marker for young plants. She has ruled a line on it at the height of half a popover pan and now even she can produce them of a uniform height and brown crisped effervescence.

Put all the ingredients milk, eggs, butter, flour measured after sifting with the salt into the blender. Blend for three minutes. If any flour has stuck to the side, push it into the batter with a rubber shaper.

Using your measure, fill each pan half full. Return the pans or cups to the oven. Bake 30 minutes. Reduce the heat to 350° and bake 10 to 15 minutes longer. Remove from pans. Make tiny slits in the side with a sharp knife. This lets the steam escape. Turn off the oven. The popovers not used immediately may be kept hot for a time without getting soggy. Good luck to you!

Cranberry Lattice Pie

2 cups cranberries　　　⅔ cup water
1 cup sugar

Put cranberries, water and sugar in that order into a saucepan. Cook till the berries all pop — about ten minutes. Cool while you line a pie plate with pastry and cut strips for the lattice. Light the oven: 450°. Put the cranberries into the pie shell, put on the lattice, the first strip going north and south and the next east and west and so on until the pie is covered. Moisten the edge of the crust a little, using a pastry brush, so that the lattice strips will stay in place. Bake for 10 minutes at 450°. Then reduce heat to 350° and bake until the crust is well browned, about 30 minutes longer.

The digger was nearly ten feet down when they got back to the field. Already many dowsers had been eliminated from the contest. Not a drop of water was running into the hole. The greatest depth guessed was twelve feet eight inches. Mr. Stanford told Mrs. Appleyard so.

"I calculated two gallons at ten and a half feet," he confided to Mrs. Appleyard in a wonderful soft deep Vermont voice several sizes too big for him. Vermont men often have such voices. The shrill nasal ones are employed by women to keep the soft-voiced men up to their work.

Mr. Stanford added: "I guess it just wasn't my day but there's water there somewhere, I vum."

"Twelve feet eight inches down, I swear," said the man in the poncho. "No question about it."

How much nicer "I vum" sounds than "I swear," Mrs. Appleyard thought in a spirit of pure partisanship.

Even if Mr. Stanford could not win, it was a wonderful day. The sun was warm now on the red and gold hills and on the purple Vermont mountains behind them. In the distance the White Mountains were like silver clouds and the clouds were like floating mountains.

"Yes," Mrs. Appleyard heard the lady with the turkey wishbone say, "it was worth coming just for the dinner." She named a town in the southern part of the state. No backhoe digger shall drag this dishonored name from Mrs. Appleyard. "Down at —— they had, you may not believe me if you don't care to, *they had a caterer!*"

"No!" said her friend in a tone of deep shock. "What did they serve?"

The awful details are still unspoken, for just then it happened.

Water began to gush into the hole.

"Four veins — no, five. I snum!" Mrs. Appleyard heard Mr. Stanford say happily as the digger raised its long neck and clanked off.

But when the measuring was done — you guessed it, so did Mrs. Appleyard — it was ten feet seven inches down and a gallon and six ounces a minute and Mr. Stanford's guess was the nearest. So he had a prize in a wallet and a free dinner — he took the ham, which he pronounced excellent, and the apple pie — and his name will forever be engraved upon the Dowsers' Cup.

"Did you see the snowbow this morning?" Mrs. Appleyard asked him.

Mr. Stanford forked in potato salad and nodded happily.

"I believe one end came right down in this field," Mrs. Appleyard said.

"I vum!" said Mr. Stanford.

Musical Cooks

DURING October Mrs. Appleyard still stayed in her own house, stoking her Franklin stoves by day and the stove in her winter kitchen both by day and by night. This art object is perhaps a hundred and twenty years old. In decorating it no pains were spared. It has cherubs' heads, egg-and-dart molding and acanthus leaves on it. There is a grating in front that opens and shows the fire. On top is an interesting piece of metal that looks as if it had been crocheted in a hurry by some absent-minded giantess. Lift it and you'll find a practical flat top with a stove lid, a splendid place to keep a soup kettle going.

The pipe from the stove wanders through the house, warming the dining room and the bedroom above it slightly. It keeps the bathroom thawed so you can't skate in it and even takes some of the chill off Mrs. Appleyard's bedroom. It is perhaps the most effective heating device ever invented — if you keep stoking it. Luckily Mrs. Appleyard has an ankle-length camel's-hair dressing gown, just the costume for night stoking. The story that her scarecrow wears it in summer is simply not true — yet.

Fortunately there were some warm days in October and it was on one of these that the music room was christened. Two years ago Mrs. Appleyard had the good luck to have a few days of comfortable illness. Cicely, instead of sending flowers, asked her mother if she would like the door of the Remember Appleyard house to use anywhere. The door is a beautiful one, the kind that has two large crosses and panels of several sizes. The pine of which it is made has been furrowed by storms since 1797. At that time it was impossible for Americans to build anything badly proportioned. Ash houses, smokehouses, sawmills, corn barns were all just right. Exactly when people acquired the taste and skill necessary for making everything just wrong, Mrs. Appleyard is not sure but she sees the results — the brick siding that imitates the most hideous bricks, the windows sullenly lurking under the eaves of little houses, the artificial stone of many colors.

"Say no more," said Cicely. "Remember your blood pressure."

Mrs. Appleyard obediently thought about the old door.

"A door," she said after a while, "can't just be nailed on the outside of a house for an ornament. It has to open into something. I think I'll make the woodshed into a music room."

The room, she explained, as she began to draw pictures of it, would be just for chamber music and playing Hi-Fi records. Cicely was relieved. She had seen her mother's Steinway inserted into the ballroom of the Museum with about a quarter of an inch to spare and she remembered the last time a piano was taken out of there, the wreckage was extensive.

Besides, she thought, this may be fantasy.

Of course she knew very well that a plan of her mother's is about as fantastic as a load of gravel. The next time she tried to make a telephone call, always an interesting project on an eight-party line, she heard her mother buying the silver-gray boards and the beams of an old barn.

"Roger Willard will be right over to get them," she told the owner.

When Cicely next saw her mother she was drawing the plans, using the same method she follows when she designs her miniature rooms. She uses sheets of thin cardboard cut on the scale of an inch to a foot. There is a sheet for each wall, one for the ceiling and one for the floor. She colors them, draws in the things she intends to hang on the walls, even shows the rugs and where the couch is going.

It took Roger Willard some months, but at last the music room was almost ridiculously like the patterns. There were the gray boards and the bluish green of the mantelpiece, a color suggesting that Mrs. Appleyard had made a raid on Williamsburg and escaped with a sample of woodwork. The bookcases were there with gilded hollow half circles over them made from an old chopping bowl. The Hi-Fi, FM and TV were chastely hidden in cupboards of gray boards. The Franklin stove was sending real smoke up the chimney and suprisingly little into the room. The cupboards beside it were full of wood and could be filled again from outside. Small-paned windows on two sides and the fanlight over the door caught sunshine all day long.

The fanlight was not exactly like the drawing. It was an improvement. Picking out her favorite hardware store to give them a nice piece of business, she showed the picture to the manager and asked if he could order one like it for her.

Well, he guessed he could but he didn't see much sense in it. There was one up over his garage that he figured would come pretty close to fitting.

That would be fine, his customer said, and could she buy it?

Well, the owner guessed not. No good to him. Most of the glass out of it. All cobwebs, no paint, but if the customer wanted to have such a piece of junk fixed up, she'd be welcome to it.

So there it is, making patterns like the spokes of a wheel on the hooked rugs, just right for the old door below it and giving Mrs. Appleyard, every time she looks at it, an extra reason for liking to be an adopted Vermonter.

The design around the door was copied from an old house fifty miles away. Mrs Appleyard saw it one day when she was at a Book Fair pretending to be an author and not a master builder. Luckily she had a pencil and the back of an envelope handy. Roger Willard carved the pattern. He used a set of tools that Mrs. Appleyard once tried for about twelve minutes twenty years ago. She then cleverly decided not to be a wood carver. She did make the plaster ornaments on the mantelpiece and above the doors. She used something she calls the lost-wax process. Someday when she is feeling strong and sadistic she is quite likely to tell how she did it.

With Patience Barlow's help she made the curtains. They look rather like Fortuny copies of old Italian brocade. The background is a greenish, grayish blue and the pattern is in dull gold and Venetian red. Two large stencils were used and it took Mrs. Appleyard and Patience about three weeks before the curtains were finished. During this time these ladies enthusiastically gave up cooking. Perhaps Mrs. Appleyard ate something besides cucumbers and yogurt but she can't remember what it was. Patience did cook herself an occasional hot meal — tea and cinnamon toast. The cooky jar was emptied and not replenished. Hungry grandchildren came and clinked the lid and looked reproachful. Friends to whom Mrs. Appleyard had said "Do drop in to lunch sometime" dropped in, saw every available table covered with newspapers, brocade and coffee-can covers containing gold and Venetian red, took a long breath of oil and Japan drier and dropped rapidly out again.

Yet there came a day when Mrs. Appleyard could think of nothing more to do for the room — except give a party for it, of course. The idea for it came when she heard a group of her favorite musicians agreeing that they would rather cook than play their instruments. Then one of them asked Mrs. Appleyard when she was going to christen the music room.

"Tomorrow night while you are still here," she said. "And every one of you must either cook or play. I promise not to play my accordion," she added. "Now tell me what you are going to cook so I can have the right things for you."

The resulting list began with a small cabbage, which Mrs. Appleyard acquired from her own garden, and ended with a quart of fine white Burgundy, which she produced from her own cellarway if not from her own vineyard. She did have to go to town for some of the items between. The only thing missing from the market was fresh mushrooms. She planned to substitute some cans she keeps for such emergencies but on the way home she stopped at an appropriate pasture. It had two palominos in it, looking especially decorative against a back-

ground of flaming maples and deep blue sky. It also had mushrooms pushing up shining ivory umbrellas through grass that was
still green, so the menu was safe.

When she got home Roger Willard was putting a small fir
tree on the roof to show that the music room was finished and
Patience Barlow was arranging autumn bouquets in big stone-
ware jars. They and others who had worked on the room were
all invited to the party.

All the cooks were men. The women preferred to stick to
their cellos and violas. There was probably psychology mixed
up in this, Mrs. Appleyard thought, but she was much too busy
to unmix any of it. After all, men cooks always need a kitchen
maid. By being one on this occasion, Mrs. Appleyard was also
able to be a gastronomical spy and find out their secrets. Not
that they were unwilling to share them but their instructions
were of the "take a little of this and some of that and cook it
till it's about right" style. Mrs. Appleyard, whose only virtue as
a cook is that she writes down promptly how she did something
that came out right, had her notebook handy and used it.

Everyone seemed happy. A group in the music room played
the Brahms Clarinet Quintet three times. Roger Willard was
sitting down — a posture unusual for him — listening to Mozart
in the living room. Other guests relaxed on the porch and
breathed in the prophetic smells of supper. There were lights
coming from the barn where people were looking at the miniature rooms and from the carriage house where someone was reading a mystery story and from the corn barn where others were
sitting around the fire.

In the kitchens every stove was in use. A violinist, whose reddish curls began to stand up all over his head as the steam rose,
was making cabbage soup on the cherubs'-head stove. A very
tall pianist, working at an electric stove, was simmering broilers

in white Burgundy and could he have another half pound of butter, please? In the summer kitchen a cellist was getting ready to bake coffee cake. He had arrived with his bowl of raised dough, tenderly wrapped in damask napkins and a pink knitted blanket. He was now dipping pieces of the dough into a mixture of preserved fruits and spices and dropping them into an angel-cake tin. He looked much more nervous than he did when Mrs. Appleyard heard him play Dvořák's Cello Concerto. She assured him that they would find a quiet, calm, warm place for the final rising of his coffee cake. She thought near the Franklin stove in the library might be the best. The flautist was busy with the salad.

Why, Mrs. Appleyard found time to wonder, do people say "flautist" which is such an ugly word instead of "flutist" which is a pretty one?

Just to be embarrassing, she supposed and decided to call this one, who was small, impish and rather like Puck in *A Midsummer Night's Dream*, a flutist. He asked her for a garlic press. Mrs. Appleyard brought it to him and they had a congenial talk about garlic. The flutist said it was good for relaxing tension and he always liked some before playing the flute. Mrs. Appleyard, fascinated with this musical secret, contributed the information that Marco Polo said the natives in the Himalayas gave their ponies garlic so they could breathe well in the thin air of the high mountain passes. She then passed on to the oboist who also wanted garlic and a sharp-tined fork with which to score the outside of a cucumber. She gave him both and put her own contribution, a chocolate icebox cake which she had just been decorating with whipped cream, into the refrigerator.

The menu resulting from these activities was:

Cabbage Soup*
Fish Mousse, mushroom sauce   Coq au Vin*
Spaghetti with Meat Balls
Coffee cake*
Tossed Salad   Cucumber Salad, Yogurt dressing*
Chocolate Icebox Cake†
Coffee   Pouilly Fuissé

Ice cream and oatmeal cookies for the children many of whom turned out to be over twenty-one.

The meal was planned for seven o'clock and was served right on time at eight. Mrs. Appleyard never could remember just how many people ate it but there was plenty — just exactly plenty — and not enough left over for a blue jay on a reducing diet. Music was laced in and around the supper with wood-smoke and people laughing. After it was all over, and with the assistance of a couple of poets she had washed the dishes, she realized that all she had eaten was cucumber salad. But after all she had heard the Brahms Clarinet Concerto in her own music room. She can eat another day.

Cabbage Soup

2 pounds beef chuck, cut in inch cubes	½ teaspoon mixed spices
bones from beef chuck	2 pounds tomatoes
2 pounds chicken necks and wingtips	6 potatoes
3 quarts water	1 stalk of celery
½ teaspoon mixed herbs	2 onions, minced

4 tablespoons fat from stock

Put the beef, the bones and the chicken necks and wingtips into a deep kettle with the water. Add the herbs and spices and let it simmer for 2 hours. Skim it from time to time to remove as much of the fat as possible. While it is cooking prepare your vegetables. Peel the tomatoes by holding them over gas flame until the skin cracks. You need a wooden-handled fork for this. If you don't have one, plunge the tomatoes briefly into boiling water. Cool them and cut them into eighths. Peel the potatoes. Small new potatoes freshly dug were used in this soup but potato balls made from larger ones will do or half-inch dice. Cut the celery fine and mince the onions. An hour before serving time remove the bones from the soup. Sauté the celery and onions until the onion is transparent in fat from the stock and add them to the soup. Then in the same pan sauté the cabbage for 5 minutes. Add it to the soup. Add the potatoes. Cook until potatoes are done — about 2 to 5 minutes. A short time before serving add the tomatoes. They should keep their shape. Rinse out the frying pan with some of the soup to get all the flavor. Salt to taste. Serve it in a large brown bowl. For ten.

Coq au Vin

1 cup chicken stock	parsley
2 three-pound broilers, cut in four pieces, wingtips removed	4 tablespoons flour with ½ teaspoon poultry seasoning
1 onion, grated	½ pound butter
1 pound mushrooms, sliced vertically	2 cups dry white wine
toasted French bread	

Begin by making stock of the wingtips and necks of the chickens. Cook it down to ½ cup. Cool and skim off fat. Grate the onion. Slice the mushrooms, caps only. The stems may be added to the stock. Cut the parsley fine. Mrs. Appleyard does this with scissors, rather than cutting it on a board with a knife or chopping it.

Put the flour and seasoning into a large paper bag and toss the pieces of chicken in it till they are well coated. Melt but do not brown the butter in a large iron frying pan. Brown the pieces of chicken on both sides and transfer them to a large fireproof baking dish. Set them into a 350° oven to finish cooking for 20 to 30 minutes. Cook the onion in the frying pan until it is transparent. Add the mushrooms and sauté them 3 minutes. Add the chicken stock and cook two minutes longer. Add this sauce to the chickens. Rinse out the frying pan with the wine. Simmer it, stirring well to get all the flavor. Add salt to taste. Pour it over the chicken. Sprinkle over the parsley. Serve with French bread to mop up the sauce. For eight.

Coffee Cake

Use a package of hot roll mix for this. Follow directions for first and second risings.

Mix 2 cups sugar, ¼ pound mixed candied fruit, ¼ pound each of currants, seedless raisins and walnuts, ¼ teaspoon nutmeg, ½ teaspoon cinnamon. Butter an angel-cake tin well. Tear off pieces of dough. Dip them into the sugar mixture and pack them lightly into the angel-cake tin. Cover and let it rise till double its bulk in a warm place. Scatter with what is left of the sugar mixture. Dot with butter.

Bake at 375° for 25 minutes. Reduce heat and bake until delicately brown, about 15 minutes longer.

Cucumber Salad, Yogurt Dressing

2 large cucumbers	2 tablespoons scissored parsley
1 bean of garlic	1 cup yogurt
¼ teaspoon white pepper	½ teaspoon paprika
salt to taste	mint leaves

Peel the cucumbers. Score the sides deeply with a sharp-tined fork. Slice them paper-thin. The scoring indents the edges of the slices. It isn't necessary but it looks attractive, Mrs. Apple-yard thinks. Add the garlic, put through the press, the pepper, salt and the parsley to the yogurt. Toss the sliced cucumbers in the mixture. Sprinkle over the paprika. Decorate with small sprays of fresh mint leaves.

Harvest Supper

ONE OF Mrs. Appleyard's favorite parties is the Harvest Supper. It is given by the PTA to raise money for the hot-lunch program. The school Halloween exercises are part of the entertainment. The combination gets people together in an atmosphere of warmth and relaxation. Summer residents, who have come for a last weekend to shut up their houses, appear. Neighbors come from around the county for what is known as an excellent meal. Children can come for half price. A child of the right size and shape often eats twice as much as his father so this is rightly regarded as one of the bargains of all time.

The stage of the Community Hall is decorated with tall cornstalks and pumpkins and bright leaves cut out of paper. The real leaves are all off the trees now. There are great piles of them, fine for rolling and rustling in, near the schoolhouse. All the brilliant reds and yellows have turned to the same dull pinkish tan. Oaks still show color but they are rare in this part of Vermont. Every year what Mrs. Appleyard thinks are evergreens prove to be nothing of the sort. They are larches. First they turn an olive-gold green, next — briefly — they are spires of bright burnt orange, and then, just before the needles fall, they are the color of cinnamon toast. There is an enormous old larch near one of Mrs. Appleyard's favorite houses, an old brown house suggesting kinship with the House of the Seven Gables though a century younger. It has enough gables, if you count the dormers, and a dark roof almost the color of the clapboards. The big larch twists up above the end of the house and its needles fall on the roof, edging the dark shingles with bright gold. Even after the zinnias and dahlias have frozen, the house, with pale blue smoke curling out of the big chimney, the one with the secret staircase around it, looks warm and welcoming as it must have to slaves on their way to Canada a century ago.

Frances Ward, the owner of the house, will be at the party tonight. She will bring her violin and she will fiddle for dancing after supper. She also plays Bach and Corelli but tonight she will be fiddling. The technique is different. Not every violinist can also fiddle the "Devil's Dream" with properly controlled wildness or inspire the dancers of "Money Musk" to be both stately and gay. Luckily Frances can and after supper and the Halloween Exercises there will be plenty of dancers on the floor. They will be sustained by the following menu:

Baked Beans*   Red Flannel Hash*
Succotash Casserole†   Fish Balls*
Harvest Vegetable Salad*
Brown Bread*   Mustard Pickle
Watermelon Pickle
Squash Pie   Cranberry Apples*
Coffee

Baked Beans

One of the first things Mr. Appleyard did when he had married his wife was to carry her off to a lonely island where they spent a week cut off from the mainland by waves like Vermont mountains and fog like potato soup. During this happy time he began converting her into being a Vermonter by breaking the news to her that he regarded beans as baked in Boston as food unsuitable for human beings.

His bride, who up to that moment had never even boiled a kettle of water, solemnly promised that the shadow of a pea bean should never cross her husband's plate. She learned that there were beans called soldier beans and others called yellow eyes. Either, Mr. Appleyard said, might be used — on the whole he preferred yellow eyes — so long as the pork with them was streaky fat and lean and if they were flavored with maple sugar, not with molasses.

Mrs. Appleyard began to realize that married life was a serious affair. By the time she reached their apartment on Beacon Hill she was able to inspire her cook, who was even more ignorant than her mistress, into baking beans that were not tough, slippery, and pallid and made unpalatable to a Vermonter by a weird mixture of molasses and tomato sauce.

Here is how Mr. Appleyard liked his beans:

Appleyard Center Baked Beans

2 quarts yellow eye beans	1 tablespoon dry mustard
boiling water	½ teaspoon ginger
1 onion	1 teaspoon ground pepper
1 cup granulated maple sugar	salt to taste, perhaps 1 teaspoon
1 pound streaked salt pork	

Cover the beans with cold water and soak them overnight. In the morning strain off the water. Cover them with boiling water and simmer until the skin wrinkles when you blow on a tablespoon of them — about 20 minutes. Drain. Put a layer of beans in the bottom of a beanpot. Add the onion. Mix the dry ingredients and scatter them in as you add the rest of the beans. Score the rind of the pork deeply. Bury it among the beans so that the scored edge just shows. Fill the beanpot with boiling water. Cover. Bake 6 hours, at 300°, adding water from time to time. Uncover. Bake until beans are done, golden brown, tender but not mushy — about half an hour longer.

These beans have a texture and flavor a little like chestnuts. Granulated maple sugar is now so hard to get that Mrs. Appleyard has used light brown sugar, a cup of it with an added tablespoon of white sugar, with pretty good results or anyway no open disapproval from her Vermont gourmets.

If, like Mrs. Appleyard, you like beans but are denied the privilege of eating salt or salt pork, you might like to try this version. She sometimes carries her own private unsalted casserole of this or that to a community supper and usually finds friends who share it.

Mrs. Appleyard's Own Baked Beans

2 cups yellow eye beans
⅛ pound butter
¾ cup light brown sugar
1 teaspoon granulated sugar
¼ teaspoon ground pepper
1½ teaspoons dry mustard
bit of bay leaf, scalded in
   water and removed

pinches of rosemary, basil,
   marjoram, orégano, curry
   powder, nutmeg
1 onion, minced
2 beans of garlic, crushed
1 cup light cream
¼ pound beef suet in
   ½-inch cubes

1 tablespoon brown sugar (extra)

Soak and parboil beans as above. Mix the butter, sugar, dry seasonings, onion and garlic and combine them with the beans. Put them into a small beanpot or into a casserole with a tightly fitting cover. Bake covered for 6 hours at 300°. Try out suet cubes until golden brown. Drain. Uncover the beans. Pour in the cream. Stir beans so that different ones are on top. Scatter suet cubes over the beans. Sprinkle over the extra brown sugar. Cook ½ hour or until the beans are tender and have absorbed most of the liquid. Serves four to six.

Red Flannel Hash
FOR SIX

Some dishes are causes, others are results, Mrs. Appleyard says. Red flannel hash is the result of a New England boiled dinner and, Mrs. Appleyard thinks, the best part of it.

There are three important points about any hash. Always chop it in a wooden bowl, not too fine. Do not use cooked potatoes — cook them especially for the hash. Have twice as much potato as you do meat. In red flannel hash be sure you have plenty of beets to give it color. Mrs. Appleyard does not include cabbage in her hash. She thinks it tends to make it slippery. However she does not insist on this point. If you like it, go ahead.

For a large frying pan:

4 tablespoons beef suet in ¼-inch cubes
1 tablespoon onion, finely minced
1 cup of meat, chopped
6 cups of freshly boiled potatoes, chopped in small cubes

3 cups of vegetables from boiled dinner: carrots, lima beans, turnips, beets, chopped not too fine
1 cup stock from boiled dinner, simmered down to ½ cup

Try out the beef suet in a large iron frying pan. Skim out the cubes. Drain. Add the minced onion and cook over low heat till straw-colored. Mix the meat, potato and vegetables well and add them to the pan. Stir briefly until fat and onion combine with mixture. Add the stock. Turn heat as low as possible. Smooth mixture but do not mash it down. Cook it until it begins to brown around the edges — about 40 minutes.

Have a large hot platter ready. Physical strength is now necessary. The frying pan is hot and heavy. With a spatula carefully loosen the hash all around the edges. Make a deep crease with the spatula across the hash at right angles to the handle. Now take a holder and bravely grasp the handle of the pan in your left hand. Tip the pan and fold the top half of the hash over the lower half. Run the spatula carefully under the lower half to be sure it is free from the pan. Place the platter over the pan. You'll need another holder at this point. Invert pan and platter. The hash will drop out and be like a glazed brown omelet with red edges. Sprinkle the suet cracklings over it. Put sprays of parsley around it. Mrs. Appleyard hopes that after you have lived dangerously with the hot pan and platter you will enjoy it.

Fish Balls (*M.O'M*)

Never having fried anything in deep fat in her life, Mrs. Appleyard falls back upon the wisdom of the good angel who helped her in her kitchen for seventeen years, told the children about leprechauns, played them the record of "The Two Black Crows" and taught them manners by example. She has since used her wit, charm, philosophy and just plain goodness on her own children and still has a supply on hand for her grandchildren. Do they appreciate their good luck? Mrs. Appleyard hopes so.

In the Appleyard family it was a grave misdemeanor to form fish balls into firm cakes. If you like them that way, better get them out of a can and relax. The Appleyards like them light, fluffy and as prickly as porcupines. This happy result is achieved this way.

2 cups of raw potatoes, diced	1 teaspoon butter
1 cup of uncooked salt codfish, picked fine	pinch of ground pepper
	1 egg, well beaten

Freshen codfish as directed on package. Have water boiling in saucepan. Add diced potatoes and codfish picked in small pieces. Cover. Cook till potatoes are soft. Drain well. This is important. Unless fish and potatoes are well drained as soon as they are cooked they will not hold together well while frying. Cover. Shake over low heat until well dried. Now, using a pastry blending fork, mash and beat the fish and potatoes until they are very light. Add butter and pepper. Beat in the beaten egg. Have fat heated to 375°. It should be about two inches deep. Dip a tablespoon into the fat, then spoon up lightly some of the mixture and drop it into the fat. Fry it one minute. Fry five at a time. Drain on paper towels. Reheat fat and fry another batch. Serves six.

Fish Hash

This seems the right place to mention that the same mixture used for fish balls also makes fish hash. This is how Mrs. Appleyard's grandmother made it. Six slices of salt pork were cut in quarters and fried gently until a delicate golden brown. The pork was removed and drained on brown paper. The fat was left in the pan — an iron frying pan, medium size. The fish hash was carefully browned like the Red Flannel Hash above, removed from the pan in the same way and garnished with the salt pork cracklings. This served six people. Of course they also had oatmeal, thick cream, eggs, three kinds of hot bread, plenty of fruit and a lamb chop if they preferred it to the hash so they would usually say yes when asked by their hostess if they had "made out a breakfast."

Harvest Vegetable Salad

This varies according to what vegetables are available. Occasionally, when frost delays, lima beans ripen before they are frozen to a mush, and tomatoes, picked not quite green, turn red on Mrs. Appleyard's windowsills. This was such a year: there was even oak leaf lettuce left in the garden to put around the edge of a huge wooden chopping bowl. In the center was a small yellow bowl containing mayonnaise mixed with sour cream. Around it were a ring of cooked beets cut in cubes, one of cooked sliced carrots, another of raw broccoli flower heads alternated with raw cauliflower flowerets. Green beans, frozen in August, made another ring. Then more beets, more carrots, finely cut celery and here and there a little heap of asparagus tips frozen in June or peas, marked A+ by Patience Barlow when she put them into the freezer in July.

French dressing has been poured over all the vegetables, parsley and chives have been snipped with a scissors and scattered here and there. Mrs. Appleyard gets the same pleasure out of one of these arrangements that she does out of painting a dish of fruit on velvet. She says it's less trouble: you don't have to frame it or hang it on the wall.

Brown Bread

Mrs. Appleyard heard the other day of a man from Texas who sends to Vermont to have brown bread without raisins made for him and flown west. If she knew his name she would ship him a loaf of hers as a tribute to a congenial spirit. She doesn't like raisins either, at least not in brown bread. Plum pudding or fruitcake or mincemeat she considers suitable situations for this nutritious fruit.

For two loaves:

1 cup rye flour	1 ¾ cup sweet milk
1 cup stone ground whole wheat flour	¾ cup molasses
1 cup stone-ground cornmeal	¾ teaspoon soda
	¾ teaspoon salt

If you have thick sour milk on hand, use 2 cups of it instead of the sweet milk and increase the soda to 1 teaspoon.

Sift dry ingredients thoroughly. Mix the milk and molasses well together. Make a hollow in the flour mixture and pour in the milk and molasses, beating it in well as you pour. Put the batter into tall, tightly covered greased tins. The easy way to get these is to inherit them. Sometimes they turn up at auctions. Do not fill tins more than two thirds full. Place them on a rack in a tightly covered kettle or use your covered roaster. Steam 3 hours. Start with plenty of boiling water as the bread will cook more evenly and quickly if you do not have to replace water during the steaming process. At the end of the 3 hours, remove tins from water, uncover them. Place them in the oven at 300° for ten minutes so the bread can dry a little. Of course the usual place for this bread is with baked beans, but don't forget that when cold it makes delicious sandwiches to go with any kind of shellfish. Slice it very thin and spread it either with sweet butter or first with butter and then with a mixture of cream cheese and horseradish.

Cranberry Apples

8 fine tart apples	2 cloves
2 tablespoons lemon juice	2 cups sugar
pinches of nutmeg and	2 cups water
cinnamon	2 cups cranberries

Wash, peel and core the apples. They should be perfect but not too large. Brush them with lemon juice and set them in a cool place while you cook the peel and cores in water seasoned with the spices. Also mix the sugar and water and bring it to boiling point. Add the cranberries and cook until they all pop. Put the apples in a shallow heat proof glass baking dish, lightly buttered. Fill centers of apples with the popped cranberries and pour 1 tablespoon of the cranberry juice over each apple. Set the dish in a 350° oven and bake. Apples should keep their shape. Now mix juice from the apple peelings — there should be ½ cup — with the same amount of the cranberry juice. Use this mixture to coat the apples as they cook. It will slide off but keep spooning it over every 10 minutes during the baking. This may take 40–50 minutes according to the kind of apples used. When they are tender, put them into a serving dish. Add a little of the cooked cranberries to any that do not look well filled. Pour all the juice in the pan over them. Chill.

These may be eaten as a dessert or used as a garnish with roast turkey, duck or goose. Grated orange rind may be sprinkled over them if you like.

After supper the children, who had been well brushed and polished for the occasion, began decorating their faces to make goblins, elves and witches of themselves. There were some of the most benevolent-looking witches Mrs. Appleyard had ever seen, including the head one who was her granddaughter Camilla. This is high promotion for Camilla: she was always an elf before. Now she is beaming because she has a broomstick and a black pointed hat with stars on it. She also wears her new glasses becauses she is a nearsighted witch as well as a genial one.

With the help of her assistant witches she casts a spell with great efficiency and the children, who have been happily dancing around the stage, are all frozen into uncomfortable positions. They have, it seems, pains in their midriffs, teeth and ears and toes. Camilla puts down her black cat, which walks among the frozen figures with a good deal of satisfaction. Perhaps, like some of the mothers, it wishes it too had a magic wand and could get peace so easily. However, the moment of quiet is soon over. A golden-haired good fairy appears. The children are unfrozen. Camilla snatches up her cat and hurries off on her broomstick. She is followed by her goblins and elves who deliver a few sly pinches and tweaks as they go. One has the impertinence to pull the good fairy's yellow curls. There is loud applause from the parents, who tell each other kindly and sincerely how well each other's children did. Of course they know whose child did the best.

Even grandmothers, Mrs. Appleyard thought as she happily listened to Frances Ward tuning her fiddle for the dancing, have a right to an opinion, I suppose.

November

Bridge Party

IT WAS a distinct surprise to Mrs. Appleyard's friends when she announced that she was going to give a bridge party. Philanthropic considerations had led her, in 1912, to give up playing this interesting game. She was the kind of player who always held poor cards — or did they just seem so when she held them? Her intentions about keeping her mind alert were good but somehow her thoughts would drift to her trousseau — this was when she was engaged to Mr. Appleyard — or to the island they were going to on their wedding journey or just to Mr. Appleyard.

There came to be a tone of well-bred patience in her partners' voices. It is not true that the term "dummy" was invented just for Mrs. Appleyard — that was simply a rumor — but it certainly suited her admirably. So well, in fact, that it took her some time to realize that when her friends asked her to make a fourth "just to help out," she would be rather more helpful if she stayed at home and read a good book.

Luckily Mr. Appleyard was not a bridge player. He preferred squash rackets, cowboy pool, golf, poker, tennis or chess. So they were married and lived happily for a time that now seems short to Mrs. Appleyard though it was more than thirty years. She became rather an attentive chessplayer but she has never gone back to bridge. She has sometimes been invited to play but not by anyone who knew her in her youth. The game is really complicated now, she hears.

"Of course she can't really be meaning to play herself," her friends exclaimed uneasily when they heard she was giving a bridge party.

They were right. It was a different kind of party and indeed a different kind of bridge, a covered one, in fact.

It was Cicely's idea really.

"The town is going to take down the East Hill Bridge and widen the road there. I think they would give it to you if you'd take it away," she told her mother.

Mrs. Appleyard, who was feeling a little let down because she had moved into her new apartment at Cicely's for the winter and everything was perfect, brightened up at once.

"I could put it across the brook," she said. "Roger told me that my old one needs rebuilding. It would probably be an economy to have a covered one."

"Of course," said Cicely who is the same kind of economist as her mother and President Kennedy and other people with vision. "Let's go and look at it."

The covered bridge was a great favorite of Mrs. Appleyard's. When she had foreign visitors, she used to entertain them by taking them to see it, telling them that it was the smallest one anywhere around.

The visitors had usually been shown the widest rivers, the tallest buildings and the busiest street corners in the world. Sometimes they had seen a mountain with the largest possible letters painted on it. (HOLLYWOODLAND, it says.) They seemed to enjoy the change of scale.

Mrs. Appleyard liked the bridge best when the elms along the river were arches of gold and maples blazed on the hillside above it. On this November morning the sky was dingy with cold, sullen gray clouds. The pastures were lion-colored with dark manes of bare maples. Mountains were a wall of dark steely blue. They seemed to have moved in closer since yesterday. Still, even in these forbidding circumstances, the bridge looked attractive.

"Cozy," said Mrs. Appleyard. "I'll have a few electric outlets put into it and we'll have tea there summer afternoons while the children are swimming. It will be shady and well ventilated at the same time."

Even if November had been a grass-growing season, no blade would have increased in height under Mrs. Appleyard's feet. She talked to the selectmen, who did not see any reason why she couldn't have the bridge — probably. (Vermont for "yes.") So long as she took it pretty quick. They planned to start work that week. She talked to Roger Willard who thought likely, he guessed, maybe it could be moved and he would get estimates.

When Cicely next saw her mother she was happily at work with pencil and paper making out a list of guests and a menu for the bridge opening. She had a picture of the inside of it showing the kingpost trusses and a harvest table heaped with food.

"You mean you plan to start cooking there in November?" Cicely asked.

"If it's Indian summer," her mother said. "If it snows, we'll eat here and just go and look at it. Anyway I've planned to cook things here and carry them down. I'll keep them hot on that wonderful heating tray you gave me. There's lots of watercress in the brook. I'm only asking eight people besides you and me," she added virtuously.

Her daughter said she hoped her mother would keep the number at eight.

"The last time you said that," she pointed out, "there were seventy-three."

"That was just for dessert," her mother said hastily, "and I didn't know a good many of them."

"If that makes it any better," Cicely said. "How can you be sure there won't be people around you don't know this time?"

"Foliage is over and skiing hasn't begun," Mrs. Appleyard said. "I'll read you the menu," she added, since the subject seemed to need changing.

Cream of Watercress Soup*

Seafood Croustade*   Cold Baked Ham

Hot Brown Bread (p. 34)

Orange, Avocado, Onion and Watercress Salad

French Dressing

Brown Betty*

Vermont Cheese   Crackers

Cider   Jug of Red Wine

Coffee

"What, not a vintage wine?" inquired Cicely.

"Not out of paper cups," her mother explained.

They did not drink out of paper cups. No electric outlets were put in the bridge and they did not eat in it. By the day of the party it was being burned where it had always stood.

"I suppose we might go over and cook hot dogs there when they burn it," said Mrs. Appleyard.

This was the day Roger Willard brought the news that moving the bridge would cost a substantial amount suitable for sending a man to the moon, about as much as it would cost to send Tommy Bradshaw to college, a purpose for which these ladies had been saving up for some years.

"We might give up sending him to college," Cicely suggested. "He always says his teachers are dopes. Perhaps he'd do better as a self-made man."

"I don't care for them much," Mrs. Appleyard said. "They always seem so pleased about it. As if everyone weren't self-made really. Only the educated ones are sometimes humble enough to know they had help. I'll tell the guests that the party will be here in the evening instead of at noon," she added.

"Why not at noon?" Cicely asked.

"Because," said Mrs. Appleyard, "evening is a better time for bridge. And as I've been pretty economical this week, I am going to buy you two card tables each with four unspavined legs."

The party was a great success. No one came except those invited. The tables were splendidly sturdy. Venetia Hopkins and Mrs. Appleyard played chess. An extra bridge player had been asked so that Cicely would not have to help by making a fourth. She was able to keep an eye on the Brown Betty and keep up her reading average of two books a day. Mrs. Appleyard's is only one but then she has to write one occasionally and that cuts into her reading time.

A cold rain fell all day. Cicely kindly made no reference to Indian summer. About the time the guests went home, the rain stopped and clouds blew away from the moon. The wind from East Hill brought a smell of wet wood smoke with it.

In her mind Mrs. Appleyard followed the course of the brook, in full flood tonight, down to her own pond. Suddenly it was spring. Purple iris and blue forget-me-nots edged the pond. The waterfall foamed so loud that she could hardly hear the wood thrushes calling. Suddenly, below the tall green wine-glass of the lady elm something rose out of the dark cedars, a silvery gray shelter from rain, from hot sun, from snow.

Well, thought Mrs. Appleyard, this one can't be burned or carried away by floods. I'll always have it now.

Mrs. Appleyard did most of the cooking for her bridge party the day before it took place. Since she had chicken stock on hand and watercress in the brook she began by getting them together.

Cream of Watercress Soup
FOR EIGHT OR TEN

1 quart fresh crisp watercress, carefully washed	pinch of nutmeg
	pinch of cayenne pepper
1 quart chicken stock	salt to taste (perhaps 1 teaspoon)
3 tablespoons butter	3 cups rich milk
3 tablespoons flour	1 cup thin cream
3 egg yolks	

She makes the stock with veal bones — 2 or 3 pounds, the carcass of a roasted chicken with any meat that clings to it,

4 carrots, washed and sliced, 2 onions sliced, 2 stalks of celery cut fine, celery tops, a tablespoon of snipped parsley, pinches of basil, rosemary and orégano. She uses a large kettle, puts in 2 gallons of water, cooks the stock over low heat for 4 hours. It should cook down to about 2 quarts. She strains and chills it, skims it when it is chilled. It ought to be stiff enough to skate on, she says, and adds that having it on hand is very sustaining.

Put the washed watercress and a cup of the stock into the blender and let it run till you have a smooth bright green purée. Melt the butter, rub in the flour mixed with the seasonings, cook until smooth, about a minute. Remove from heat, stir in the other 3 cups of stock a little at a time. Stir in the purée. Cook over hot water 15 minutes. Scald the milk and cream. Stir them into the watercress mixture. When you are ready to serve the soup, beat the egg yolks. Add some of the soup to them, a little at a time, stirring well, until you have about a cup of egg mixture. Stir this into the soup. Cook until the egg yolks thicken, about 2 minutes. Do not cook too long or it will curdle. It may stand over hot but not boiling water until it is ready to serve.

Mrs. Appleyard likes Euphrates sesame seed crackers with it.

Croustade of Seafood
FOR EIGHT OR TEN

The croustade was also made the day before. It is simply a loaf of home-baked bread, baked according to Andrea Morini's rule but in a round enameled iron casserole instead of in a regular loaf pan. On the afternoon of the party Mrs. Appleyard sliced off the top of the round lightly browned loaf and removed the soft part of the bread. (Don't worry about its being thrown away. She dried it and used it for stuffing another day.) She then buttered the inside of the croustade and the inside of the lid with softened sweet butter. Just before she filled the croustade she set it into a 350° oven to heat for about 5 minutes while she was making the filling.

Seafood Filling

Seafood, flash-frozen as it leaves the ocean, is often better than fish in fish counters, which is often, Mrs. Appleyard regrets to remark, frozen anyway, though partly thawed to an uninteresting limpness. Fish is really mostly water, held together by a few bones. When it thaws, liquid runs out of it leaving it dry and tasteless. Unless you caught it yourself, fish straight from your freezer has the most flavor and the best texture.

For a large croustade, use:

¼ pound butter	½ pound shrimp, peeled and
2 cups light cream	deveined
1 teaspoon paprika	½ pound scallops
¼ teaspoon nutmeg	½ pound oysters
salt to taste	1 pound fillet of haddock, cooked 7
4 egg yolks, beaten	minutes in rapidly boiling
1 pound lobster meat,	water and flaked
cut up, not too fine	4 tablespoons sherry
2 tablespoons brandy	

Use a large enameled iron frying pan. Melt the butter over low heat. Scald the cream and the dry seasonings. Add some cream to the beaten eggs and then the egg mixture to the cream. Add all the fish to the melted butter. Toss over medium heat, till the edges of the oysters start to curl, about 3 minutes. Add the cream and egg mixture. Cook till it thickens and the sauce coats the back of the spoon. At the last minute add the sherry and brandy. Fill the croustade. Serve.

Guests cannot eat this standing up with a fork. They need a table and knives for cutting. Mrs. Appleyard has some small tables that look like Vermont verde antique marble and seem to be about as strong. They are cheering to men, who would be miserable sitting down with plates in their laps. Of course that harvest table in the bridge would have been even better but then — well, let's not brood about it. Think about the salad.

Avocado Salad

This is one of those combinations for which there is no definite rule. Perhaps you prefer it without the onion. In any case it should be mild onion and sliced very thin. Slice the avocado and put it in the bottom of the salad bowl. Squeeze lemon juice over it and cover it with sections of grapefruit and orange and the onion so that it will not turn dark. Since there is plenty of fruit juice in the bowl your dressing should be only oil mixed with whatever seasonings you like. Mrs. Appleyard sometimes adds a little ginger, besides mustard and paprika, and decorates the bowl with a little crystallized ginger. She sometimes puts chicory around it but she likes watercress best.

Brown Betty

In a moment of enthusiasm and forgetting that she is now a kind of Vermonter, Mrs. Appleyard labeled this in her notebook "Perfect Brown Betty." She apologizes for her excitement and says it's pretty good, especially when made with her neighbor's McIntosh apples.

2 cups cubed homemade bread (no crusts)
3 cups pared and thinly sliced apples — 4 large Macs or 6 medium

1 cup white sugar	2 tablespoons butter, in small dots
½ teaspoon nutmeg	grated rind and juice
¼ teaspoon cinnamon	of one lemon
⅛ teaspoon cloves	2 tablespoons butter, melted

Into a straight-sided buttered baking dish, a French soufflé dish or a Swedish enameled iron dish that will hold 1½ quarts, put a layer of your cubed bread. Mix apples, sugar and spice and cover bread with a layer of it. Dot with butter, add a little lemon juice and rind. Put in more layers, alternating bread and apples, till the dish is well heaped. Finish with the cubed bread. Pour over the melted butter. Cover. Bake at 375° for half an hour. Uncover. Bake until apples are tender and crumbs are brown — about half an hour longer. Serve at once with thick cream or vanilla ice cream. Like a soufflé, it will collapse if it stands.

Deer Season

WHEN deer season began, November ceased to be a quiet gray month. Men who wore dull grays and browns the rest of the year happily blossomed into crimson shirts checked with black, into turquoise quilted jackets and tartans never seen by any Scot. Scarlet caps covered the bald spots of bankers as they strolled the streets of Montpelier with guns under their arms. Business sagged into its annual lethargy. Lawyers, doctors, merchants, chiefs had all gone hunting. Also, more inconveniently, had garage men and plumbers. So, Mrs. Appleyard supposed, had rich men, poor men, beggar men, thieves. Also, she thought, with the tingle of the spine that means a mystery story coming on — murderers.

She did not mean the slayers of ten thousand deer but those of the other hunters who are found dead in the woods every year in their bright caps and shirts. Some of these killings are accidental, she supposes. However she realizes that most of the guns she sees will kill neither men nor deer. What most men like about Deer Season is getting out in the woods with their sons and brothers. They are having the happiest hours of the year and they will hurt no one as they take part in this American ritual.

Some of their ancestors came to this country for religious and political reasons but others came because they were eager for land and for the freedom to go hunting. In England the killing of a deer was a privilege of the rich and well fed. The poor and hungry could be hanged for it. If you were a thirteen-year-old juvenile delinquent, you could also be hanged for stealing a silver spoon. Or on the other hand you might be sent to the colonies and become the distinguished ancestor of dashing deer hunters. No matter if you were a colonial governor and were painted by Copley, when she heard your gun go off, Mrs. Appleyard would be pro-deer.

The morning deer season started, Roger Willard came to tell her about the big buck whose tracks she had often found near her pond. Once she had seen him on the hill at sunset, rearing up against a silver-green and orange sky to eat wild apples off one of her trees. One day she was walking near the old cellar hole, the site of the first house in Appleyard Center. There are scraggly lilacs there and Lombardy poplars and bright red roses and apple trees, descendants of those planted a century and a half ago. There was also the buck and he nearly knocked Mrs. Appleyard down as he cavorted out of the cellar hole and into the woods.

"This morning," said Roger, "I got to your house about seven. The road was full of cars with guns sticking out the windows. New York cars — quite a few of them."

There is no way to report exactly the tone in which Roger said "New York cars." It is somewhat as if he said "rattlesnakes," accepting them as a manifestation about which nothing could be done.

"A couple from Massachusetts," he added more tolerantly. After all Massachusetts is in New England and Mrs. Appleyard used to live there. "They were parking cars just about anywhere and beating it for the woods. I went round back of the

barn to see if the buck had left tracks around the pond and there
he was, flat up against the barn, watching those Yorkers. You
know the red paint on the back of the barn has faded and worn
off in spots and he kind of melted in it. There was a little mist
rising off the pond — that helped some too, I guess. Anyway
they didn't see him and I swear he looked as if he were laughing
at them. Either he didn't see me or he knows the difference
between a gun and a Stillson wrench. He didn't hurry a mite,
just watched the Yorkers stravaging off into the woods, guns
and plaid pants and red caps and all. Then he had a good drink
out of the pond and went along, not very fast, to the old cellar
hole, having a nap there now, I wouldn't wonder. You think I
ought to paint that side of the barn? There's still some Venetian
red in the barrel."

"No," said Mrs. Appleyard who was delighted to think of the
buck using this background for protective coloration while the
Yorkers, armed to their dentures, trudged through the woods.

Of course, to do them justice, many of them spent much of
the day sociably drinking by the roadside. She saw one trio
playing a few hands of bridge. Or was it poker? Not having
been asked to make a fourth, she is not sure but she feels that the
practice should be encouraged.

She toyed with the idea of putting her outdoor fireplace at
the disposal of hunting parties. For a price, naturally: to raise
money for the PTA. She would have gourmet foods and vintage
wines on sale, pine tables for eating or bridge, a supply of cross-
word puzzles, paperbacks of her own mystery stories and cots
with tartan rugs.

That will keep them out of the woods, she thought, and went
on to plan some good sleep-producing menus.

The Elizabethans served the right sort of meal. Once when
the Earl of Leicester entertained the Queen, there were two

hundred courses. One was lamb "cooked to resemble venison."

I might give the hunters collops of lamb, thought Mrs. Apple-yard. There wouldn't be time to make imitation venison pasty. I'd let them cook the collops themselves. I'd have chefs hats for them — plaid, of course. "Now," I'd say, "just take some currant jelly — "

At this point in her meditation, the telephone rang.

It was Venetia Hopkins reporting that her gun had brought in a haunch of venison. She did not mean that she had killed a deer. She can't even bring herself to shoot a woodchuck that has just eaten most of her green peas. In deer season, Earl Lester (not related to Queen Elizabeth's friend) borrows her gun, a very fine one, and if he gets his deer, he gives Venetia a piece.

Mrs. Appleyard rather likes the phrase "his deer." It suggests that a large buck has Earl's social security number tattooed on it and is leaping around waiting for Earl to shoot it.

"I'll hang it till the weekend and if you'll come over and help cook it, we'll have a party."

Mrs. Appleyard, who is inconsistent enough to like to eat venison when it has become an impersonal piece of meat, says: "Fine. We'll cook it to resemble venison. I'll be right over to plan the menu."

Menu for Deer Season

Celery   Olives   Radishes
Clear Beet Soup†
Roast Venison, Currant-Orange Sauce*
Kasha with Mushrooms*   Green Beans, Garlic Croutons*
Red and Green Peppers, Sautés*
Lemon Soufflé*   Foamy Sauce*
Charmes Chambertin 1953

Roast Venison

Not being obliged to make lamb masquerade as venison, Mrs. Appleyard cooked the venison as she would lamb. It had been hanging for two days in the freezer room. It stood there for two days longer in the covered roaster with the ventilators in the cover open. It weighed 4¼ pounds, all clear meat, no bones. Mrs. Appleyard, after a brief glance into her crystal ball, decided to cook it at 250° and allow 25 minutes to the pound or until the thermometer she had inserted in it registered 145°. She rubbed it all over with melted butter, dusted it very lightly with flour seasoned with pinches of mixed herbs, cinnamon and nutmeg, put it uncovered on a rack in a pan in the oven and left it alone for an hour and three quarters. She says a hot oven dries and toughens venison.

If you feel in the mood to take more trouble and have an eight-pound roast here is another method.

Marinate it for two days in the covered roaster. Pour around it: 1 quart of red wine (Zinfandel), 1 quart fizzy cider.

Add:

6 cloves	5 cloves garlic, put through press
1 teaspoon each, allspice, nutmeg and cinnamon	1 teaspoon mixed herbs, thyme, rosemary, orégano
3 onions, sliced thin	3 cups carrot sticks
bay leaf	

Turn it twice each day. Remove from marinade. Cover it with seasoned flour and slices of beef suet. Put it on a rack in the roaster. Put about a cup of the marinade in the pan. Add more as it cooks away. Cook uncovered at 250° to 145° if you like it rare, about 4 hours for this size piece, or to 155° if you

like it better done but do not overcook it. Gravy may be made
from the juice in the pan. Brown 2 tablespoons of butter, work
in 2 tablespoons of browned flour, remove from heat. Stir in 1
cup of the hot juice from the roaster. Add ½ glass of currant
jelly.

In either of these methods if the roast does not look brown
enough to suit you, run it very briefly under the broiler. Let it
cool slightly while the soup is being eaten. It carves better if it
is not hot from the oven.

Currant-Orange Sauce

1 cup red wine	juice of 1 orange
1 tablespoon thin orange peel, finely cut	½ cup orange marmalade, made from Seville oranges
1 tablespoon thin lemon peel, finely cut	1 glass currant jelly

Mix the wine, orange and lemon peel and orange juice. When
it boils, add the marmalade and the currant jelly and stir until
they melt. Set aside in a warm place until it is needed.

Kasha with Mushrooms

Kasha is one of Venetia's specialties. It is a confusing vegetable to many people. Mrs. Appleyard looked it up in the dic-
tionary and found it defined as barley groats. You may use
groats if you like. Follow the directions on the package. The
kind Venetia used, however, is a kind of cracked wheat. She
buys it from a Syrian shop where they part with it suspiciously.
Apparently something — possibly her blond hair and blue eyes
— make them think she is not a Syrian. She always feels slightly

nervous while buying it, as if a real Syrian might come along and, with one imperious gesture, make her hand it over.

Sometimes she uses a kind packaged under the name of Wonder Wheat or some misspelling of that name. The package contains an envelope full of herbs and spices. It is the opinion of both Venetia and Mrs. Appleyard that these condiments should be discarded or perhaps they could be used to melt snow off the front walk. The charm of kasha is that its own delicate flavor absorbs and complements other flavors. Mrs. Appleyard sometimes buys whole-grain wheat and grinds it herself. This sort of kasha has to be soaked in cold water for 2 hours before the first cooking.

Whatever kind you use, cook it for 5 minutes over high heat, strirring it constantly. Use about 2 cups of water to one of kasha. Then cook it over boiling water for at least half an hour. Turn off the heat and leave the kasha over the hot water. Just before you serve it, set the water under it boiling for 5 minutes.

The mushrooms used with it were caps only, sliced vertically, tossed in butter with finely minced onion for 5 minutes and added to the kasha before its last 5 minutes of cooking. For eight people allow a quart of cooked kasha, half a pound of mushroom caps, a teaspoon of minced onion, two tablespoons of butter.

Green Beans with Garlic Croutons
FOR EIGHT

The beans were Mrs. Appleyard's own frozen beans from her garden. Packaged French-cut frozen beans may be used.

2 packages beans   garlic croutons
½ cup heavy cream   2 tablespoons sour cream
            salt, pepper paprika, to taste

Cook the beans in the top of a double boiler in a small amount of boiling water, about 2 tablespoons to a package. Keep stirring with a fork so that the ice in them will melt as fast as possible. After 6 or 7 minutes, the water should have all cooked away. Add the sweet cream. Set the beans over hot water until serving time. They improve while standing.

In the meantime make the garlic croutons. Cut 3 slices of homemade bread or Anadama white bread into quarter-inch cubes. Toss them in 3 tablespoons of melted butter until they are delicately browned. Sprinkle them with 1 teaspoon garlic powder. Set aside in a warm place. At serving time add the sour cream and seasonings to the beans. Put them in a hot dish. Serve with the croutons sprinkled over them.

Red and Green Peppers, Sautés

Plain green peppers will do but if they are partly ripe, showing some red and orange, they look cheerful. Allow half a good-sized pepper for each person to be served. Split the peppers, carefully clean out seeds and white pulp. Cut the peppers with scissors into long narrow strips. Toss these in melted butter or in part butter and part cooking or olive oil until the edges are brown. Do not overcook. They should be slightly *al dente*. Venetia cooks them in a scarlet and ivory frying pan and serves them in the same pan.

Lemon Soufflé
FOR EIGHT

The lemon soufflé went into the oven when the guests sat down to eat their soup. It takes only a few minutes to mix it and this Mrs. Appleyard did while Venetia was serving the soup and persuading the guests to stop admiring the table and sit down.

This soufflé needs a large straight-sided dish, or two smaller French soufflé dishes will do. In either case before you start beating your eggs, light the oven at 325° and set into it a large dripping pan with a rack in it and about an inch of hot water. Mrs. Appleyard, earlier that day, had made a collar of wax paper to extend the height of the soufflé dish. She uses paper clips to fasten it.

No — she says in response to an impertinent question — she has never found a paper clip in the soufflé but try Scotch tape if you like.

The ingredients are:

8 eggs separated in two bowls,   2 cups powdered sugar, sifted
the yolks in the larger one   4 tablespoons lemon juice
grated rind of 2 lemons

Beat the egg whites stiff. Beat in, a tablespoon at a time, a cup of the sugar. Without washing the beater, beat the egg yolks till thick and lemon-colored. If you use an electric mixer you can get an assistant to beat the yolks while you do the whites. Add the lemon juice and rind to them, still beating. Beat in the rest of the sugar. Fold in the whites. Be gentle but thorough.

Put the mixture into the soufflé dish. Clip on the paper collar. Set the dish on the rack in the pan of hot water in the oven. The soufflé should be ready in 40–50 minutes. This will serve eight generously and how else do you want to serve them?

Foamy Sauce

Mrs. Appleyard has the ingredients for the sauce all ready and when dessert time comes, she makes it. While she performs this congenial task, the guests clear the table. Guests are wonderfully well trained these days. Mrs. Appleyard thinks that one of the happy features of modern times is that no impatient retainer is breathing hard down your neck, ready to snatch your plate before you have finished. Miraculously, on this occasion both soufflé and sauce are ready when the guests are back in their places.

The sauce consisted of:

½ cup butter, creamed	3 egg yolks
1 cup powdered sugar	1 teaspoon vanilla
2 tablespoons sherry or rum if you prefer	

Have the butter already creamed in the top of a double boiler. Mrs. Appleyard uses rather a deep one into which the eggbeater fits well. Set the butter over hot, not boiling water. Beat in first the sugar, a little at a time. Then beat the egg yolks well and add them. Keep beating. Add the flavorings. Beat some more. At the end of 7 minutes, if you arm is still working, the sauce should be light and foamy. Have a warm pitcher that pours well ready. Scrape every drop of sauce into it with what Venetia calls a spendthrift's enemy. Mrs. Appleyard calls it a miser's friend. Actually, if we are going to be literal, it's a rubber scraper.

This dessert was so popular that after the first refined screams of excitement and a few manly growls of approval, it was eaten in a sort of trance. A cook's best compliment, Mrs. Appleyard thinks.

Thanksgiving

IT SEEMED to Mrs. Appleyard that the guns had hardly stopped cracking for deer season when Thanksgiving arrived. She and Cicely served a co-operative meal. The turkey, mashed potato and the giblet gravy were cooked in Cicely's large kitchen. The pies, the vegetables and the cranberry sauce were cooked in Mrs. Appleyard's apartment. By Thanksgiving time she had become so congenial with her new electric unit that she often turned on the proper burners at the right speed and also got them off again without scorching anything.

She still feels rather as if she were piloting a jet plane and it continues to be a happy surprise that the refrigerator and the oven work side by side in perfect harmony, the same current keeping the ice cream cold and the oven hot. She also feels that people smart enough to think up such comfortable co-operation ought to be able to stop shaking fists full of bombs at their neighbors.

"We could just turn it over to the women, I suppose," said her grandson, Tommy Bradshaw, with just a slight tone of skepticism in his voice, "but who will make the pies?"

"I'd trust Mrs. Roosevelt and Mme. Khrushchev to take care of the bombs," Mrs. Appleyard said. "I daresay neither of them has a really light hand with pastry," and she went on rolling out hers. Perhaps this is as good a place as any to tell how she treats that substance.

2000-Layer Pastry

If you like your pastry pale, tough and tasteless, do not follow this rule, which produces a sort of puff paste, tender, brown and flaky. It is easy to make and is better made by amateurs than by experienced pie makers, who are inclined to thump with the rolling pin. You ought not to hear pastry being rolled out, Mrs. Appleyard says.

She learned this method from her grandmother. Her own contribution is a mathematical one. An essential feature of the process is that you keep cutting the rolled pastry into three pieces, turning your board 90 degrees, piling the pieces on top of each other and rolling the paste out again. The first time you do this, you have three layers, the second nine. They increase in numbers so fast that if you cut, pile, turn and roll seven times, you produce 2187 layers. This is enough, Mrs. Appleyard thinks. She has had approximately 20,000 on occasions and once, out of curiosity, she rolled it out ten times which produced — if her arithmetic is correct and please check it and let her know if it is — 59,049 layers. It did not seem to make much difference in the result.

Take:

4 cups all-purpose flour, sift it 3 times. Measure it. Use what is left beyond 4 cups for flouring your pastry board and rolling pin.

Extra flour for rolling out, as little as possible. Use a pastry-board cloth and rolling-pin cover if you have them or put lightly floured wax paper between rolling pin and paste.

1 cup butter, very cold   1 cup lard, very cold
1 cup ice water

Chill beforehand your water, chopping knife and spatula. Mrs. Appleyard keeps a large wooden chopping bowl in her freezer room and uses it to mix her paste in but she has managed with a large chilled pottery bowl.

Put the flour, butter and lard into your bowl. Chop until butter and lard are well distributed through the flour in pieces no bigger than your little fingertip. Add half a cup of the ice water, all at once. Work it well in with your chopper. Add the other cup. Work it in. You now have your paste. Get it out of the bowl and on your floured board with your chopper and spatula.

Roll paste out gently into an oblong about twelve inches long. Cut it in three pieces. Lay end pieces on top of middle one. Turn the board ninety degrees. Roll out paste again, never touching it with your hands, until you have repeated the process seven times. You now have 2187 layers of cold air trapped in the paste.

Mrs. Appleyard now cuts it into chunks the right size for the pies she is planning to make, wraps each piece in wax paper and shapes it into a ball as she wraps it. This is the nearest she comes to touching the paste with her hands. She puts the balls of it into the refrigerator and takes them out the next day and rolls them out as she needs them.

When the heat of the oven suddenly strikes the cold air trapped in the paste, the air expands making the pastry rise to puffy lightness.

After the dinner had been cooked and served from the two kitchens, Cicely and her mother agreed that neither felt as if she had done anything at all. They decided that no house is complete without a kitchen unit in the living room. That is if there is also a living unit in the kitchen, not to mention a table long enough to seat twelve people in front of a big fireplace. Cicely's house provided all these items as well as a red damask tablecloth faded to the color of old Italian brocade for the table, white openwork compotes for mounds of fruit, white ironstone plates and platters embossed with sheaves of wheat. Her mother produced old blue Canton to serve pie on.

The guests were Hugh Appleyard and his family. They have come home from Brazil, where they found a suitable place for the new capital, and are now turning their attention to the United States. Now that Nicholas (eleven months) has joined the organization his grandmother feels sure that the streets of Boston will be cleared of automobiles and given back to the cows, that cities she is too polite to name will have water suitable for drinking, that unspoiled Vermont will remove car graveyards from the lush green foreground of its best mountain views and that our nation's capital will be moved to Colorado. Just give Nicholas time — he certainly has the energy.

THANKSGIVING MENU

Cream of Spinach Soup*
Montpelier Crackers, Split, Buttered and Toasted*
Roast Turkey with Link Sausages*
Chestnut stuffing   Giblet Gravy*
Whole Cranberry Sauce
Green Beans with Mushrooms*   Glazed Carrots†   Mashed Potato
Pumpkin Pie*   Mince Pie*
Vanilla Ice Cream   Cabot Cheese
Coffee   Cider   Pouilly Fuissé Latour 1955

Cream of Spinach Soup

Make this just as you make the Cream of Watercress Soup (p. 44) substituting spinach for the cress. It may be made the day before you serve it all except for the addition of the egg yolks. Reheat it in a double boiler and add the beaten yolks just before you serve it.

Toasted Montpelier Crackers

As Mrs. Appleyard said in *The Summer Kitchen*, she uses the real names of products when she thinks it will help her readers. These crackers have been made by Cross in Montpelier since 1828 and the standard has never been lowered. They may be ordered through the Maple Corner Store, Calais, Vermont. Receipts for using them are on the box. They are fragile and you may find a few crumbs. Use every single one in meat loaf, stuffing or with bread crumbs in au gratin dishes.

When you use them with soup simply split them, butter them generously and put them under the broiler four inches or more from the flame. Remove them, a few at a time, as soon as the butter is a pale golden brown and move the others towards the spot where they brown the most quickly. They should not be dark brown. This takes only a few minutes so watch them all the time. It may be done in the oven but Mrs. Appleyard thinks it is easier to get the right shade of pale gold under the broiler where you can see what's going on all the time. In any case do them ahead of time. They are better if they stand and cool for a while. Of course Mrs. Appleyard has scorched her quota, but the chickadees that come to her feeder relish every crumb.

Roast Turkey

This was a Vermont turkey and just as broadbreasted as if it had come from New Hampshire, New York or Utah. It weighed, ready to stuff, about fourteen pounds. It had never been frozen and it had been kept not in the refrigerator but in a cool room for two days in a covered roaster. Whether a turkey has been frozen or not it is important to have it at an even temperature all through before you stuff it. Be sure to get the giblets and neck out of a frozen turkey as soon as you can so that there will not be an icy spot left in the center. Cooking and mincing the giblets for gravy is something you can do the day before the turkey is to be roasted and you will be glad you got the task out of the way.

Cicely allowed 22 minutes to the pound at 275° and she cooked the turkey uncovered on a rack in a dripping pan until the meat thermometer, thrust into the second joint close to the body, registered 185°. She figured that it would need about 5 hours cooking time. During the last 2 hours she draped links of sausage over the turkey. She had already brushed it all over with melted butter before she put it into the oven. The sausages help to baste it and are delicious themselves with this long slow cooking. When a turkey was thus decorated, Mrs. Appleyard's English father used to call it the Alderman in Chains.

This alderman had enough parsley around it for a wreath for a winner in a Greek race. That's what they used — parsley.

καλὰ σέλινα means beautiful parsley. Mrs. Appleyard, who is teaching herself Greek in her spare time, learned this just in time to tell it to her grandchildren, who brought her an enormous bunch of parsley from her own garden. They promptly offered to make her a wreath of it but she decided that on the whole it would be more becoming to the turkey.

Chestnut Stuffing

Cicely and her mother had stuffed the turkey the night before. Mrs. Appleyard has recently learned a fact of life that she wishes she had known long ago. It is not necessary to shell chestnuts. They come in cans, all cooked. Or — if you are lucky enough to have a good Italian grocery at hand — you can get dried ones. You soak them overnight and cook them until they are soft. Either way is so much easier than that routine of cutting crosses on the shells, of toasting and tossing the nuts in a buttered frying pan that chestnut stuffing is no longer a hard-fought battle.

For this batch Cicely allowed:

3 cups bread crumbs, made of homemade bread, dried and rolled into rather coarse crumbs	1 cup Montpelier cracker crumbs
1 teaspoon mixed herbs	1 small onion, finely minced
½ pound sausage meat	2 eggs, lightly beaten with ½ cup milk
24 chestnuts, each broken into 4 or 5 pieces	

Mix all together. *Never* taste it after you have put in the raw sausage meat. There is still such a thing as trichinosis in the world. Cicely likes a dressing that is rather dry in texture. Add more milk if you like yours moist. You may also use ¼ lb of butter, melted, if you prefer it to the sausage meat.

This is a very lightly seasoned dressing because otherwise you would not taste the chestnuts. If you are not lucky enough to find them, this may be made as a plain dressing in which case you would probably increase the amount of herbs. Remember that the sausage meat has sage in it and that will supply part of the flavor.

Cranberry Sauce

The Appleyards like cranberry sauce with the berries popped and not strained. Mrs. Appleyard buys Massachusetts cranberries and cooks them exactly the way it says on the package. For eight people she uses two packages and cooks them the day before they are to be served, heaps them in her best Sandwich glass compote and sets them in a cool place.

Giblet Gravy

The day before you plan to make the gravy, simmer the gizzard, heart and neck until they are tender, 2 or 3 hours. The last 20 minutes add the liver. Mince all the meat fine, discarding bones and gristle. Use a wooden bowl and a chopping knife. Set the chopped giblets in a cool place. Save the water in which they were cooked in a separate bowl.

The next day when the turkey is almost cooked, take:

4 tablespoons of fat from the roasting pan	pepper from the grinder
1 small onion, finely minced	paprika, salt to taste
minced giblets and meat from neck	2 cups stock from giblets
4 tablespoons flour	2 cups rich milk
	2 tablespoons finely scissored parsley

In a large iron frying pan put the fat and sauté the onion in it. Add the minced giblets and cook over low heat stirring constantly until the mixture begins to brown. If it has absorbed all the fat, add another tablespoonful. Mix flour and seasonings and sprinkle over the mixture, blending them in well. Add gradually, while stirring, the stock. When the mixture begins to thicken, blend in slowly the milk. (In the city use 1 cup milk and 1 cup thin cream.) This may now stand until you are ready to serve it. Heat it up, put it in hot bowl, sprinkle parsley over it.

Green Beans with Mushrooms
FOR EIGHT

2 packages frozen French-cut beans	1 tablespoon flour
1 teaspoon minced onion	½ teaspoon paprika
2 tablespoons butter	salt to taste
½ teaspoon nutmeg	½ cup cream
1 pound mushrooms, caps cut vertically, stems sliced thin	2 tablespoons sherry (optional)

Every now and then Mrs. Appleyard tries to have a Thanksgiving or Christmas dinner without this vegetable but her grandchildren, hardened gourmets when still in their high chairs, protested. Make these ahead of time and keep them in a double boiler till they are needed. They improve with standing.

Cook the beans in a small amount of water until they are tender but not mushy. Do not overcook. Put them in the top of a double boiler. Sauté the onion in the butter till it is straw-colored. Add the mushroom caps and stems and cook 4 or 5 minutes, stirring well. Sprinkle over the flour mixed with the seasonings, blend it in. Do this over very low heat. Add the cream, let it get hot but not boil. Add the mixture to the beans and stir well.

Just before serving reheat, add more cream if necessary. Add the sherry. Serve.

Variations on a theme:

Perhaps this is as good a place as any to mention that this combination of mushrooms, onion, butter, cream and seasoned flour may also be used with:

Broccoli	Lima Beans
Brussels Sprouts	Shell Beans

Mix the mushroom sauce — that's what it really is — with the cooked vegetable. Let the mixture stand over hot water till needed. Mrs. Appleyard likes the flavor of sherry with the green beans and lima beans but not with the other vegetables. You may like them all better without.

THANKSGIVING PIES

In Mrs. Appleyard's youth her grandmother always had a large chicken pie as well as the turkey. There used to be three other kinds of pie too. Mrs. Appleyard has fallen far below this standard. She considers chicken pie an event in itself and she made only two kinds of pie for dessert — mince and pumpkin.

Mince Pie

If you have a large hungry family, a big covered crock and a cool place to keep it in, it is worthwhile to make mincemeat yourself. Do it at least a week before Thanksgiving. It mellows as it stands. Vermonters sometimes use venison for the meat but beef is excellent in it.

3 pounds round of beef, simmered till tender, about 5 hours and chopped, rather fine	2 pounds seedless raisins
	2 pounds currants
	1 pound seeded raisins
1 gallon fizzy cider	1 tablespoon cinnamon
Tart apples, twice as much bulk as you have meat, measured after they are pared and quartered and after the meat is chopped	1½ tablespoons nutmeg
	¼ teaspoon clove
	2 teaspoons allspice
	1 tablespoon extract of lemon
1 pound suet, chopped	2 lemons, juice and grated rind
1 pound citron, chopped	3 cups brandy
¼ pound each candied orange and lemon peel	2 pounds sugar
	1½ cups stock from meat

When you chop the meat, remove any pieces of gristle. Do not put meat through the grinder. Use a wooden bowl and a real chopper. While you are chopping the meat let the water in which it was boiled cook down so that you have about a quart of good stock. Also put the cider on to cook until the gallon cooks down to 2 quarts. Measure the chopped meat. Fix twice as much chopped McIntosh apple. Chop and mix in the suet. Moisten the mixture with a quart of the cooked cider. Cook the citron and peel in the other quart for ten minutes. Strain. Add them to the meat. Add currants, raisins, spices, lemon extract, lemon juice, rind and sugar. Add the meat stock. Put the whole mixture in a heavy kettle. Cook for 2 hours over very low heat. Stir carefully from the bottom now and then. Moisten occasionally with the rest of the cider. During the last half hour the mixture should be thick enough so it will absorb the brandy. Do not add the brandy if the mixture is too moist. As it stands it should dry slightly and absorb the mixture. Add more brandy if needed just before you make the pies.

If you do not feel in the mood for this adventure you have Mrs. Appleyard's permission to do what she plans to do this year: buy S. S. Pierce's mincemeat, heat it slightly and add some brandy the day before you use it. Cover and let it stand in a cool, not cold, place overnight.

Actually if she were not writing this book she would be making mincemeat herself. She says there is something restful about it. During much of the process you can be writing letters, making a miniature Chippendale chair, reading Gibbon's *Decline and Fall of the Roman Empire* or just watching evening grosbeaks eating sunflower seeds. Mince pie contains everything necessary to the nourishment of the human system. So do sunflower seeds, but on the whole Mrs. Appleyard prefers mince pie. The house smells wonderful and breathing the spicy steam from the cooking mincemeat is good for you.

"In what way?" inquires one of her grandchildren, a scientific type.

"It's good for — well, for sinus trouble," Mrs. Appleyard says.

"But you don't have any," objects her relative.

"That's why," his grandmother says firmly and goes on to the subject of

BAKING MINCE PIES

You have plenty of pastry on hand, of course. It may be in a package, in which case follow directions exactly and you will get a perfectly edible pie in which Mrs. Appleyard wishes she could take more interest.

She herself has suitable portions made the day before (as on p. 60) in the refrigerator. They are wrapped in wax paper. The larger balls are for the bottoms of double crust pies or for pie shells. The smaller ones are for top crusts.

Flour your board slightly, also your rolling pin. Gently roll out a circle of paste at least an inch larger than your pie tin. Add a few extra dots of butter. Place your tin face down on the paste and mark a circle an inch larger than the tin around it. Cut out your circle. Save the scraps left over. Touch the paste with your hands as little as possible. Using a cold spatula and pancake turner, fold your circle in quarters, and lift it to the pan. Unfold it. Press it against the sides of the pan. You'll have to use your fingers for this. Put the lined pan into the refrigerator while you roll out the top crust. Chill the scraps too. Now roll out one of your smaller balls. Fold in quarters. Snip it with scissors in three places to make gashes through which steam can escape. Light the oven: 450°. Fill the pan generously with mincemeat. It will settle while cooking. With a pastry brush, moisten the edge of the lower crust with ice water. Put on the top crust. Fold the lower edge up over the top edge and press crusts lightly together with a fork. Return pie to the refrigerator for 5 minutes while you roll out the scraps you saved. Cut the rolled paste into strips. Twist two strips together and lay the twist around the edge of the pie. Make a bowknot of any pieces left and lay it on top of the pie.

The whole thing is going to puff and brown delicately and melt in the mouth. It is not going to remind anyone of our great and admirable plastics industry.

Start the pie on the lower shelf of the 450° oven and bake 30 minutes. Move it to the top shelf. Reduce heat to 350°. It may take another half hour to brown it enough. Serve it hot with vanilla ice cream and wedges of Vermont cheese. If there is any left, it's also good cold.

Mrs. Appleyard has been known to bake a mince pie the day before and have it cold and also have one hot. The cold pie was a tribute to Mr. Appleyard's ancestors who brought plenty of frozen pies with them when they came to Vermont from Massachusetts with an ox team over a blazed trail.

It took Mrs. Appleyard about a quarter of a century to realize that she could have her pie hot if she liked and that the operation Deep-Freeze customers could enjoy theirs too.

She also learned from Mr. Appleyard's mother how to make

Pumpkin Pie Filling

This is also something that you do the day before you are going to bake your pie.

Mrs. Appleyard likes to use fresh pumpkin from a small sweet "pie" pumpkin from her own garden. She says this is largely a sentimental idea and that to be perfectly honest she can't tell it from canned pumpkin properly treated.

The treatment consists of buttering a large iron frying pan and cooking the pumpkin pulp — either freshly steamed or canned — until the natural sugar in it caramelizes and it is a deep golden brown in color. It should be as dry as mashed potato. This process takes your complete attention: no chess, no bird watching, please. Stand right there and, with a large wooden spoon, turn the pumpkin over and over so that every part of it comes in contact with the hot pan from time to time. Do it over medium heat. You are trying to make it a uniform brown not a kind of palomino with black spots.

From time to time steam will puff out of it. Stir those steaming spots well from the bottom. Drying out pumpkin in the oven is not a substitute for this top-of-the-stove process. In the oven the pumpkin just dries on the outside and is still moist inside. It takes only about 20 minutes to cook 2 cups of watery pumpkin down to the 1½ cups of the dry golden substance that you need for baking two pies.

Mix:

1½ cups caramelized pumpkin	1 cup cream
2 tablespoons flour	1 teaspoon cinnamon
1 cup sugar	½ teaspoon ginger
1 teaspoon butter	½ teaspoon nutmeg
3 cups rich milk	2 eggs

Put the cooked pumpkin into a bowl. Sprinkle it with the flour. Add sugar. Stir till the flour vanishes. Butter a saucepan. Pour in the milk. Scald it but do not let it boil. Add the cream and the seasonings. The Appleyards like it lightly spiced so that they can still taste the pumpkin. Increase the seasonings if you like the pumpkin concealed by a dark smog of spice. Add clove and allspice, chile tepines and curry powder for all Mrs. Appleyard cares — it's your pie, isn't it? ("Relax," says Cicely at this point.)

Her mother relaxes and says that you mix the sugar with the pumpkin, pour the hot milk and cream and spices over the pumpkin mixture and then add the well-beaten eggs.

You are supposed to have two pie shells ready. (For pastry see p. 60.) They should be nicely fluted around the edge or with a braided strip laid all around the edge. Do not fill the shells too full: three quarters of an inch is about right. The filling will expand slightly in baking. Bake only what you will use that day. Both filling and pastry will keep in the refrigerator until you need them. Put one-inch strips of gauze, slightly moistened, around the edges of the pies. This will keep them from browning too fast before the filling is cooked.

Bake in a preheated oven at 450° for half an hour. Reduce the heat to 325° and bake them until the crust is well browned and they just shake in the middle when moved — about 15 minutes longer. Or test the filling with the blade of a silver knife, delicately inserted. When the pies are done, it comes out clean.

Old Home Day

JUST because Mrs. Appleyard has officially changed her residence from Woodbrook Green in Massachusetts to Appleyard Center in Vermont it does not mean that she feels no responsibility for her native state. She still has to check up on the Symphony from time to time, visit the gentlest yet firmest dentist in the world, have the heels of her shoes made straight and her hair made crooked and buy a hat that will be like her other hats, yet different. Accordingly she was much gratified when the McNabs asked her to visit them for a few days. The people who bought her house were delighted to take the McNabs along with it and give them kitchen privileges so she would be a visitor in the house where Washington once slept.

When she finished packing her car the contents may safely be called unique. Who else travels with seven favorite cookbooks, frozen vegetables from a Vermont garden, a Burberry coat thirty-three years old, four pens with which no one else in the United States including Puerto Rico can write, eight pounds of fruitcake, Volume Two of the *Decline and Fall of the Roman Empire*, materials for making tinsel pictures and a large box containing what are simply called The Papers?

These are filed according to a system peculiar to their owner in envelopes of various shapes and sizes. Seeing them, librarians shudder briefly and then brighten up, for they remember that Mrs. Appleyard once thought of joining their profession — but didn't. If she had, some library, like her box, might contain an envelope marked "Ideas — not for anything special." Perhaps the escape was not narrow but it was certainly fortunate.

There was a light frost, crystallized dew really, the night before Mrs. Appleyard started south. It steamed off the sunny sides of fence posts and telephone poles but lay in the shadows of pointed firs marking their silhouettes in silver on the lion-colored grass. Fir trees themselves had their own dark needles pointed with sparkling needles of hoarfrost, each one a rainbow. Every blade of grass, every dried stalk of mullein or golden rod or milkweed was its own private prism, its own burning glass.

Burning, she thought. Something has really burned.

She saw through smoke the blackened shell of a barn. Hay bales still steamed. Tools saved from the fire had been hastily piled in an untidy heap. A few desolate cattle stood near it quietly and their owner stood hopelessly looking at them. His hands were thrust into his pockets. His coat collar was turned up against the raw, smoky air. The place used to look like a Currier and Ives print. Now it was Vermont Tragedy, one too often repeated. The owner might collect insurance, but the life that had gone into building up his farm was blowing away with the smoke.

The two hundred miles of road slipped quietly away. The car seemed to know every turn. It was only two o'clock when it stopped in front of the square white house on Woodbrook

Green. Mrs. Appleyard gave a brisk look around the green and saw that everything was normal: small boys scuffled in the sport locally known as pig-piling or hung upside down on gates. Small girls told them what they ought to be doing. This display of wisdom was checked by the appearance of Mrs. Appleyard. Both sexes converged on her car and began to unload it. Soon a train of native bearers had carried everything to the front porch and sat there eating Vermont apples.

They dashed back to the green as the sightseeing bus zoomed past the statue of General Washington. Visitors who come to see the sights of Woodbrook Green are innocently unconscious that to young Woodbrookians these foreigners are one of its sights. Their numbers, costumes and cameras are carefully checked. Their habit of glancing listlessly at the church steeple and appraising it as "cute" is noted for imitation later. Their questions are politely if inaccurately answered.

Mrs. Appleyard looked on in pleasure. Like the visitors she had forgotten that she too is one of the sights. Suddenly one of the group left the shadow of Washington's horse and plunged across the green. In no time at all she had Mrs. Appleyard's hand in a warm, adhesive clasp and was saying: "When the children told me who you were, I just had to come and tell you how I *love* your books. I always feel so *safe* when I'm reading one."

Mrs. Appleyard, who writes what she has always supposed was a spine-tingling type of mystery story, was not quite sure if she had received a compliment. However, like any author, she was made happy by the idea that people read her books or indeed used them for any purpose — to keep a door open, hold up other books, hold down papers, prop up a window. Everything that wears a book out is good. Sometimes a reader loses a library copy and has to replace it. Mrs. Appleyard gazed in a benevolent glow at the possible consumer of literature and thanked her for her kind words.

"What are you writing now — or is it a secret?" her reader asked coyly.

"Just a cookbook and I really must unpack the manuscript," Mrs. Appleyard said, detaching her hand before writer's cramp set in.

"Now don't put any arsenic in the soup!" said her reader, shaking a finger as she started back for the bus.

This piece of advice gave Mrs. Appleyard several ideas but she decided not to file them in that mysterious envelope. She merely picked up the box containing The Papers and made her entry, an easy matter since on Woodbrook Green no one locks doors. She could hear that someone was exercising kitchen privileges.

The dishwasher was making a noise like waves dashing against a lonely lighthouse in a northeast gale. The whistling kettle whistled. The blender was blending and the mixer was mixing. The washing machine groaned under its load and disgorged the soap it did not need upon the floor. It looked as if it were standing in a meringue. Stewart McNab (eighteen months) had paved a section of the floor with muffin tins and was filling them with soapsuds. This takes good co-ordination but Stewart is a remarkable child, as indeed, by some coincidence, are all Mrs. Appleyard's grandchildren, legal and adopted.

The kitchen was deliciously perfumed with chocolate. Three layers for a cake were cooling on the table. The beaters of the mixer were darkly immersed in fudge frosting. Moira McNab, who was operating the mixer, had her back to the kitchen and her face to the window and such chrysanthemums as had survived the dimpled hands of young nature lovers.

It was one of them, Stewart McNab in fact, who first saw

Mrs. Appleyard. Having no bagpipe handy with which to greet her, he picked up a roll of aluminum foil and blew a loud and soapy blast through it. Moira spun around and found Stewart and Mrs. Appleyard happily beaming upon each other. With his bright red cheeks and bright brown eyes, Stewart could be used to advertise any brand of soap or cereal. As if to prove it, he flung himself in his new shirt of the McNab tartan right into the suds-meringue and came up with a package of bite-sized crunchy rainbow goodness which he offered to Mrs. Appleyard.

Both she and Moira were laughing by this time.

"I'm sorry you have such a noisy welcome," Moira said, turning off some of the instruments of the orchestra.

"I love it," Mrs. Appleyard truthfully stated. She added, to Stewart, "Bhan oidhch an oidche na'm bu ghillean na ghillean," and received a suitable reply through the aluminum trumpet.

In case you have not brushed up on your Gaelic lately, this remark — Mrs. Appleyard says — means: "The night is the night if the lads were the lads." It refers to the time when some McNabs, always an active, decisive clan, it seems, were planning an outing to cut some of their neighbors' heads off. As they were discussing the matter over a haggis with usquebaugh, the McNab of that ilk said to his twelve sons, "Bha'n oidch' an oidche na'm bu ghillean na ghillean" and of course the night *was* the night and the lads were the lads so the story had a happy ending — for the McNabs anyway. Judged by Stewart's appearance, they must have been a fine sight in their tartans of orange red and reddish orange and two shades of green, with their sporrans and their dirks and sprays of heather stuck in their bonnets.

I ought to make Stewart a sporran, Mrs. Appleyard thought. I wish I hadn't let that coonskin coat get made into so many

Davy Crockett hats when they were in style. It would have been just the thing.

"One or two of the neighbors are coming in for dessert to-night," Moira said.

"You mean I'm going to get some of that chocolate cake — wonderful!" said Mrs. Appleyard. "I brought some white fruit-cake. It doesn't keep as well as the dark kind so we'd better use some tonight. It would be too bad if it spoiled. What can I do to help?"

Moira said that there wasn't a thing. She would mop the floor and they'd have supper early so she could get Stewart to bed and then Mrs. Appleyard might like to rest. Mrs. Appleyard realizes that nothing makes a visitor so popular as taking long rests and she was so tired after her drive that, soothed by a few paragraphs of Gibbon, she went sound asleep. Two hours later she became conscious of people being very quiet in the front hall and of doors being carefully shut. Such stillness is always peculiarly resonant so she got up and was dressed when Moira knocked at her door.

The pseudo silence suddenly ceased. Mrs. Appleyard emerged from her room into waves of talk and laughter and firelight, into a delicious blend of coffee, Chanel No. 5, hot chocolate sauce and white wine punch. Everywhere she looked — in the North Parlor and in the library, in the kitchen where men, true to the prerogatives of their sex, stood in all seven doorways while wives dodged around them, in the dining room where candle-light glowed upon a galaxy of desserts — were graduates of her kitchen and its privileges.

For a moment it was touch and go whether Mrs. Appleyard would burst into tears or not. Fortunately the Carroll twins hurled themselves out of the crowd and fell upon her just in time so that she banged her ankle bone sharply against a fine

old Boston rocker. A combination of pain, joy and surprise —
the twins were supposed to be in Oregon — braced her to reveal
merely joy.

She took a long breath and rapidly decided which was which.
Yes, Sam had an extra dimple and Pete a small scar on his forehead acquired in a fall down the front stairs, so she attached the
correct names to them. Always an original thinker, she did not
mention that they had grown even though their blond crew
cuts and blue eyes were unexpectedly high in the air.

Sam said: "I remember that dress."

So did everyone who had known her five years, Mrs. Appleyard supposed. Her friends often say: "I always liked that
dress," in a way that seems to imply that they must have seen
the design in *Godey's Lady's Book* for 1868.

Pete Carroll, more contemporary in mood, said politely, "And
I love your shoes."

So does Mrs. Appleyard.

It was a happy day when she discovered Celestial Swans ("the
shoes of featherdown that float or fly"). They are comfortable,
they are chastely chic, they build morale. It is obvious that the
feet in them belong to a Republican, an Episcopalian (occasionally a Unitarian), to a Friend of the Symphony, to a reader
of the *Atlantic Monthly* (through bifocals), to a member of the
Horticultural Society, to an admirer of Picasso (she thinks he's
modern) and to a member of the English Speaking Union. It is
not true that she had to show her birth certificate to the sales-
man. Why should she when on her wrist is a gold chain dripping with little gold disks with her grandchildren's initials and
birthdays on them? She sees her dentist twice a year. She does
not know a psychoanalyst. She owns a Vermont tweed suit
and a scarf made of five minks. One of them, in the battle of
life, has probably lost an eye.

Celestial Swans come in many colors and textures. Mrs. Appleyard could have exhibited a fine variety but she chose the sedate well-polished blue pair with the silver buckles. She was much pleased when the twins got down on the floor and tried to see their faces in them.

Their mother, Allison Carroll, detached them from this task and led Mrs. Appleyard to the dessert table, so she could see it while it was a still life. They were none too soon. Blades of shining silver already approached the succulent array of cakes, tortes, cheese cakes and trifles. There was ice cream and sauces to put on it, but ice cream had changed its social position in Mrs. Appleyard's lifetime. It no longer sits coldly upon the pinnacle of gastronomy.

She can remember when it came only from a well-known caterer's and so seldom that special plates were used for it. When the first plate was set down, the children all began to shiver and start their teeth chattering. Their favorite kind was macaroon with orange sherbert. Macaroons baked within an hour came along with it. This combination was eaten in what was known as the ice-cream silence.

Soon dawned the day of the home hand freezer. People followed rules from Philadelphia or the White Mountains, happy places where the inhabitants were supposed to live chiefly upon this delicacy. The result of several hours' cranking came to the table in a sturdy cylinder skidding around in a blue Canton dish. On top of it was a tiny upward-pointing finger of ice cream showing where the crank was while the freezer had been whirled for an hour in ice and salt. Sometimes ice cream tasted of salt but children ate just the same.

Mrs. Appleyard's father used to say: "Those children would eat glue if you froze it!"

Actually, the truth of this remark was not tested until his

great-grandchildren's youth. By that time ice cream contained little of such indigestible substances as cream and fresh fruit. It is now often constructed of good health-giving milk solids, gelatin (a form of glue), dried eggs, emulsifers, cornstarch, lecithin with artificial colors and flavors. These are guaranteed by the United States government, which seems to know a lot about such things, if that's any virtue.

However, it is still possible to buy ice cream made out of cream. There are a few things that the atomic age has not yet spoiled. Mrs. Appleyard hereby confers a gold medal on a few of them: Howard Johnson's ice cream (her favorite is pistachio), Bailey's coconut cakes, Baker's cooking chocolate, Gilchrist's golden macaroons (still baked fresh every hour), Underwood's deviled ham, Royal Riviera pears and Cross's Montpelier crackers. This being a beautiful morning when blue and white snow is bright under a white and blue sky, when maple trees are fans of white coral lightly dusted with crushed diamonds, when pointed firs are white pyramids outlined with invisible green, she is in a pleasant mood and she is not going to mention what has happened to a lot of other foods: just read the labels for yourselves.

With this sinister and sadistic suggestion, she turns her thoughts again to the dessert party. It is a good kind of party, she thinks. Neither hosts nor guests have to give their children knockout drops so as to be there in time: they can bring them along. If it is a co-operative party, like this one on Woodbrook Green, no one has to work very hard although it is evidently a point of honor, Mrs. Appleyard observes, that the desserts should be handmade and not in any blithe fifteen minutes. The kind made out of a package and tasting like the package was conspicuously absent from the table.

"I feel as if I were at a party in a Jane Austen story," Mrs. Appleyard stated. "Syllabubs, quivering jellies, trifles, floating island! Who could ask for anything more?"

Indeed she found it necessary to ask for less. A real helping of all these delights would have run to 5000 calories, she estimated roughly. By special permission she was allowed to pave her plate with a mosaic of small cubes of many colors. With plenty of white wine punch this menu was stimulating at the moment and soothing later.

Dessert Party Menu

Almond Ring*   Upside-Down Caramel Custards*
Glazed Strawberry Cheese Cake*   Pistachio Marron Trifle*
Floating Island*   Fudge Layer Cake with Marshmallows*
White Fruit Cake*   Coffee

Almond Ring

Mrs. Appleyard has given out this information before but as she is still asked for it, she repeats it here. She is proud indeed of the alumna (Woodbrook, K.P. '58) who succeeded in turning out a perfect ring in spite of three children and a thesis to type for her husband.

Spry for greasing mold	1 cup sugar
2 Zwieback rolled very fine, sifted, rolled again	6 ounces almonds, blanched, chopped fine or ground
whites of 5 large eggs	through medium cutter
1 teaspoon almond extract	of grinder
8 candied cherries	

Use a circular mold that will hold a quart. Don't use a fluted one or you will rue the day. The mold should be perfectly smooth. A glass one is best but they are not easy to find.

Begin by greasing the mold thoroughly with Spry. There must be no bare spots. *None*. Not *any*. (Is that clear?) Pour in your powdered Zwieback and tip the mold around till every bit of it is coated. Light oven: 325°. Beat egg whites to a good froth. They should be slippery and sticky rather than fluffy. Add almond extract. Fold in alternately sugar and chopped almonds. Pile lightly and evenly and bake for ½ hour or till the top looks like a macaroon. Remove from oven. Press cherries lightly on top. Let stand exactly one minute. Loosen with spatula around the outside edge, pushing spatula gently underneath as far as it will go. With a thin flexible table knife, loosen it carefully around the inner edge. Invert the ring at once on a cooky sheet. Even with the most careful handling, you may find that a small piece has stuck to the mold. Grieve not but tailor it back into place neatly. Now invert the ring again on your serving plate. This will bring it macaroon and cherry side up. Mrs. Appleyard sometimes blanches and browns a few extra almonds and alternates them with the cherries. With it she serves in a separate bowl vanilla ice cream with frozen peaches and raspberries but other flavors go well with it too.

Fudge Layer Cake with Marshmallows

It seems pretty unfair to Mrs. Appleyard that her daughter Cicely first advised her to go on a diet and then asked her to write the rule for "that chocolate cake — you know, the one with the marshmallows lurking under the frosting." Mrs. Appleyard knows all right and it would not take much persuasion to get her to put on her cherry-colored smock and start baking

one of the things; not to mention retiring into a corner immediately afterwards and eating most of it.

Ah well! Into each life some rain must fall and out of each
life a certain number of chocolate cakes had better fall too.
Just be sure this one lands right side up.

2 cups cake flour, sifted
  before measuring
3 teaspoons baking powder
4 squares Baker's chocolate, un-
  sweetened: melted with 2 teaspoons water over hot water
1 cup brown sugar
1¼ cups milk

3 egg yolks, well beaten,
  large eggs
1 teaspoon vanilla, or — if you'd
  rather, 3 drops of peppermint
½ cup butter
1 cup white sugar
3 eggs whites, beaten stiff
24 marshmallows

Light oven: 350°.

Sift flour three times with the baking powder. Grease two
9 × 9 layer tins. (Increase quantities by one half if you make
three layers: use five small eggs.) Flour pans very lightly, just
the thinnest veil. To the melted chocolate add the brown sugar,
half a cup of the milk and two of the egg yolks. Cook this mixture over hot water stirring all the time till it is like thick custard.
Remove from heat and cool. Add flavoring. Cream the butter
and the white sugar, add the remaining egg yolk, well beaten,
with the rest of the milk, add the cholocate mixture alternately
with the flour, beating well. Fold in the stiffly beaten egg
whites. Spoon lightly into the pans and bake until it shrinks
from edge of the pan and springs back in the middle when
touched with the finger — about 35 minutes.

Remove from pans. Pave each layer neatly with marshmallows which you first cut in halves horizontally and dip briefly
into cold water. While the cake is cooling and amalgamating
itself with the marshmallows, make:

Fudge Frosting

⅓ cup light cream	2 tablespoons butter
4 squares Baker's unsweetened chocolate	1 teaspoon vanilla or 3 drops of peppermint extract
1 egg	2 cups confectioner's sugar

Put the light cream and the chocolate in the top of the double boiler and stir until chocolate melts. Cool to lukewarm: stir in the egg unbeaten. Beat in the butter. Add the flavoring. Add the sugar, 2 cups, or more if necessary to make it the right consistency to spread. Put the layers of the cake together — they should be almost cool. Have triangles of wax paper on your serving plate. Place the cake where the points meet. Swirl the frosting over the cake. Remove the papers. No doubt someone will be at hand to lick the surplus frosting off them and scrape the pan.

If you flavor the cake with peppermint, you might like to try covering the layers with white peppermints instead of marshmallows.

"Couldn't they be any other color?" inquires one of Mrs. Appleyard's grandsons.

They could indeed, a whole rainbow. However, if Mrs. Appleyard gets absent-minded about that diet, they will be white. Marshmallow or peppermint, pink, yellow or green, if it is half as good as Moira McNab's masterpiece, all will be well.

Upside-Down Caramel Custards
FOR SIX CUSTARD CUPS

1 cup white sugar	4 eggs, well beaten
1 quart milk, part cream	1 teaspoon vanilla

Put a few drops of water in each cup. In an iron frying pan, caramelize the sugar over medium heat. Have the milk and cream heating over hot, not boiling water. Do not scald the milk or you will have trouble when you add the caramel. Be sure to stir caramel thoroughly and get all the lumps out of it. It should be a rich dark golden brown syrup. Put a little into the bottom of each cup. Add the rest very slowly and carefully to the warm milk. If you are not careful, it will foam up and go all over the stove. (How did Mrs. Appleyard find out this interesting fact? We can't imagine.) Stir well. When there is no undissolved caramel in the milk, set the mixture aside to cool while you beat the eggs. Beat them well, then pour the caramel mixture over them and beat some more. Add the vanilla. Light the oven: 350°. Put a rack and some hot water in a baking pan. Fill the custard cups. Set them on the rack. Bake until custard is set — about 25 minutes. If you put the mixture all in one dish it will take almost an hour to bake. Serve cold. The caramel makes the sauce for it.

Glazed Strawberry Cheese Cake

1 cup wheat germ, mixed with
   ½ cup sugar
¼ teaspoon nutmeg
1 pint cottage cheese
⅓ cup light cream
½ cup heavy cream
2 teaspoons vanilla

1 8-ounce cream cheese
4 eggs, separated
1 tablespoon flour
1 cup sugar
1 large box frozen strawberries, defrosted
1 glass currant jelly

1 tablespoon instant tapioca

Use a 9 × 13 Pyrex oblong dish. Butter it well and coat it with the wheat germ mixed with the ½ cup of sugar and the nutmeg. Save about ⅛ of the mixture for topping.

Light oven: 300°.

In the mixer put the cottage cheese and the light cream and beat till smooth. Add the heavy cream, vanilla, cream cheese, egg yolks, flour and sugar and blend well by hand. Beat egg whites stiff but not dry and fold them in gently.

Put mixture in the coated dish. Top it with the remaining wheat germ mixture. Bake one hour. Cool.

For the glaze:

Strain 1 cup of juice from the defrosted strawberries. Add 1 glass currant jelly and cook till jelly is melted. Add instant tapioca. Cook over hot water till clear — about half an hour. Cool until it begins to thicken. Top cheescake with the drained whole berries. Add glaze spooning it over each berry. Chill.

Pistachio Marron Trifle

2 dozen lady fingers	½ cup candied fruit (orange
½ cup currant jelly	peel, lemon peel, citron)
24 marrons in syrup	½ cup peach brandy
12 almond macaroons	½ cup pistachio nuts

Custard:

6 eggs	4 cups scalded milk
½ cup sugar	1 teaspoon almond extract

Raffetto's marrons either in vanilla or brandy-flavored syrup were as good as ever last time Mrs. Appleyard had them. However, at the moment she has taken to making her own and she tells how on p. 291. The pistachios are shelled. She mentions this because a very sophisticated and elegant friend of hers encountered them in the shell and almost wrecked one of the extremely efficient homegrown set of teeth that she has had for a certain number of years. Her host, hearing the crunching sound, commented admiringly: "I would certainly like to see what you would do with a peck of steamed clams in the shell."

Mrs. Appleyard makes her own peach brandy but perhaps you spent your summer in some more intellectual way such as sailing your boat or trudging through the Louvre, so she advises you to buy a bottle. She says it's better than hers anyway. Or a little Cointreau will do.

Make the custard first so it will be cooling while you arrange the trifle. Beat the eggs until yolks and whites are well blended. Use a wire whisk or a fork. Beat in the sugar. Pour the scalded milk over the mixture, stirring all the time. Cook over hot but not boiling water until the mixture thickens. This takes about 10 minutes and the mixture must be stirred often from the bottom of the pan. Remove it from the hot water as soon as the custard coats the back of the spoon. It will curdle if it is left too long. Add flavoring. Chill. The friend whose trifle Mrs. Appleyard is describing colors the custard delicately with a little green coloring. She says this makes it taste more like pistachio. Mrs. Appleyard does not guarantee this psychology but says that the trifle looks very handsome in a big glass and gold bowl.

Arrange lady fingers thinly spread with currant jelly around the inside of the bowl. Put in a layer of marrons, quartered, six macaroons cut in eighths, some of the candied fruit. Mix the syrup from the marrons with the peach brandy or Cointreau and sprinkle it over everything, put in another layer of ladyfingers and repeat the process till the bowl is filled. Pour the custard over everything and sprinkle the top with the pistachios. Set the bowl in a cold place for several hours. Whipped cream may be used as a decoration for the top just before serving but it isn't really necessary.

Floating Island

This innocent dessert used to be a favorite with children. Could it be that children were more innocent than they are now? At present it seems to be grownups who like it. This should be served in a large rather shallow bowl so there will be room for plenty of islands.

Meringue:

8 egg whites	1 quart milk, scalded
⅓ cup sifted granulated sugar	½ cup sugar
½ teaspoon vanilla or almond	

Custard:

scalded milk from the meringue recipe	8 egg yolks
½ teaspoon vanilla or almond	½ cup sugar

Make the meringue first. The egg whites should be cold and put into a well-chilled bowl. Beat them to a stiff froth and beat the ⅓ cup of sifted sugar into them. Put the milk into a shallow pan, add the vanilla and half a cup of sugar, let it come to a boil. Drop in heaping tablespoons of the meringue. Use half of it and poach the "islands" over low heat for 3 minutes on each side. Remove them with a skimmer and drain on a paper towel. Repeat with the other half of the meringue.

Now the custard:

Mrs. Appleyard has heard from several readers that the remark "coats the back of the spoon" annoys them. They say they can't tell where it is coated and that it makes them nervous. Anyone in this critical mental state, Mrs. Appleyard says, had better use a candy thermometer and cook the custard to 175°.

She herself finds the back-of-the-spoon technique less nerve-racking, says it makes her feel more like a Norn or a wise woman of the tribe. Well, everyone to her taste.

Use the milk in which you poached the meringues. Taste it. Add more flavoring if needed. Strain it through a very fine sieve on the beaten egg yolks. Put the mixture into the top of a double boiler. Cook it, stirring carefully until it coats — excuse it, please: to 175°. This happy moment might occur in about 5 minutes. Pour it into that cool shallow bowl. Mrs. Appleyard uses a Chinese one with green and yellow dragons on it. Put on the islands. Sift a little sugar over them. Chill till serving time.

White Fruitcake (S.H.L.)

½ pound each candied citron, orange peel, lemon peel, and cherries
½ pound pitted dates, cut fine
2 pounds seedless Sultana raisins
½ pound dried figs cut fine with scissors
1½ pounds blanched almonds, slivered (keep 24 whole for decorating)

juice and grated rind of two lemons
2 teaspoons almond extract
½ cup brandy
1 pound each of butter and sugar
4 cups flour
12 eggs
½ teaspoon nutmeg

Put fruit and almonds in a bowl. Pour lemon juice and rind, almond extract and brandy over it. Let it stand while you cream the butter very smooth and work in half the flour. Separate the eggs. Beat the yolks till lemon-colored and beat in the sugar. An electric mixer is a great help in such a project. Light the oven: 300°. Sprinkle the rest of the flour and the nutmeg over the fruit mixture. Beat egg whites stiff. Combine in a large bowl the flour-butter and egg-sugar mixtures. Fold in alternately the floured fruit and the egg whites. Put into greased and lightly floured tube pans. Bake till testing straw comes out clean, about 4 hours. If in one large pan without a tube, it will take longer — perhaps 5 hours. Reduce heat if it browns too quickly.

This is perhaps the right moment for Mrs. Appleyard to express her opinion on the subject of straws for testing cake. A dry clean straw is undoubtedly the best cake tester but where do you get them? The old-fashioned way was to pull one out of a broom. It was washed perfunctorily or not at all. Mrs. Appleyard has seen this method practiced but it never appealed to her.

Luckily her garden — a rather elaborate name for her two hollyhocks, phlox of many colors, chiefly magenta, and such cinnamon pinks as the deer left during November — grows a sturdy variety of grass, Tall Timothy, to be exact. Only the toughest kinds of plants can survive Mrs. Appleyard's inky thumb. She harvests her Tall Timothy with care, leaving plenty for next year, peels it and dries it. It is not only cleaner than a broomstraw — it is straighter, smoother and stronger. She also uses it for picture moldings in her miniature rooms when she has to frame anything. She never sweeps anything with it. She keeps it in a red glass vase from the Chicago World's Fair of 1892, right above the kitchen sink. Help yourself, any time.

December

Apartment Warming

WHEN she used to live alone in the house on Woodbrook Green, Mrs. Appleyard's friends were always telling her she ought to move into a nice little apartment. They did not approve of her version of living alone, which was to fill the house with medical students and their wives and give them kitchen privileges. It is true that two charming young couples "without encumbrance," as landlords so kindly put it, came to live with her when the men were medical students and that when they went away, as competent and impressive doctors, they took with them seven active children including twins. No doubt an apartment would have been more peaceful but not nearly so much. fun.

One mathematical fact not always understood by the general public, though it's really very simple, is that as soon as a child can crawl it begins to make friends. Modern children are bright and frighteningly healthy with vitamins and anti-this-and-that shots and all that good advice from Dr. Spock and they begin to crawl early. So if you have seven children on the lawn you soon have fourteen. And then more. It gets to be rather like that 2000-layer pastry of Mrs. Appleyard's. Only the numbers increase faster because mothers come too.

It is only fair to say that some of them simply dash in and state: "You wouldn't mind my leaving Archibald here, I hope," and, pausing not for a reply, make a beeline for the League of Women Voters while Archibald is still hitting high C. It is remarkable, Mrs. Appleyard says, how quickly a child stops screaming after his mother has gone; how soon he turns to snatching up any flowers imprudent enough to open their petals that morning.

Of course in December he is more likely to be whanging a fire engine against a Chinese cabinet. It was in spring that someone heard Mrs. Appleyard utter the inhospitable wish that tulips had thorns. She says that in a leisure moment (when was that, Mrs. Appleyard?) she has designed a childproof garden, bright with rugosa roses, cactus, barberries and thistles, those large thistles with the very long spines. When it was pointed out to her that she was the one who was so good at pulling out thorns with tweezers, she invented the Child Picker.

This machine is rather like a cotton picker, only larger and stronger of course because children are so hard on machinery, which would pick up small flower snatchers and drop them into a child pound. One wall of this enclosure would have a row of buttons on it. The child would be able, by pushing the proper ones, to get chewing gum, chocolate bars, lollipops, Mrs. Appleyard's oatmeal cookies and other soothing and adhesive substances.

Traces of these could be removed by his mother when she returned from her civic work. Luckily for such a project, Mrs. Appleyard had a coronary and put in a downstairs bathroom. Several of the mothers of Woodbrook Green say they don't see how they ever got along without it.

The Child Picker would also have an attachment for removing velocipedes, tricycles, scooters and stuffed tigers three feet long from steps, walks and porches. Mrs. Appleyard says there would be a fortune in such a machine. Questioned closely, presumably by someone who wanted to get in on the ground floor as to just how stock in the Child Picker would compete with — say — that of a breakfast cereal loaded with tranquilizers, she replied that mothers would pay well to get the children back, or anyway the velocipedes.

"Why would they?" asked her possible financial associate who just happened to be the father of some of the stickiest of the children who were riding around in circles screaming.

He seemed to have a point there so Mrs. Appleyard took up painting on velvet.

She had always said she would sell the house on Woodbrook Green when the right people came along. After she had been leading her pleasant communal life for ten years, the right people did and soon afterwards she arrived in Appleyard Center preceded by a van containing a number of things. She had wondered how the truck would get into her yard. It turned out to be quite simple, really. The driver backed the trailer in knocking down two gateposts and plunged across the lawn, which was like green velvet only mushier, making its own road.

The men then swiftly put the furniture into the carriage house, dropping an eighteenth century girandole here, a Chippendale mirror there and drove back to Massachusetts.

Mrs. Appleyard was now a year round Vermonter.

As soon as she had mended the mirrors, using the lost-wax process to replace some eagles, which she thinks must have been eaten by the movers, she began to plan her apartment.

In summer rugged Vermonters sleep under blankets and send annoying postcards saying so to such tropical spots as Boston. Really prudent residents use electric blankets, with a few un-wired ones at hand in case the current goes off. Naturally every summer night Mrs. Appleyard thought of winter and she joy-fully accepted Cicely's invitation to have an apartment in her warm house. There were two bedrooms and a bath and her mother, she said, could do whatever she liked with them.

Seeing her mother's eyes flash with delight at this remark, Cicely was not much surprised one morning to find Roger Willard making a large hole in one wall of the house.

"Your mother says this is going to be a sun trap for her bed-room," Roger informed her. "There's going to be one in the living room too. Bay windows, I call 'em."

Roger also insulated floors and covered them with cork tiles, painted woodwork white and walls a delicate sea-blue-green, built shelves for china and cupboards for saucepans. He also told Mrs. Appleyard what programs to watch on TV and gave her some useful suggestions for baking drawn from his experience as an army cook. ("Take 100 pounds of flour, 58 pounds of water and a pound of yeast . . .") He also found what was wrong with the power steering of her new car ("some dope put the cover on crooked when he checked the oil") and fixed the antenna of her FM radio. Nor is this all, but perhaps it is enough to show why Mrs. Appleyard enjoys his company.

Naturally he was present when her electric kitchen was put in place. This ingenious device has three burners, an oven, a broiler, a double sink and a refrigerator with a freezer compartment all in about the same space occupied by an ordinary chest of drawers.

She planned a menu for her apartment-warming that would demonstrate its happy versatility.

Seafood Chowder*   Toasted Montpelier Crackers
Ham Mousse*   Mustard Sauce*
Corn Pudding*   Tossed Salad (p. 147)
Deep-Dish Apple Pie*   Vanilla Ice Cream
with Vanilla Ice Cream   or   with Chocolate Sauce*
Coffee

She was up early the day before the party. She was planning to make the Ham Mousse, the pastry for the pie and the chocolate sauce. She has recently worked out a way to make it so that it can either be heated up or served at room temperature. It does not get sugary and too thick but stays so it can be poured easily if you just keep it on top of the stove where your grandchildren can get it when necessary.

She had even got out her package of chocolate and had found — as Cicely deduced later — that she didn't have enough. That indeed was as far as the preparations for the apartment warming went.

It was a wonderful day as she started for River Bend, a day with the mercury almost touching zero and a coating of fresh diamond dust over snow that had been melting the day before. Every tree had its shadow sharply cut out of thin blue glass lying on the ground below it. Barns glowed red against the snow. The ring of mountains was a dark blue wall, white topped against the cloudless sky. At the schoolhouse the new flag with its fifty stars looked brighter than any flag Mrs. Appleyard had ever seen as it echoed the red, white and blue theme in its own key. Blue jays flashed screaming across the snow. The sun was bright on the heads of a flock of red polls.

The Appleyard Center roads were freshly sanded but as she crossed the town line she found glare ice. She slowed to a cautious crawl keeping far to the right, close to the snowbank. She had almost reached the top of the long hill that twists for two miles down into River Bend when a truck came speeding towards her in the middle of the road. The driver had room to pass but he jammed on his brakes and skidded towards her in a fierce deadly curve.

So Mrs. Appleyard spent the evening of her apartment warming in her favorite hospital. She had a poached egg for supper and some excellent prunes. In a few days she and her cracked ribs returned to Appleyard Center. Her car was demolished so she has not been back to River Bend yet to get the shrimps for the chowder. However, since this is a cookbook and neither a clinical study nor a report to the State Police, she supposes there is no reason why she should keep secret the way she makes the dishes on her menu.

Seafood Chowder
FOR EIGHT

¼ pound beef suet	3 tablespoons cold water
3 medium onions, minced	8-ounce tin of frozen lobster
6 medium potatoes, sliced thin	1 pound shelled, cleaned and
½ teaspoon garlic powder	frozen shrimp
1 teaspoon mixed herbs	2 8-ounce tins of minced clams
¼ teaspoon nutmeg	3 cups rich milk
1 teaspoon paprika	2 cups light cream
3 pounds haddock fillets, frozen	sliced lemon
2 tablespoons flour	Montpelier crackers

An electric skillet is good to make and serve this in but a big gaily colored enameled iron frying pan will do.

Cut the suet into very small dice and try them out in the frying pan over low heat until they are crisp and a light golden brown. Remove them with a skimmer and drain them on brown paper till you need them. Cook the minced onions in the fat until onion is transparent and straw-colored. Pare the potatoes. Slice them less than a quarter of an inch thick. Pour 1½ quarts of boiling water into the skillet. Put in the potatoes and mix them well with the onions. Sprinkle in the seasonings, except the parsley. Lay in the haddock fillets cut into 4-inch pieces. Cover pan but let some steam escape. Cook about 15 minutes. Water should cook down to about a quart. Now turn off heat. Put the flour in a cup. Add the cold water to it, stirring till smooth. Salt to taste. Strain it through a fine strainer into the mixture. Stir it in well.

The basis of your chowder is now ready and you may set it aside in a cool place to mellow. Several hours will do no harm. Just before you serve it, heat it to boiling point and add the lobster and shrimp, which have slowly defrosted in the refrigerator. Cut the largest pieces of the lobster in medium-sized pieces. Leave shrimp whole. Add the minced clams. Check the time. When liquid boils again, cook mixture 5 minutes. Heat milk and cream so they are just scalding. Add them to the mixture. Taste it and add more seasoning if you like. Do not let the chowder boil after you have added the milk or it will curdle. Put in the suet cubes. Add the minced parsley.

Pass the lemon slices and Montpelier crackers, split, well buttered and delicately browned with it.

Ham Mousse
FOR EIGHT

1½ tablespoons plain gelatin	¾ cup cream
2 tablespoons cold water	2 teaspoons dry mustard
¾ cups hot water	1 teaspoon horse radish (optional)
3 cups ground ham	⅛ teaspoon cayenne

Soak gelatin in cold water 5 minutes. Dissolve in hot water, stirring till it is free from lumps. After grinding the ham — be sure there is no gristle or fat in it — pound it in a mortar till it is smooth. Add gelatin and the seasonings. Whip cream till stiff and add it. Have a mold ready with cold water and ice cubes standing in it. Empty it and put in mousse. Chill in refrigerator for at least 3 hours. When unmolding, set the mold for about 10 seconds into hot water, wipe dry and invert it on serving plate.

Mustard Sauce (C.B. & M.C.)

1 pint heavy cream	salt to taste
½ cup sugar	⅔ cup vinegar
4 tablespoons dry mustard	2 egg yolks

Heat half the cream and the sugar over hot water. Add mustard and salt mixed with the vinegar. Beat egg yolks slightly. Add some of the sauce to them, about 3 tablespoons, one at a time, mixing well. Add the egg mixture to the sauce. Stir it in carefully and cook until it thickens slightly — 2 or 3 minutes. Cool. Before serving, whip the remaining cream and fold it in.

Everyone will say: "*What* makes this mustard sauce so delicious? So much better than mine?"

Mrs. Appleyard, having asked these questions, has gratefully received the directions above.

Corn Pudding

This is best of all made from corn picked fresh from the garden, but either corn from the freezer or whole Golden Bantam from a can may be used successfully.

6 tablespoons melted butter	3 eggs
¾ cup cornmeal	2 cups rich milk
1 cup boiling water	2 teaspoons baking powder
1 cup corn	

In a baking dish that will hold a quart and a half — Mrs. Appleyard likes an old brown Bennington one best — melt 2 tablespoons of the butter. Scald meal with boiling water, right from the kettle. Stir it well with a spoon with holes so there will be no lumps. Add the rest of the butter. Stir till it melts. Beat eggs lightly, add the milk and beat some more. Add the baking powder, beat the mixture into the cornmeal. Add the corn, cut from the cob, or slightly thawed if frozen, or drained if in a can. Stir well. Have the oven ready at 375°. Put the mixture into the warm, buttery baking dish. Bake 35–40 minutes.

Reduce heat to 350° after the first 10 minutes. It should be golden brown on top and have a brown crust on the bottom of the dish.

Mrs. Appleyard likes it cooked so that the center is still rather soft. Other members of the family cherish the brown crust especially but they seem on the whole rather amiable about eating it the way they get it.

Deep-Dish Apple Pie

Make 2000-Layer Pastry (p. 60) the day before you plan to make your pie and set aside a ball of it of suitable size to cover a large dish. This is Mrs. Appleyard's favorite apple pie. There is no problem about the under crust being properly baked because there isn't any. If you choose a dish about twelve inches across and not too deep — three inches perhaps, you get a good proportion between apple and pastry.

2 cups sugar	12 tart Vermont apples
1 teaspoon cinnamon	1 tablespoon butter
⅛ teaspoon cloves	juice of ½ a lemon
1 teaspoon nutmeg	½ teaspoon grated lemon rind

Mrs. Appleyard suggests that you measure the spices carefully and mix them evenly through the sugar. She says it's better not to use any than to scatter them casually about. Perhaps you may prefer different proportions of nutmeg and cinnamon but anyway measure them and don't overspice. You should be able to taste the apples.

Pare the apples. Quarter them. Remove cores and seeds. Slice rather thin. Butter the dish well. Put in a layer of apples, sprinkle them with spiced sugar, repeat layers of apples and sugar till the dish is full. Dot the top layer of apples with butter, sprinkle with lemon juice and rind and any sugar there is left. Apples should be well heaped up because they will settle.

Roll out the pastry gently and cut a circle of the size needed, a little larger than the dish. Moisten the edge of the dish slightly. Fold the circle of paste in quarters, gash it with scissors. Lay it on the dish, centering it carefully, and unfold. Pinch the paste into a neatly fluted border. Take any scraps of paste left and roll them out into an oblong. Cut this into narrow strips. Twist them into a chain and lay it around the pie just inside the fluted edge. Mrs. Appleyard uses the last scraps to make bowknots. She makes two loops and lays them on one side of the pie, then two tails with the ends cut diagonally and a piece across the middle to conceal the place where ends and loops join. Then she makes another for the opposite side of the pie. When the paste rises and puffs, it looks as if the bowknots had really been tied.

After indulging in this innocent pastime, she chills the pie for a few minutes while she is heating the oven to 450°. Put in the pie. After the first 10 minutes reduce the heat to 425° or less if it seems to be browning too quickly. Bake it until it is puffed and delicately brown. Serve it either hot with vanilla ice cream or cold with cheese.

Perhaps someone doesn't eat pie. Mrs. Appleyard with her genial Puritan inheritance can hardly understand this but there are such cases. If one arises give the customer some of the ice cream and

Chocolate Sauce

4 tablespoons butter	1 cup hot water
4 squares Baker's unsweetened chocolate	2 cups sugar
	2 teaspoons vanilla

In the top of a Dutch iron enamel double boiler, put the butter and melt it over low heat. As it melts, add the chocolate and stir till it is melted. Add gradually the hot water. Then stir in the sugar. Cook over low heat, stirring all the time, until every grain of sugar is melted and the sauce thickens — about 5 minutes. This will keep at a good consistency over hot, not boiling, water for some time and will keep so that it can be poured at room temperature. Just before you serve it, add the vanilla.

Well, you can see that Mrs. Appleyard's intentions about her apartment warming were good. If she gets a new car and road conditions seem favorable, she still intends to go to town and get those shrimp and make some chowder.

Candlelight

Perhaps Appleyard Center is not really busier at Christmas time than New York or Boston. Probably, Mrs. Appleyard admits, it just seems so. Everyone is taking part in the holiday. They are all cutting their own Christmas trees, hauling their own Yule logs, making their own wreaths. When you hear Christmas carols, it is not because they have been piped into a shop to promote customer acceptance: the 4-H club is practicing them, sometimes more than one at a time. The sound of sleigh bells is rarer than in New York, where they are broadcast from every shop in magnificent silvery peals, but when you hear them, they are real sleigh bells, two at least, and they are on a real horse. He does not look much as if he had dashed out of a Currier and Ives print and the bells have a deliberate, almost serious sound. He is a sedate brown horse with a thick winter coat. It harmonizes well with the ancient buffalo robe that his master has wrapped around himself and the boys.

Less in period are the boys in their cowboy suits. Davy Crockett hats and guns in belts hardly seem to Mrs. Appleyard appropriate symbols for a New England Christmas but of course, she says, our culture is a complex one, and if it had been left to the passengers on the *Mayflower* we wouldn't have Christmas at all. She notes with pleasure that the boys are as red-cheeked and bright-eyed as if they came out of an advertisement for one of the tastier forms of toothpaste and that they have their skating boots with them. Frank Flint has dammed up the brook back of his house and the water has spread out and frozen into a pond that looks greenish blue against the snow. Shrill screams are coming from it, making it sound rather as if blue jays were skating, but it is only happy children. Girls do most of the screaming. A pond full of boys never sounds quite so excited.

It reminds Mrs. Appleyard of Rockefeller Center — it's so different. No one is waltzing to "The Beautiful Blue Danube." No one is looking on. Everyone is scrambling over the ice in white jackets and red ones, white boots and black ones, caps, mufflers and mittens of all colors. None of these costumes was designed by *Vogue* but the occupants don't seem depressed about it.

Close to the pond is Frank's red barn. In the barnyard a big bay horse, a small white and brown pony and some Black

Angus heifers are out in the winter sunshine. Their winter coats look as thick and plushy as if they had been woven on one of those machines that make mink by the yard. They seem to be quietly enjoying the skating. Dogs of course are skating too, or anyway pretending they are as they run and bark among the skaters. There are three Norwegian elkhounds, two bandy-legged beagles and a golden cocker. A black saddle horse and a silvery gray burro are hitched to the fence. The burro is adding his braying laugh to the noise from the pond. The horse preserves a dignified silence.

The sun slipped suddenly behind the hill, leaving snow glowing on the mountaintops and turning white birch trunks pink. The moon's coppery gold disk floated up out of Frank's sugar place.

It's going to be a fine evening for the carol singing and for the Davenport's Open House, thought Mrs. Appleyard. I must go and pack my marzipan.

When they got to the church, Fairfield Davenport already had fires going in both the iron stoves that send their long pipes stretching through space and warming it. The stoves were a modern improvement made about 1830. Up to that time people used foot stoves with coals in them or — even more primitive — a freestone in a wooden box with holes in it. You heated the stone in the brick oven and carried it to church in a box. Mrs. Appleyard rather wished she had brought Remember Appleyard's freestone. The fact that heat rises occurred to her.

The old square pews were beginning to fill with people dressed in their warmest clothes. Like the cattle in their winter coats, they looked a size or two larger than usual. Candles lighted the church warmly downstairs and their reflections sparkled in the many-paned windows in a pattern of black and white and gold. Above the high pulpit was a misty, smoky twilight.

Through it Mrs. Appleyard could just make out the letters on the wall: "Remove not the ancient landmark that our fathers have set."

Most of the woodwork in the church is of unpainted pine that has mellowed to a soft brown, but the pulpit, the top edges of the pews and the gallery are all painted a misty blue rather like the smoky air above them. The last time it was painted was before Mrs. Appleyard was born. Her husband, then ten years old, remembered how he and his father, as a gift to the church, mixed blue paint as near as they could to match the old and made everything fresh and clean. An earlier generation of Appleyards had hewed timbers for the building and sawed primeval pines into boards for the pews.

They certainly, Mrs. Appleyard reflected, chose the hardest pine they could find.

The seats were now well filled. Joyce Madden sat down at the organ and the carol singing began. The service was a simple one. Fair Davenport read the Christmas story from St. Luke, pausing often for an appropriate carol. Most of them were sung by the whole congregation but there were some for the choir alone. Mrs. Appleyard however sang them all but not so anyone could hear. She is, fortunately, an internal singer. Every word and note is clearly formed in her mind but the outer voice is someone else's, one of her grandchildren's perhaps or a daughter's or a neighbor's. She knows them all as well as if they were woodwinds in the Symphony, piccolos, flutes, oboes, clarinets and the loud bassoon.

After the singing in the church was over, the 4-H Club and a few valiant parents went singing around the village. They walked to the very edge of it where Robin Viereck lives with only his Nubian goats and his fiddle for company. He came out onto the porch with his fiddle and played while they sang. The goats came out too and tap-danced to "God rest ye merry, gen-tlemen." When the carols were over he struck into "Portland Fancy" and everyone square-danced in the snow.

Back in the Davenports' big red house the ladies of the village were helping Eleanor unpack and set out the different things that had been brought to the Open House. Eleanor herself must have been working for days to make the wonderful display of sugar cookies in all the Christmas shapes — stars, trees, angels, sheep and shepherds. She had made brandy balls too and tiny meringues; not to mention, of course, feeding her family, making the house beautiful for company and conducting choir re-hearsals. By the time the carol singers began stamping snow off their boots, the long table was ready. These were some of the things on it.

Sugar and Spice Cookies*   Pecan Brandy Balls*
Oatmeal Lace Cookies*   Marzipan Fruit*
Dark Fruitcake*   Swedish Cookies*   Baked Fudge Brownies*
Hot Spiced Cider*   Coffee

Sugar and Spice Cookies

From the following rule, Eleanor Davenport confided to Mrs. Appleyard, she had made ten dozen cookies.

2½ cups flour
½ teaspoon nutmeg
pinch of allspice
1 teaspoon cinnamon
¼ teaspoon cloves
½ teaspoon baking powder
1 cup butter

1½ cups sugar
2 eggs
½ cup flour for rolling out, less if possible
2 tablespoons cream
pink and green sugar for sprinkling

Make the cookies in the mixer. Do not substitute anything for the butter or neither flavor nor texture will be right. Sift the flour three times. Measure it, sift it again with the spices and baking powder. Cream the butter, add sugar gradually, beating all the time. Mix eggs and cream together and beat them in well. Stir in the spiced flour. Chill the mixture one hour. Light oven: 375°. Remove enough dough for a batch of cookies. Keep the rest chilled. Roll it out using as little flour as possible. (Mrs. Appleyard finds it helpful to cover the rolling pin with a paper towel. She fastens it on with Scotch tape.) Cut the cookies in fancy shapes. Put them on a buttered baking sheet. Handle them with two spatulas. Sprinkle some with green sugar, some with pink. Bake about 8 minutes. Do not over-bake.

Pecan Brandy Balls (N.F.L.)
MAKES THIRTY-TWO

½ cup butter	1 cup pecans, finely chopped
¼ cup granulated sugar	1 tablespoon brandy
¾ cup flour	½ cup confectioners' sugar

Cream butter, beat in sugar, flour, nutmeats. Add the brandy. Light oven: 300°.

Press mixture into a square pan 8 × 8. Cut it into 32 pieces. Make each piece into a ball. Sugar your hands lightly with confectioners' sugar while you do this. Put the balls on a lightly greased cooky sheet. Bake 30–35 minutes. They should not brown except where they touch the pan. Remove from the oven. While they are still warm roll them in confectioners' sugar. Cool. Roll them in confectioners' sugar again, using extra if necessary. Keep them in a tightly covered tin box between layers of wax paper. These keep well, so they can be made two or three days before they are used. They do not, however, Mrs. Appleyard notices, keep well at the party. So make plenty.

Oatmeal Lace Cookies (P.B.)

As soon as Mrs. Appleyard saw these she realized that her friend Patience Barlow had been at work. Mrs. Appleyard invented the formula for these about a quarter of a century ago. With her grandchildren's interests at heart she still makes an occasional batch. Some of them are larger than others. Some are usually slightly scorched around the edges. It is Patience who turns them out uniform in size and shape and of a golden lacy color and texture that Benvenuto Cellini might have equaled if he'd felt in the mood and had enough gold on hand.

Mrs. Appleyard was recently given a present that she is much pleased with, a copy of the latest edition of *Clara Carpenter's Cook Book*. For Clara Carpenter, Mrs. Appleyard feels a kind of awe and veneration. Mrs. Appleyard — it seems hard to believe this — was a small child once and her grandmother, Mrs. Elmore, went to Miss Carpenter's cooking school.

The food that emerged from Mrs. Elmore's kitchen, which had a polished range rather like a baroque pipe organ, a sink of Vermont soapstone and tables covered with red and white damask, was excellent but then, according to Mrs. Appleyard, it was so before Mrs. Elmore ever crossed Miss Carpenter's threshold. Apparently Miss Carpenter conferred a sort of mystic Phi Beta Kappa upon her graduates. The possession of it enabled them to sit serenely at Louis Quinze tables in their libraries with sunlight, tempered by stained glass, falling upon rubber plants and marble busts. They were dressed in black satin basques trimmed with velvet and jet. Their caps were of velvet and rose-point lace. They read the works of W. D. Howells and Mrs. Humphry Ward while in their kitchens young ladies who had recently been treading the heather in the highlands broke Lowestoft cups and made Lobster Newburg and vol-au-vents of chicken and oysters under Miss Carpenter's inspiration.

Mrs. Appleyard admits that this picture is slightly idealized. Her grandmother was supposed just to relax among the bric-a-brac. Her daughters considered that at her advanced age (about five years younger than Mrs. Appleyard's at present) this was how she ought to spend her time. Actually, as soon as her daughters left the house to attend to their whist, charities, golf and music Mrs. Elmore would put on a layer or two of aprons and interpret Clara Carpenter to her minions. Moreover it was she who rolled out the pastry for vol-au-vents.

Miss Carpenter's cookbook was a dingy green volume then. Now it has burst into pale pink and turquoise blue. Mrs. Appleyard was much flattered to find included in it, though without mentioning the source, her rule for oatmeal lace cookies exactly as it was given in a book called *Mrs. Appleyard's Kitchen* in 1942: not exactly fame but certainly a nice tribute.

Time however has marched on and that's not exactly how Patience Barlow and she make the cookies now. They have kept experimenting and this is their present formula.

    1 cup butter, melted   2¼ cups regular rolled oats
    2¼ cups light brown sugar   1 tablespoon flour
    1 tablespoon white sugar   1 egg slightly beaten
    1 teaspoon vanilla or, if you prefer, ½ teaspoon almond extract

Before you begin to mix them please note that: quick-cooking oats will not do. You can get regular ones if you insist. The sugar must be light brown. It may be called Golden Brown on the package. That is all right but dark brown will not do. Use butter: margarine will not do. Don't try to make half the rule unless you beat the egg, measure it and use half of it. A messy business and what do you do with what's left? Throw it away? Not in New England. (It seems rather elaborate to get a veal cutlet, so you can dip it in egg and then in crumbs, doesn't it?) Anyway you'll be sorry you did not make the whole batch. They keep well in a tightly closed box between layers of wax paper. Don't try to make them on a hot, humid day with a falling barometer. A clear, crisp blue and white morning is what they prefer.

In a saucepan large enough to hold the whole mixture, melt the butter over low heat. When it starts to froth a little, stir in the sugar, brown and white. Remove pan from heat. Stir in the oats and the flour. Let the mixture cool for at least 5 minutes. This is important. Add the beaten egg and vanilla. Light oven: 375°. Set the mixture in a cool place while the oven is heating and while you fix your pans.

Patience Barlow has baked these circles of golden lace on various kinds of cooky sheets. Heavy ones are best, she says. Better still are old-fashioned iron dripping pans. Grease them lightly with the paper the butter was wrapped in and a small amount of butter. After the first batch is baked it will not be necessary to grease the pans again. Mrs. Appleyard used to keep three pans going. She now finds that two will serve to keep her mentally active.

Put the mixture on the pans by teaspoonfuls, pushing it off the spoon in small circular lumps, leaving plenty of room for the cookies to spread. Seven or eight is about all most pans will take. Fill a second one as soon as the first is in the oven. It takes about 7 minutes to bake them. Watch them carefully. They should be deep golden brown on the edges.

Getting them off the pans needs a little deftness. Let them

stand one minute. Use a spatula and a small pancake turner. Keep testing the edges with the spatula. When the edge of a cooky turns up easily, slide the pancake turner under it and remove it to a large platter. Don't put cookies on top of each other. As soon as they are completely cool, put them in a large tin box with a tight cover with layers of wax paper between and try to hide it from your grandchildren till dinnertime. This rule makes about fifty-two cookies but the smell usually attracts volunteers who are glad to help by eating any that are scorched or broken. If you get forty-six into the box, you have done well.

Marzipan Fruit

Last year Mrs. Appleyard made marzipan fruit for her grand-children. This year they took over the shaping and coloring of the fruit so all she had to do was to supply the marzipan. She made it the day before it was to be used.

The ingredients are:

2 6-ounce packages shelled almonds	3 egg whites, unbeaten
3 cups confectioners' sugar	1 tablespoon soft butter
¼ teaspoon cream of tartar	3 teaspoons pure almond extract
extra confectioners' sugar	

Blanch the almonds. Skin them. Dry them on cooky sheets covered with paper towels in a 250° oven for 15 minutes. Put them on fresh paper towels and let them cool. They must be thoroughly dry. Grind them. This can be done by putting them through the finest attachment of your meat grinder. Mrs. Apple-yard prefers to use her small active Dutch coffee grinder. It makes a noise like a jet plane and reduces a handful of almonds to dry powder in 15 seconds. You can do only a small amount at a time but in a few minutes you will have about 3 loosely packed cups of almond powder.

Now mix the remaining ingredients into what is really un-cooked fondant. Sift the confectioners' sugar with the cream of tartar. Work in the egg whites one at a time, add the butter and the almond extract. Then mix in the powdered almonds. A pastry blending fork is a good tool for mixing the fondant. Next dust a board with confectioners' sugar, dust your hands lightly with sugar and knead the marzipan thoroughly. It should be quite stiff. Wrap it in wax paper and chef's foil and set it in a cool place.

Next day fix your palette of vegetable coloring — Mrs. Apple-yard uses a large white platter for this — and get out your paint-brushes, which should be kept especially for this purpose. Have at least three brushes and three glasses of water to wash them in. Change the water frequently so that your colors will stay clear. Put first on your palette red, yellow, green and violet. Mix orange (red with yellow), carrot color (yellow with a touch of red), pear color (green with a very little red), brown (red and green), strawberry color (red with a touch of yellow).

Shape the marzipan into apples, pears, bananas, strawberries, carrots, peaches, peapods — half open and showing the peas — and potatoes.

Have at hand whole cloves, bits of candied angelica for leaves and strawburry hulls and a mixture of sugar, cocoa and cinna-mon to roll the potatoes in. If angelica is not available, cut the strawberry hulls out of heavy green paper. In either case fasten the hulls on with the small ends of toothpicks dipped in green or brown coloring. Toothpicks are also useful in modeling.

Apples. Dilute yellow coloring and paint them all over. Put a little green around the stem end. Paint one cheek red. Add a few red stripes. Use a clove for the blossom end.

Pears. Dilute yellow and paint all over. Paint one cheek with your pear green and touch the other with red. Use a clove for the blossom end. Fasten on leaves with a brown stem.

Carrots. Paint with carrot color. Touch top with green. No leaves or stem.

Tangerine Oranges. Make little pits all over the surface with the fine point of the toothpick. Paint deep orange color all over. No leaves or stem.

Peaches. Paint yellow, not diluted. Paint one cheek with red just touched with violet. Fasten on leaves with brown stem.

Bananas. Paint with diluted yellow. Stripe and dot with brown and touch end with green.

Peas. For both the partly opened pod and peas inside, use diluted green.

Strawberries. Paint all over with strawberry color. Dot with green seeds. Fasten on hulls with green toothpick stems.

Potatoes. Make depressions with the blunt end of the toothpick. Touch these with brown. Do not paint the rest of the potato, but roll each one in the sugar, cocoa and cinnamon mixture.

Mrs. Appleyard packs assortments of these art objects in strawberry baskets lined first with chef's foil and then with crumpled green tissue paper. She says you can produce a basketful rather quickly, if you organize your workers so that one makes potatoes, for instance, and another specializes in strawberries. However she never seems to have much luck with the assembly line technique, partly perhaps because she doesn't much like to practice it herself. After all, Christmas is hardly the time when an overseer should march up and down among the workers cracking a whip. Her marzipan factory will probably remain inefficient.

However, the results look gay and taste good, the way they did when she was a child. This is not true of the handsome basket she bought for models. By a strange coincidence marzipan made of cracker crumbs, flour, dried egg whites, corn syrup and artificial flavoring does not taste like the real thing. Obviously Mrs. Appleyard has been indulging in the morbid pastime of reading labels on packages. Let us turn to happier things such as

Dark Fruitcake

Mrs. Appleyard ate a piece of fruitcake and said to her daughter, "Why, this tastes like my grandmother's Huckleberry Gingerbread!"

"That," said Cicely, "isn't really so very peculiar. Your granddaughter Camilla made it from your grandmother's rule."

Mrs Appleyard never felt prouder than when she thought of Camilla at eleven years old mixing the following ingredients:

4 cups sifted flour	½ teaspoon soda
1 pound seeded raisins	1½ cups butter
1 pound currants	3 cups sugar
¼ cup citron	6 eggs, separated
½ cup walnut meats (optional)	½ cup dark molasses
1 teaspoon nutmeg	1 cup milk (or ½ cup strong
1 teaspoon clove	coffee and ½ cup brandy)
2 teaspoons cinnamon	

Sift flour. Measure it. Flour fruit and nutmeats (if used) with half a cup of it. Sift the rest three times with the spices and soda.

Cream butter, work in sugar, sifted. Beat well. Add egg yolks, beaten thick. Mix molasses with whatever other liquid you use. (Mrs. Appleyard uses brandy and coffee.) Add liquid alternately with the flour. Add the floured fruit. Beat egg whites stiff and fold them in.

Bake in a large round graniteware pan, lined with buttered brown paper and waxed paper for 3 hours at 275° for the first hour and at 250° the rest of the time. Have a pan of water on the bottom of the oven. This keeps the bottom of the cake from cooking too quickly. You may also bake it in separate loaf pans. It will not take quite so long. The cake should shrink from the sides of the pan and one of Mrs. Appleyard's special cake testers should come out clean.

Baked Fudge Brownies

For a 9 × 13 pan:

1½ cups butter (3 sticks)	3 cups sugar
6 squares chocolate	1½ cups flour
¼ cup warm water	6 eggs, lightly beaten
3 teaspoons vanilla	extra sugar (about ¼ cup)
1 8-ounce can walnut meats, broken	

Melt butter, add water, chocolate. When chocolate is melted and well mixed with the butter add the sugar, beat well, cool. Flour the nuts with ½ cup of the flour. Beat eggs with wire whisk so that they are well blended. Light oven: 350°. Add eggs to the chocolate mixture, beating well. Add the flour and the nuts. Put the mixture in a lightly greased and floured pan. Scatter the ¼ cup of sugar over the top. Bake until it shrinks from the pan, is crusty on top and firm to the touch in the center:

about 40 minutes. Do not overbake. Chill. Mark into 48 squares. Do not try to remove brownies from the pan until they are really cold.

Swedish Cookies

To make these get a Swedish cooky press and follow the rule that comes with it exactly. Mrs. Appleyard thinks this piece of equipment well worth having. The cookies are delicious and a large number can be made in a comparatively short time, much more quickly than if they are rolled and cut.

Spiced Cider

To a gallon of cider allow:

| a 4-inch stick of cinnamon | ½ teaspoon allspice |
| 12 whole cloves | ½ teaspoon cinnamon |

Let the cider stand with the spice in it for at least half an hour. Bring it to the boil in a large kettle but do not boil it. Ladle it into pottery mugs. A gallon serves sixteen.

The stamping of snow off feet, the piling of overshoes in the woodshed and the heaping of coats on a big harvest table kept up for a long time. So did the sampling of refreshments and the laughter and talk around the fire in the back parlor. The doors of the front parlor were still closed. At last Fair Davenport slipped away. Eleanor turned off all the lights. Only one candle and the flickering fire lighted the room as Eleanor sat down at the piano.

People stopped talking and all eyes were on the folding doors. As they opened, everyone took a long breath. You could smell the tree before you saw it, breathe in the scent of balsam warming in the glow of a hundred candles. The tree filled half the room. The silver star at the top almost touched the ceiling. The branches were as dark and fresh as if it were still standing in the woods. Some of the mysterious darkness of the woods came into the room with it. There was nothing on it but the silver star and the candles. Their sparkling light deepened the shadows.

Eleanor began to play "Silent Night." Voices joined in; a few, then more, then everyone was singing. Even Mrs. Appleyard murmured almost audibly, "Sleep in heavenly peace," and felt that she would. The candles burned only till the carol was over. Fairfield put them out before they came too near the prickly resinous needles. The tree was so beautiful, Mrs. Appleyard thought, partly because — like a sunset, an eclipse of the sun or a rainbow — its moments were so few. A whole city of electric lights could never give the same sense of wonder.

Outside it was so clear that the sky was blue behind the floating moon. Crisp snow squeaked under people's feet. Smoke from the Davenports' Yule log, part of a big sugar maple, rose straight into the blue air, a column of silver. Loops and sprays and wreaths were dark against the white houses of the village. Lights were bright on trees in the windows and trees outside in the snow.

Christmas had begun.

Bradshaw Christmas

CICELY BRADSHAW's Christmas celebration is a mingling of so many traditions that it made Mrs. Appleyard dizzy when she tried to diagnose where they all came from. Her own childhood had provided well-stuffed stockings with tangerines in the toes and the hiding of presents, sometimes in such strategic places that they were not found till spring. She used to help to hang wreaths of holly in the windows and Christmas was not legal unless there were branches of holly back of the copy of the family Gainsborough and other favorite pictures. No tree. Trees were not English and Mrs. Appleyard's father was.

It was from the Appleyards that the custom of cutting your own tree from your own land reached the Bradshaw family. Mr. Appleyard used to have one shipped from Appleyard Center to Woodbrook Green and Mrs. Appleyard recognized on Cicely's tree some of the ornaments that he used to hang on the branches. She was however unprepared for everyone in the Bradshaw family having his own small tree besides the big one. "Everyone" includes Eric, the Norwegian elkhound, Laddie, the golden cocker, and the two tortoise shell cats. One of the trees was a rubber plant embellished with sprays of silver leaves. There was a crystal tree sparkling with emeralds, rubies and sapphires. Another one turned its tinseled branches and played

what Mrs. Appleyard rather thought was "Silent Night." It
was made in Japan and its maker had a different opinion: "Tune
— Holly Night," the label on the bottom said. This was the canary's tree. He accompanied the tune — whatever it was — with
valiant trills.

Mrs. Appleyard had introduced the crêche into their family
Christmas and she was glad to see that the Bradshaws had one
too. Not all her innovations became traditions. One year, inspired by *Life* Magazine, she had bought a large number of soda
straws and had threaded yards of string through them to con-
struct for Cicely an icosahedral star. Rather to her surprise it
came out looking much like the picture, but it did not become a
permanent feature of the Bradshaw Christmas. Mrs. Appleyard
is willing to bet a certain number of soda straws, enough to
make another star, in case you are interested, that she is the only
reader of *Life* who made an icosahedral star and had it eaten by
a Norwegian elkhound. Somehow Eric's tree, so neatly trimmed
with dog-biscuit bones, was not enough for him. Dogs, Mrs.
Appleyard remembered from her youth, used to like chewing
string on Christmas day. Eric certainly chewed the most string
of any dog she knows.

Homemade wine from dandelions, elderberries, choke-cherries
— each brewed in its season — were her granddaughter Cynthia's contribution to the Christmas festivities. There was even
a rich fruity old port (several weeks old) made from Mrs.
Appleyard's own beets. But who, she wondered, introduced the
gingerbread house into the family? And how did fifteen-year-
old Jane instinctively know how to make it? At fifteen Mrs.
Appleyard had never even made fudge. She is lost in wonder,
love and praise at the ease and deftness with which her granddaughters carry out such projects.

Cicely says that it's perfectly natural: that the children always helped her and that after a while she left it to Cynthia and that when she went to college, Jane took over.

"And I'll make it when Jane goes to college," said Camilla who at the moment was building a house out of lumps of sugar stuck together with pale blue mortar. Mrs. Appleyard has no doubt that Camilla will become a gingerbread architect at a suitable time.

While the gingerbread house was being baked, Mrs. Appleyard attended to her own Christmas tree. Earlier in the year she had been reading *Buddenbrooks* and she was charmed with the description of their Christmas tree, which was trimmed with white lilies and white candles and tinsel. As soon as her tree, a small but perfect balsam, was brought in, she started to town to find the lilies. She already had plenty of tinsel and a string of tiny white electric candles with white bulbs. Cynthia, who had a sort of built-in divining rod where her mother's tastes are concerned, had given it to her. Mrs. Appleyard had seen sprays of lilies, straight from Hong Kong, in the supermarket. The only trouble is that the days had drifted happily by since she had seen them. In fact when the manager told her that there had been none since Easter, she realized that of course he was right. She bought an armful of white roses.

The sun had gone down by the time she had finished trimming her tree and it was dark in the bay windows where the tree stood on an old chest of fiddleback maple. When she turned on the lights the tree seemed to blossom suddenly with stars and silver and roses. Even if the Buddenbrooks would not have recognized its ancestry, they might, she thought, feel a sort of magic about it, something that said, "All is calm — all is bright."

When she turned it on for the family there were gratifying shrieks of surprise and Cicely conferred the supreme compliment by announcing: "This must be a tradition from now on."

Mrs Appleyard did not plan to compete with the tremendous meal the Buddenbrooks always had at Christmas. She could not remember the details and someone had borrowed (courteous for stolen) the book. She knew there was carp simmered in red wine but she did not quite see how she was going to get a carp.

At Christmas time there was fishing through the ice going on only a quarter of a mile away but this is not, Mrs. Appleyard feels, a womanly occupation. Men, she thinks, fish through the ice more to get away from women than for the sake of the fish they catch: she will not intrude upon their icy privacy. Not even if some one had stolen carp from Versailles and domesticated them in Crystal Lake would Mrs. Appleyard be present when a red flag ran up to announce a catch. Making plum pudding in a warm kitchen is more in her line. There must be plenty because something delightful had happened. Hugh and his family, all six of them, were coming and also Henry and Valerie Haddam, summer neighbors, had driven east for Christmas and would come to dinner.

"So that will make fourteen of us," Mrs. Appleyard said. "What shall we have so that it will be like Thanksgiving only different? I love having two kitchens, and with so many people there'll be lots to help so it will be easy. Shall we have a boar's head? Or a suckling pig? Or shall I try for a turkey as good as the last?"

It was decided that turkey is best for a family party. This is the menu they built around that now domestic bird.

Peanut Butter and Bacon Appetizers*
Stuffed Celery*   Chicken Liver Pâté — Melba Toast*
Sesame Seed Crackers
Roast Turkey (p. 64)   Giblet Gravy (p. 66)
,Cranberry Apples (p. 35)   Candied Sweet Potato*
Mashed Potato   Cauliflower and Green Beans*   Hollandaise*
Plum Pudding*   Hard Sauce*
Cynthia's Dandelion Wine*

Stuffed Celery

For the filling: equal amounts of cream cheese and Swiss Colony Blue Cheese blended together with enough light cream to make the mixture soft enough. Use only the best and crispest stalks. Save the rest and the tops for soup. These can be made ahead and kept in a cool place till needed. One thing you can say for old-fashioned Vermont houses — there are always plenty of cool spots in them. The remarkable thing is that there are also warm ones.

Chicken Liver Pâté — with Melba Toast

You need a blender to do this. You can, of course, put the livers through the finest attachment of your meat grinder and pound them in a mortar but Mrs. Appleyard rather doubts if you'll feel like doing that two days before Christmas. Better forget the whole idea and buy some French pâté de foie gras or Sell's Liver Pâté, one of those things she likes to mention that keep the same quality over the years.

For the Melba toast, which can be drying out while you are making the pâté:

Trim the crusts off homemade bread sliced thin. Cut the crusts off. Cut each slice into four triangles. Put them in large pan into a 200° oven and leave them until they are light golden brown, dry and crisp. It takes about 2 hours.

For the pâté:

1 package (8-ounce) frozen chicken livers, defrosted several hours in the refrigerator
¼ teaspoon mixed herbs
½ teaspoon white pepper
1 teaspoon minced onion
2 tablespoons butter, extra, for sautéing

½ cup chicken stock (or water)
2 tablespoons butter, softened
¼ teaspoon nutmeg
1 teaspoon sugar
½ pound mushrooms (use caps only) chopped rather fine

Melt butter. Sauté mushrooms until tender. Remove them and keep them until later. Sauté the onion one minute. Add more butter if needed. Add livers, defrosted so they can be easily separated. Cover tightly. Cook over medium heat 3 minutes. Uncover, turn livers over, cover again and cook 2 minutes longer.

Into the blender, put water or stock, seasonings, softened butter, the livers and all the scrapings from the pan. Blend until smooth. Mrs. Appleyard does it three times, a minute at a time. It should be like very thick cream. It will stiffen as it chills. Stir in (do not blend) the chopped mushrooms. Mrs. Appleyard uses a small rubber scraper to get the pâté out of the blender and she packs it in a wide-mouthed jar such as a peanut butter jar. After it has chilled for several hours it will be just right to spread on the Melba toast.

Peanut Butter and Bacon Appetizers

These are for the children. Appetizers is an inaccurate description. Actually they are more like something thrown to a pack of hungry wolves to placate them.

Cut rounds of Pepperidge Farm bread with a small cooky cutter. The corners make excellent bread crumbs. Toast the rounds on one side lightly and then spread them generously with real peanut butter. You make it — surprise! — out of peanuts. Did you ever read the label on a modern jar of peanut butter? Well, don't let Mrs. Appleyard spoil your Christmas. If you don't feel like grinding peanuts yourself, you can buy the old-fashioned kind from your nearest Co-op store, pure peanut butter with no homogenized oil added.

Cut bacon into small squares. Cook them slowly till they are translucent. Put the canapés on a cooky sheet. Top each one with a square of bacon. Just before serving time, put the cooky sheet under the broiler and cook them until the bacon is crisp — 2 or 3 minutes. Watch them — the charcoal stage arrives rather quickly. Serve hot.

Cauliflower and Green Beans (O.H.P.)

Festive looking is cauliflower in a wreath of green beans. Begin by making some garlic croutons. Cut 3 slices of home-made bread into small cubes. Brown them in 2 tablespoons of butter, sprinkle with ½ teaspoon of garlic powder.

Cook a perfect head of cauliflower. Mrs. Appleyard does this in one of those French vegetable steamers that fold up or spread out to fit various sizes of pans. The pan must be covered tightly.

The cauliflower should be tender in about 20 minutes of steaming unless it is very large. Test the base with a sharp vegetable knife. It should go in easily. For a large number of people it is better to do two good-sized heads.

At the same time cook frozen French-cut beans. Allow two packages to a large head of cauliflower. Cook them in a small amount of water, which should be boiling when you put in the beans. Cover them at first. After 3 minutes, turn them over so that the frozen top parts will have a chance to melt. Cook another 3 minutes. When all the ice is melted, add 2 tablespoons of butter and cook uncovered until all the water cooks away. Watch them carefully. They will be done in 2 or 3 minutes. Remove from heat, cover and let them stand until you are ready to serve the cauliflower. Put it on a hot circular dish. Reheat the beans briefly and make a wreath of them around the cauliflower. Scatter the croutons over them. Serve with Hollandaise.

Hollandaise Sauce

½ cup butter	1 tablespoon lemon juice
yolks of 2 large eggs	½ teaspoon grated lemon rind
pinch (⅛ teaspoon) of cayenne pepper	

This sauce, Mrs. Appleyard says, is usually considered hard to make but if you follow directions carefully it is really less trouble than most sauces. To make it you need courage and a French wire whisk. If you have a stove where you can absolutely trust your flame to produce the lowest possible heat evenly and steadily, you may make it over direct heat. Mrs. Appleyard, who is brave but not rash, does it in the top of a double boiler over hot, not boiling water.

Use only the best butter. Divide it into 3 pieces. Put the egg yolks, unbeaten, the lemon juice and rind and the cayenne into

the top of the double boiler over the hot water. Start beating
with your wire whisk and add the first piece of butter. Keep
beating and as the butter melts, add the second piece. The sauce
will start to thicken. As the second piece of butter disappears
add the third one. Here's your danger point. Just as this last
piece of butter melts — keep on beating all the time — remove
the sauce from the heat. It will curdle if it's left a minute too
long. Don't have hysterics if it does because it can be brought
back by beating in a little cream — a teaspoonful or more. Be
sure the cream is well chilled. Put the sauce into a warm, not
hot, bowl and serve it immediately.

Sweet Potatoes, Candied and Brandied with Cashew Nuts

Allow one medium-sized potato for each person to be served.
Parboil 20 minutes. Mrs. Appleyard does this in a vegetable
steamer. Peel potatoes. Slice them lengthwise in halves. For
eight potatoes allow ¾ cup brown sugar, ⅓ cup hot water, ⅓ cup
brandy, ½ cup cashew nuts, 2 tablespoons butter. Melt the
butter in a large iron frying pan. Add the brown sugar and
hot water and cook until the syrup is quite thick — 2 or 3 minutes. Put in the potato slices, cut side down, and cook them
gently in the syrup 3 minutes. Turn them over. Baste with the
syrup. Set the pan into the oven at 350° and cook until the
potatoes are tender and the syrup thick, about 30 minutes.
Sprinkle brandy over them and the cashew nuts, broken. Put
pan over the heat for a minute and let the syrup boil up. Arrange potatoes on a hot serving platter, pour syrup and nuts
over them.

Sherry may be used instead of brandy or both may be omitted.
Peanuts or pecans may be used instead of cashews.

Plum Pudding *(A.C.R.)*

This pudding is made several weeks before Christmas. It keeps well in a cool place right in the molds in which you steamed it and needs only a short period of steaming when you serve it.

2 cups dried French bread crumbs
1 pound beef suet, ground fine
½ pound almonds, blanched and
   ground
½ pound citron, diced
½ pound seedless raisins
¼ pound candied cherries
½ pound currants
1 teaspoon each of cloves,
   cinnamon, allspice

½ a nutmeg, grated (1 teaspoon)
2 tablespoons rose water
juice of 1 lemon
1 cup sherry
2 tablespoons rum
10 eggs
2 cups sugar
1 cup flour

Dry the French bread, using the inside of the loaf only, and roll it into very fine crumbs. Mix it with the suet, ground almonds and the fruit. Sprinkle the spices over the fruit. Pour over the rosewater, lemon juice, sherry and rum and let it stand overnight. (Rosewater is not easy to find now but you can still get it from S. S. Pierce.) The next day separate the eggs, beat the yolks till they are thick. Beat in the sugar. Beat the whites stiff but not dry and fold them into the yolks, then fold the whole mixture into the fruit mixture. Scatter the flour over the whole thing and fold it in.

This makes several small or two large puddings. Steam them in coffee cans, brown bread tins, melon molds, anything that has a tight cover that fits over the can. Most modern cans unfortunately either have a cover that is damaged when opened or a projecting edge that makes it impossible to get the pudding out intact. A melon mold is really the best container.

Butter the molds well. Fill them not more than two-thirds full. The pudding expands as it steams. Set the molds on a rack in a large kettle with a tightly fitting cover. Pour in boiling water almost to the level of the rack. Steam the puddings 5 or 6 hours, replacing water as needed.

In serving hers Mrs. Appleyard likes to decorate it with a sprig of holly. Luckily she has friends in Corvallis, Oregon, where the handsomest holly grows, so when she had steamed the pudding long enough to reheat it — about half an hour — she put it on a silver dish, poured brandy over it, lighted the brandy and brought it in with blue flames flickering around the holly.

Don't forget that the dish will be hot, she says. Plum pudding is not especially improved by being dropped. What made her think of this cooking hint? Well — never mind.

Luckily Camilla is a great weaver of holders. She made her grandmother some appropriate green and red ones for Christmas, so on this occasion all went well.

Hard Sauce

½ cup best butter   1 teaspoon vanilla
1 cup powdered sugar, sifted ½ teaspoon cinnamon
½ teaspoon nutmeg

Butter should be at room temperature. Cream it. Work in the powdered sugar. Add vanilla. Beat well, using a pastry-blending fork. Put sauce into a Sandwich glass dish, swirling it around artistically. Sprinkle with spice. Chill so it will hold its shape. Remove from refrigerator a little ahead of time. It should be hard but not like granite.

Getting dinner on Christmas Day was a leisurely process. Most of Mrs. Appleyard's part of it had been done beforehand and she spent most of the day reading her new Christmas books in large intemperate gulps. She also at intervals contemplated her favorite present. It was handmade for her by Hugh's oldest son, Bruce, and consisted of a set of Napier's Bones.

In case you are not very familiar with this device, you resemble Mrs. Appleyard more than you might think. It is intended to help in mathematical calculations. Its inventor also thought up logarithms. Then one thing led to another and after a while we had the slide rule and giant computers and spent our time sending chimpanzees and men in orbit and planning to send a man to the moon. No one admires our astronauts more than Mrs. Appleyard. In fact she is planning to go to tea with her cousins in Australia by capsule some day and come back on the third round. Still she wishes people would leave the moon alone and just go on happily and incorrectly rhyming it with June.

Even equipped with Napier's Bones, there is not much chance of Mrs. Appleyard's inventing anything catastrophic. All she knows about logarithms is that the log of 1000 to the base of 10 is 3. Napier figured out that it was 2.7182181828 — but someone else decided that 3 was easier to use. This view — all mathematicians will be glad to know — is heartily endorsed by Mrs. Appleyard.

Napier's Bones as made by Bruce consist of nine strips of Vermont maple, each nine inches long and an inch wide, nicely sanded and polished. They are marked out into inch squares and the multiplication tables from one to nine are neatly printed on them. All the marks are burned in with an electric pencil. Ornamental — yes, and useful too for anyone who writes cookbooks and who might want to plan a meal for six instead of for eight. Just get out your Napier's Bones.

Mrs. Appleyard came up for air between calculations and asked Cicely what time she planned to serve dinner. "We asked the Haddams for six, didn't we?"

Cicely began to murmur statistics, not simple things about three fourths of a cup of flour. For these a real computer was needed: "Tommy skiing will pick up Cynthia, five-thirty. Hugh, skating, will bring Camilla six-fifteen. Persuade eight children to brush hair, dress, wash. Turkey weighs twenty pounds. Haddams asked for six will be two hours late . . . twenty-five minutes to the pound . . . when will droppers-in drop out? . . . how long to mash potatoes for fourteen . . . extra plates . . . high chair . . . We'll serve the turkey at eight-ten," she concluded.

"Then I'll make Hollandaise, triple rule, at five minutes past," Mrs. Appleyard said and sank restfully into another book.

The house smelled wonderful — of balsam and roasting turkey and woodsmoke from blazing birch logs. The musical tree from Japan was very excitable: the slightest motion near it, such as the cats batting their catnip mice, made it twinkle out "Holly Night."

English is a confusing language: it might just as well have said "Wholly Night."

Thankful that she did not have to label a musical revolving Buddha in Japanese, Mrs. Appleyard put another log on the fire.

Cicely's computations worked perfectly. By eight-ten the dinner was ready and the family and guests were there to eat it. Candles burned on the long table, light sparkled on all the Christmas trees. The canary seemed delighted with his tree and gratefully sang an obbligato every time it tinkled. Outside the dogs were chewing the bones so neatly wrapped in Christmas paper and tied to their trees. The cats had now given up inhaling catnip and were seriously at work with their velvet paws batting silver balls. They broke only two.

Henry Haddam sat at one end of the table and served vegetables. Hugh carved the turkey at the other end.

He carves as well as his father, Mrs. Appleyard thought.
High praise.
Cynthia filled glasses with her own wine — dandelion or beet.
Ah that beet wine of 1961! What a vintage! Or is it a rootage?
Anyway it made Mrs. Appleyard's ears ring: obviously a root-
age to remember.

Cynthia's Dandelion Wine

Choose a bright warm May morning when dandelions look
up out of the grass like small hot suns. Pick 4 quarts, flowers
only. By the time you have done that you will have stood on
your head all you want to and will be willing to work in the
shade for a while.

To 4 quarts of dandelion blossoms allow:

1 gallon boiling water	2 packages frozen raspberries
juice of 6 lemons	3 pounds granulated sugar
	2 yeast cakes

Wash and scald a two-gallon crock with a cover. Put the
flowers in and pour the boiling water over them. Let them stand
in a cool place overnight. In the morning strain liquid from
the flowers, squeeze all the juice out of them through a strainer.
Put the juice on to boil with the lemon juice, raspberries and
sugar. Boil 20 minutes and pour it back into the crock. Let
cool till lukewarm, then add yeast. Cover and let the juice fer-
ment until it stops hissing — about ten days. Strain through
filter paper into scalded cider jugs. Let it stand three days to
settle. Tops should be on but not tightened. Strain once more
through filter paper into clean quart bottles. Let it stand for
another day to be sure it is clear. Filter again if necessary. If

not, cork the bottles tightly. Leave them in the cellarway till
Christmas.

The Hollandaise did not curdle. The plum pudding blazed
blue and was scorching hot. No one dropped the platter. The
Hard Sauce was just cold enough. Mrs. Appleyard did not make
the coffee, it was excellent.

It had been a perfect day, she thought: sunshine on snow,
grandchildren, red carnations, neighbors dropping in, books,
Jane's gingerbread house, telephone calls from distant children,
Cicely, warmth, music, Hugh's family skating on the millpond,
cards from two hemispheres, Double-Crostics, Napier's Bones,
laughter. Who could ask for anything more?

December–January

Epact of Turkey

ONE OF THE few restful aspects of Christmas vacation, Cicely Bradshaw says, is that the children, to use an elegant phrase, eat off the turkey. The Bradshaws all, including the cats, like turkey best when it's cold. This convenient taste somewhat makes up for the fact that on any given day each of the children wishes to be driven twenty or thirty miles in a different direction. Skiing beckons one, ballet another, sacred ties of old friendship (two weeks old at least) a third. The fourth would like to shop for a new skirt "and one or two other things," a remark with sinister implications.

Such projects leave little time for cooking even if one had the inclination. Mrs. Appleyard certainly lacked it. She was perfectly happy eating yogurt with apricots and doing double crostics. Her excuse for taking up this occupation rather than writing a book or painting on velvet or cooking or shortening any of her well-known skirts is that her mind needed stretching. She also admitted that if she laughed, coughed, sneezed or even whistled, her ribs reminded her of her brief but emphatic contact with that green truck. Besides, she said, she had to entertain the insurance adjusters, dignified, cleancut young gentlemen in dark suits, plain dark ties, white shirts and beautifully polished shoes. There is something very soothing about a medium-sized black shoe in which you can see your face — in case you want to, of course.

Actually the less Mrs. Appleyard saw of hers the better she was pleased. Having her nose cracked did not improve her appearance so much as she had hoped. If it had been really broken she supposed it could have been set Greek or Roman or Early Aztec but it simply had its usual undistinguished lines with, around it, areas still faintly black and blue, not to mention yellow and green. She is definitely a type that looks better by candlelight — she hopes.

Still, even though she has not been in the mood to make the turkey into esoteric *plats du jour* in case any gourmets dropped in, she realizes that there are people who like turkey some other way than cold. For such restless spirits she suggests a few menus that will keep them occupied till New Year's.

The days just after Christmas belong, she says, neither in December nor in January. They are part of the epact, which is the excess of the solar year over the lunar months of the calendar. This is the kind of thing she learns from double crostics and she feels it is her duty to make the information readily available. What you eat during this period is, naturally, an epact of turkey — what is left over from Christmas and will, with ingenuity, last until the New Year.

You cannot be sure what time the family, working so hard at play, will get home, but you can be certain they'll be hungry. These dishes can be fixed ahead of time and served quickly. They are planned for six. If your family is larger than that, act accordingly. You will have done your duty by the turkey all the sooner and you will be able to enter the hamburger-and-hot-dog phase with a clear conscience.

1.

Turkey with Broccoli and Mushroom Sauce*
Mashed Potato Cakes*   Beets Appleyard*
Brown Betty (p. 47)   Hard Sauce (p. 130)

2.

Turkey Salad*   Tomato Conserve*
Baked Stuffing*   Spinach Appleyard*
Mince Pie (p. 68)   Vanilla Ice Cream

3.

Creamed turkey and oysters   Peas
Toasted English muffins*
Pineapple Upside-Down Cake*   Foamy Sauce (p. 58)

4.

Turkey Soup*   Thin-Scalded Johnnycake†
Tossed Salad*   Crackers and Cheese*

MENU I

Turkey with Broccoli and Mushroom Sauce

dark meat of turkey, sliced	3 tablespoons milk, rich, or light cream
cooked broccoli flowers,	4 tablespoons bread crumbs
2 pkgs, frozen	1 tablespoon butter
1 cup Mushroom Sauce (p. 169)	2 tablespoons grated cheese

Slice turkey neatly. Put cooked broccoli flowers in a lightly buttered shallow baking dish. Cover them with the turkey slices and then with the mushroom sauce to which the milk has been added. Sauté bread crumbs in butter and spread them over the sauce. Sprinkle grated cheese over the top. Do this ahead of time. When you serve it, put it over medium heat until the sauce starts to bubble, then run it under the broiler till the cheese starts to brown.

Mashed Potato Cakes
SIX CAKES

2 tablespoons butter   2 tablespoons flour
2 cups cold mashed potato made with real potatoes and cream and butter

Flour your hands slightly. Roll the potato into six balls of uniform size. Flatten them. They should be about ½ inch thick. Have the flour, seasoned as you like it, in a thin layer on a plate. Have the butter melted over low heat in a large iron frying pan. Dip both sides of the cakes in the flour. Shake off what does not stick readily. Place them in the buttered frying pan and cook them until they are well browned on both sides. This will take at least half an hour and may take longer. They will have to be moved around the pan at intervals so that they will be evenly browned. The moving and the turning are both delicate operations, best done with a spatula and a short-handled pancake turner. Cakes should be turned only once.

Beets Appleyard

2 beans garlic, crushed	1 tablespoon lemon juice
grated rind of one lemon	3 tablespoons sugar
1 can juice from beets	2 tablespoons butter
⅓ cup red wine	1 tablespoon minute tapioca
2 tablespoons cider vinegar	1 can of shoestring-cut beets

Soak the garlic and lemon rind in the beet juice, wine, vinegar and lemon juice for one hour. Strain juice, add sugar, butter and tapioca. Cook in the top of a double boiler until sauce is thick and clear. Add the beets. Set aside till serving time. Reheat. If sauce seems too thick, add a little more wine, heated.

MENU 2

Turkey Salad

3 cups turkey, white meat, cubed	½ cup chow-chow pickles,
1 cup celery, cut very fine	finely chopped
1 cup French Dressing (p. 190)	2 sliced, hard-boiled eggs
1½ cups Mayonnaise (p. 265)	12 large stuffed olives
	lettuce

Cut the turkey into rather large cubes. Cut the celery very fine. Mrs. Appleyard does this by cutting well-washed stalks into quarter-inch strips and then cutting strips into quarter-inch cubes. She uses scissors, says this is neater than chopping and really no more trouble.

Mix celery and turkey and marinate in French dressing for at least one hour. She uses her own mayonnaise but your favorite brand will do. She also usually has some of her own pickle on hand but if it has all vanished, she uses Crosse and Blackwell's Chow-Chow pickles. In either case chop the pickle rather fine. Get Boston Market lettuce if possible. This is easier to do in New York than in Boston. It is more than likely that you will have to use iceberg, so named apparently because it has all the flavor and texture of the part of an iceberg that is above water.

Asked how the bottom seven-eighths tastes, Mrs. Appleyard froze not but replied imperturbably, "Salty and fish with just a hint of whale oil," and added a request for at least a spray or two of watercress, chicory and parsley around the edge of the salad bowl.

At serving time drain off the French dressing. Save it: there are many ways in which a little marinade can be useful. Stir half the mayonnaise into the turkey mixed with the celery and the pickle. Mask the mixture with rest of the mayonnaise. Decorate with the sliced hard-boiled eggs and the stuffed olives, also sliced. Surround with salad greens. Keep cool till ready.

(Good advice for the cook as well as the salad, Mrs. Appleyard says.)

Spinach Appleyard

Mrs. Appleyard prefers spinach out of a cellophane bag, or frozen spinach even to spinach from her own garden. She has never succeeded in washing spinach so there is no sand in it. She supposes that professional spinach washers must have enormous automatic washers in which the spinach swirls gently in a green centrifugal forest, spinning out sand as it goes. Perhaps next summer —

"Please do not try that in my new dishwasher," Cicely said firmly on hearing this speculation.

On the whole a reasonable request, Mrs. Appleyard thought, and continued to buy her spinach in cellophane.

1 teaspoon onion finely minced	2 tablespoons thick cream
2 bags washed spinach	2 tablespoons butter
¼ cup water, hot	pinch of nutmeg

Croutons:

4 slices homemade bread ¼ inch thick	2 tablespoons butter ½ teaspoon garlic powder

Begin by making the croutons. Cut the crusts off the bread. Cut it into ¼-inch cubes. Melt the butter, toss the croutons in it till they are golden brown. Sprinkle the garlic powder over them. Remove with a skimmer and set aside till needed. In the same pan put the onion and cook until it is transparent and yellow. Rinse out the pan with ¼ cup hot water. Swish it around to get all the flavor and pour it into the kettle in which you plan to cook the spinach. Chop the spinach, rather coarsely. Mrs. Appleyard does this in a big wooden chopping bowl and an old-fashioned steel chopper. There should be just enough water in the kettle to cover the bottom of it. Have it boiling hard. Add the chopped spinach. Cook it 5 minutes, chopping while it cooks. By this time it should be tender and a bright light green. Remove it from the pan to a hot dish, leaving the water. Cook this down to about a tablespoon. Add the cream, butter and nutmeg, heat and pour this over the spinach. Sprinkle croutons over and serve.

Baked Stuffing

Get this ready earlier in the day and set the dish in the oven about the time you start chopping the spinach.

Mrs. Appleyard has a habit of making more stuffing than the turkey will hold. She saves it and combines it with stuffing left in the turkey.

1 cup stuffing from turkey	½ cup hot water
2 cups stuffing (extra)	1 tablespoon butter
½ cup giblet gravy	1 egg, well beaten
1 tablespoon butter, in small dots	

Put stuffing in bowl. Mix gravy and hot water. Add 1 tablespoon butter. Cool slightly. Add beaten egg and add the mixture to the stuffing. Dot the top with butter. Bake at 375° about 25 minutes.

The exact contents of the dish can vary with what you have on hand — a little mushroom sauce, a few chestnuts or cashews or a little diced celery go well in it. Life is a lottery, so is a casserole: be valiant.

Having given this advice and also having encountered a good many casseroles where the makers had shown no hesitancy, Mrs. Appleyard wishes to make it clear that her remark was addressed to the eaters.

Tomato Conserve

4 quarts ripe tomatoes, measured whole	1 cup seedless white raisins
	½-ounce stick cinnamon
sugar	6 medium-sized tart apples,
3 oranges	peeled, cored and cubed
3 lemons	

If you make this in winter, substitute 2 large cans of tomatoes for the ripe tomatoes. They will be better than anything except tomatoes from your own garden.

Peel the tomatoes by holding them by a wooden-handled fork over the gas flame until the skins pop and sizzle. Peel off skin. Slice tomatoes and cut them up, not too fine. Pour off about a quart of the juice. Keep it to drink, chilled, or use as soup. If you are using canned tomatoes, use just as they come from the can.

Measure tomatoes and add an equal quantity of sugar. Slice oranges and lemons very thin. Cut slices in eighths. Use kitchen shears for this. Add the orange, lemon, raisins and stick cinnamon to the tomatoes and put them on to boil. Use a large kettle. Put the sugar into a 250° oven in a shallow pan. When the tomato mixture starts to bubble, add the heated sugar. Cook 5 minutes, stirring well from the bottom of the kettle. Cover, turn off heat. The second day, reheat and boil 5 minutes longer. The third day reheat (cheer up — this is the last time!) once more. Peel, core and cut the apples into small cubes. As soon as the conserve starts to boil, add the apples. Cook until they begin to soften. By this time the juice should crinkle when tested on a cold saucer. Stir conserve well from the bottom of the kettle always while it is boiling and especially during this last day's cooking. Remove the stick cinnamon. Put the conserve into sterilized jars. Steam them 10 minutes on a rack in a covered kettle to seal the lids.

MENU 3

Creamed Turkey and Oysters

8 ounces oysters, frozen
2 cups breast meat of turkey
3 tablespoons butter
½ teaspoon minced onion
caps from ½ pound mushrooms, sliced,
   or
4-ounce can of mushrooms, caps only
3 tablespoons flour

2 cups rich Vermont milk (known in the city as thin cream)
2 pimentos
1 green pepper
1 cup heavy cream
2 egg yolks
½ cup white wine
juice of ½ lemon (1 tablespoon)

½ cup chicken or turkey stock, jellied

Let the oysters thaw out gently in the refrigerator ahead of time. Slice turkey rather thick and cut it into fairly good-sized pieces. Melt butter, sauté the onion and the mushroom caps in it until onion is straw-colored. Sprinkle in flour, stir well. Reduce heat. Add the milk slowly, blending it in well. When sauce is smooth increase heat and simmer mixture for 5 minutes. Add the turkey, the pimentos cut in small strips, the green pepper cleaned of seeds and cut in very thin strips. Add the cream. Simmer a minute longer. Transfer everything to the top of a large double boiler and let stand till you are ready to serve it. Then heat mixture over hot, not boiling water. Beat the egg yolks, add wine and lemon juice, beat all together. Stir 3 tablespoons of the hot sauce into the egg mixture, one at a time, blending sauce well into the eggs and then add this mixture to the turkey mixture. Cook, stirring well for 5 minutes or until it thickens. Remove from heat. During this last 5 minutes bring the jellied stock to a boil in a small saucepan. Add oysters. Cook them until the edges curl. Add them and the stock to the turkey mixture.

Toasted English Muffins

Split muffins, butter generously, run them under the broiler. Soon done: soon charcoal too. Have this done by someone who can give all his time to it.

Pineapple Upside-Down Cake

Mrs. Appleyard's favorite weapon for this dessert is an iron frying pan large enough to hold 7 slices of pineapple. Dressier enameled pans may also be used, she admits, but most of them are not big enough.

½ cup butter	1 large can (7 slices) of pineapple
2 cups light golden brown sugar	small jar maraschino cherries

Melt butter in frying pan. Stir in sugar and melt it. Arrange the pineapple slices in the pan. Put cherries in their centers and in the spaces between slices. Add a tablespoon of the cherry liquid. Set the pan in the oven: 375°. Make the following batter and when butter and sugar mixture begins to bubble, pour it over them.

Batter:

1 cup milk	2½ cups cake flour, sifted 3 times
1½ cups sugar	and measured
6 tablespoons melted butter	2½ teaspoons baking powder,
3 eggs	sifted with flour
1 teaspoon vanilla	

Mix milk, sugar, butter, eggs and vanilla. Beat with an egg-beater until they are well blended. Beat the mixture into the sifted flour and baking powder. Keep on beating till the batter is smooth. Pour over the hot bubbling fruit and bake until a testing straw comes out clean.

Turn the cake upside down on a platter big enough to hold it. This takes courage, speed and a strong wrist. Good fortune attend you!

Serve the cake with thick cream, vanilla ice cream or with Foamy Sauce (p. 58).

MENU 4

Turkey Soup

carcass of a 20-pound turkey (it was stuffed with chestnut and sausage stuffing. The roaster contained the juices that had run out of it, thick as molasses and almost as dark)

2 onions   2 carrots sliced

celery tops and outer stalks

The day before you plan to make the soup, break up the carcass and put the bones and any meat and stuffing that clings to them into the roaster. Add wingtips, all the skin, onions, carrots, celery tops and stalks. Cover bones with water and simmer 5 or 6 hours. Strain off liquid — there should be about 2 quarts. Remove any scraps of meat from bones and add them to the broth. Chill it well.

The next day you will need:

any leftover giblet gravy	2 tablespoons flour
2 tablespoons turkey fat, skimmed from the broth	1 teaspoon burnt onion powder
1 onion finely grated	⅛ teaspoon each of pepper, clove, cinnamon, allspice
stems from 2 pounds mushrooms, sliced thin	1 teaspoon mixed herbs
	½ teaspoon paprika

1 teaspoon instant coffee

Skim all fat from the broth. Save it. Mrs. Appleyard wants it for the birds that come to her feeding station. They love her cooking. One of their favorite entrées is Yorkshire Pudding with turkey fat on it. However she will let you have a little for the soup. Simmer the skimmed broth down to 1½ quarts. Add giblet gravy to it. Melt the 2 tablespoons of turkey fat and sauté the onion and the mushroom stems in it. Mix flour with the seasonings. Sprinkle it in, blend over very low heat. Add broth gradually, stirring well until soup is smooth. Simmer until it thickens. Serve.

If you would rather have a clear soup, a sort of turkey consommé, omit the giblet gravy, the fat and the flour. Add 2 tablespoons of sherry.

If you like a blander soup add a cup of rich milk to the mixture just after you add the broth.

Any one of the three versions will brace you up for the New Year.

Tossed Salad

One of the most unusual things about New York, Mrs. Appleyard says, is the tossed salad. Whether you eat at some humble cafeteria or at a restaurant where the headwaiter makes your teeth chatter with fear, you are awarded the same mixture of ground-up iceberg lettuce, chicory, radishes, well-matured carrots, stringy celery and pallid tomatoes. No one has told Mrs. Appleyard just how this gastronomic miracle is achieved, but she knows what she would do if she had to make several tons of it every day. She would get a large truck with a revolving cement mixer, have it equipped with special knives and make the salad as she drives along, handing out buckets of it to her clients. Occasionally she would replenish the mixture with tomatoes too far from home or determined branches of celery. In another cylinder she would make the peculiarly tasteless dressing that is always applied to the salad. Not having suitable ingredients at hand, she has not completely worked out the rule yet but she rather thinks it has a cornstarch base flavored with water, gum tragacanth, mineral oil and monosodium glutamate. A great many people in New York have high blood pressure for some reason. Perhaps she could collect statistics on that point while she was on her delivery route. She would have to be up bright and early anyway to accommodate all her customers. There must be thousands.

"What would you do the rest of the day?" inquired her daughter.

Mrs. Appleyard said that for one thing she would have to make the imitation vinegar that goes into the dressing. She had forgotten that she would need that. Then of course in the afternoon she would have to collect all the salad that had not been eaten the day before. She had never, she says, actually seen one of those wooden salad bowls empty.

"Probably," she added, glowing with creative imagination, "that's what you start with next day . . ."

No doubt she will work out the whole cycle efficiently in time. At present she is sticking to an old-fashioned method.

She takes:

4 beans of crushed garlic	½ teaspoon sugar
6 tablespoons olive oil	⅛ teaspoon cayenne
Boston Market lettuce	1 teaspoon dry mustard
romaine	½ teaspoon pepper from the grinder
fresh watercress from the brook	1 teaspoon paprika
1 tablespoon cider vinegar	1 tablespoon minced fresh parsley
1 tablespoon lemon juice	1 tablespoon chopped chives
salt to taste	

Parsley and chives both grow all winter in a sunny window if they are kept well watered.

Several hours before you toss the salad, crush the garlic and pour the olive oil over it. Wash the lettuce, romaine and watercress. Dry it between clean dish towels. Put it in the crisper of the refrigerator. Have a big salad bowl ready. Mrs. Appleyard prefers a china one. She says that wooden ones, unless they are plastic coated, are hard to keep clean. Whatever kind you use, you'll need lots of room for tossing.

Mix the vinegar, lemon juice, salt, sugar and spices in a big wooden salad spoon and put the mixture into your salad bowl. Add the strained garlic oil a tablespoon at a time, mixing well with the salad fork after each addition. Lay the spoon and fork crossed over the dressing. This is to keep the salad greens from being soaked in the dressing. Now add the greens. Tear up the romaine and the lettuce rather coarsely. Sprinkle the minced parsley and chives over them.

During the crisis just before serving time, Mrs. Appleyard appoints some conscientious guest, usually a man, and asks him to toss the salad gently at least twenty-eight times. The idea, she explains to him, is that every leaf should be coated with the dressing and that no dressing should be left in the bottom of the bowl. He almost always, whether his chief interest is basketball, golf or skiing, does an excellent job, perhaps better than could be done with a patented concrete mixer.

Crackers and Cheese

No doubt you have your favorite kinds of both. Mrs. Appleyard's are Vermont or New York State cheddar cheese aged about a year, Swiss Colony blue cheese and Borden's Liederkranz. Almost all cheese is improved by standing at room temperature a while before it is served.

She realizes that some changes are improvements. She thinks that most of her grandchildren's generation have more sense of belonging in the world than she had at their age. She knows that radio has made good music better known and appreciated than it has ever been before, and she loves to have it drifting into her room from the top of Mount Washington. She has no yearning to go back to horse-drawn vehicles. She likes drip-dry clothes and electric blankets. Still she is glad that Montpelier Crackers are the same as ever.

January

International New Year

A cook, Mrs. Appleyard says, has to be a prophet too. A cook is constantly predicting things. Sometimes the prophecies are rather simple: "We are going to have hamburgers for lunch" or "The potatoes will be done in twenty minutes." Sometimes there are more complicated situations with conditions attached: "If you bring home some trout, I'll cook them for supper with bacon." Then there are frightening moments where the voice of doom states: "If you slam the oven door, the cake will fall . . . Another minute and the toast will burn."

This type of prophet has the annoying habit of being always right. If she says there are going to be hamburgers for supper, small indeed is the chance that you will find yourself eating sweetbreads and mushrooms sous cloche with a side dish of lobster Bordelaise and crêpes suzette for dessert. Yet people tolerate her utterances, perhaps because she constantly assures them that they can count on a future even if it's only to last twenty minutes. Also it is a future where, if you do right, you can expect something good and — usually — get it: so different in this way from the home life of Job, for instance.

Of course cook-prophets are usually women. Men are more apt to look back into the past: "I never liked tripe . . . Mother made delicious cornbread . . . Where did you get the albatross for this stew? I had that for lunch."

Mrs. Appleyard knows, of course, that the best cooks are men. So are the best politicians, mathematicians and dressmakers. Unfortunately the best men are not always cooks.

Putting on a chef's hat and scorching steak in the backyard does not make the scorcher a cook any more than delivering one smashing checkmate makes a woman a chess player. It is the daily battle with fire and saucepan that makes a cook. Men cooks have one striking ability, which is always to have a kitchenmaid at hand. To her go such tasks as peeling onions, scouring burnt saucepans and washing the eggbeater. She is, lucky squaw, also allowed to grate cheese and crush garlic. And Old Man River, he just keeps cooking along.

At this moment in Mrs. Appleyard's reflections, her daughter Cicely was called to the telephone and began to act as prophet in her own right.

"Of course we will," Mrs. Appleyard heard her say. "If you'll take four, I'll take the other five. They'll help cook? Wonderful — we'll make it international. Sleeping bags on the floor, dinner for everyone New Year's Day. Mother will love it — won't you, Mother?"

Mrs. Appleyard agreed, on principle, to love blindly whatever was going on. She was quite pleased to learn that her affections had been plighted merely to having nine foreign students to dinner and that there would be only five sleeping bags to step over on the living-room floor.

"Pamela Hoyt says she'll find out what they can cook and we'll plan a menu tomorrow and I'll do the shopping," Cicely said.

"Are they men or girls?" her mother asked.

"Both."

"Fine," said Mrs. Appleyard, "we'll have some kitchenmaids." The menu involved was:

Tarts* with Caviar or Purée de Foie Gras
Olives   Radishes   Celery
Grønkålsuppe*
Crown Roast of Lamb, Kasha Stuffing*
Tiny Onions and Peas with Mustard Sauce*
Cole Slaw   Scotch Oatcake*
Paradise Jelly*   Artichokes Hollandaise*
Baked Alaska*   Cheese Fondue*
Beer   White Wine   Red Wine   Coffee

Mrs. Appleyard contributed only enthusiasm, Paradise jelly and Baked Alaska, all American products. Cicely and Pamela with a certain amount of international diplomacy reduced the menu to things that could be cooked in Vermont and translated the quantities into American weights and measures. They persuaded the Viennese delegate that it was not practicable to serve shaslik the way his mother used to make it since she began by marinating it for three days. They soothed the Swiss delegate when he encountered Swiss cheese, so called, and convinced him that no international insult was intended. They even persuaded him to see what he could do with Vermont cheddar.

The French Cordon Bleu was charmed by a visit to the Golden Dome Market. She was happy to find real French purée de foie gras and caviar and tins of pearl onions and tiny French peas because they were familiar. She was just as pleased to find pastry in a package because it was strange. She would invent something, she said.

"My mother will love you," Cicely told her.

Of course Mrs. Appleyard did — and all the others too, and the hustle and bustle and the different accents and the sleeping bags on the floor. They were not there when she went to sleep. The students had stayed at the Hoyts' to see the New Year in. When she got up in the morning, there were two bags on the floor of her living room, which is also her winter kitchen, an all-purpose room in fact. The bags contained one blonde and one brunette, she noticed as she stepped over their feet on her way to take her bath. The blonde turned out to be the French Cordon Bleu and the little shy brown chipmunk was German. Both spoke beautiful English, embarrassingly better than American English. Mrs. Appleyard tried her French and German on them. She so delighted them by her ineptness that they were soon friends.

Gretchen was assigned to Cicely's kitchen to make cole slaw and Marie-Claire stayed in the winter kitchen. Mrs. Appleyard was delighted to observe that with a Cordon Bleu in charge the men became the kitchenmaids. She always knew there was something special about that school.

It took all day to get the dinner ready. Mrs. Appleyard took full notes on the menu. Here they are.

Hors d'Oeuvres (French)
Pastry tarts, with foie gras

Marie-Claire made the pastry according to the directions on the package. She translated them into French for Mrs. Appleyard's benefit and made the project sound excitingly exotic. She rolled the pastry out deftly and, with Mrs. Appleyard's small crimped cooky cutter, swiftly produced fluted circles and put them on a baking sheet. Then she made the same number of circles and cut holes out of the centers. She wanted the inner edges fluted too, so Mrs. Appleyard went into a brief trance and invented an appropriate instrument — a ginger-ale bottle cap with two nail holes punched in it. Marie-Claire moistened the bottoms of the tart shells slightly with a pastry brush and placed the open-centered circles on top of them. The small circles cut out were also placed on the baking sheet to be used as lids for the tarts. She chilled the tarts for 5 minutes while the oven was heating to 450°. She baked them for 5 minutes, then reduced the heat to 375° and baked them until they were puffed and delicately browned, about 12 minutes longer. At serving time she filled some with the purée de foie gras and some with caviar. This was to show that she was broad-minded and admired the Russians for whatever was admirable about them. Of course, as Mrs. Appleyard well knew, the caviar had not been nearer Russia than Gloucester, Mass., where some ingenious Americans had dyed cod roe black. Still, imitation is a compliment and with onion, sour cream and a dusting of hardboiled egg yolk it was good enough so that Mrs. Appleyard wishes she had some right now.

Grønkålsuppe
DANISH SOUP (J.H. and B.L.)

a hambone with some meat on it	2 cups chopped green cabbage
2 potatoes	2 carrots
bunch of green onions with the tops	¼ cup chopped parsley
3 stalks of celery with the tops	3 tablespoons flour

1 cup cream

Boil the hambone until the meat falls from the bone, at least one hour. Remove bone. There should be about 2 quarts of liquid. In it put all the vegetables chopped, not too fine. Cook until they are tender, about 40 minutes. Pour cold water slowly on the flour, mixing well, and rub it through a fine strainer into the soup. Bring soup to a boil, add the cream. Cool for several hours. Reheat when you serve it. It will be quite thick. A little hot water may be added if you like.

At this time add what seasonings you like, freshly ground pepper, a pinch of mixed herbs, a pinch of cinnamon. It is supposed to be even better the next day. Mrs. Appleyard cannot vouch for this because there wasn't any left. She thinks that with garlic bread and a salad it would make a whole meal.

Crown Roast of Lamb
Vienna with help from Turkey

This rule is for eight. The international party somehow grew into sixteen so there were two roasts in Cicely's big oven.

8 link sausages
1 cup kasha (cracked wheat)
1 pound mushrooms, caps only
1 medium onion, minced
¼ teaspoon pepper
salt to taste
pinch (each) of paprika and thyme
16 rib lamb chops

3 tablespoons butter
⅛ teaspoon nutmeg
6 tomatoes, halved
3 beans garlic, crushed
1 tablespoon minced parsley
1 cup bread and cracker crumbs,
 mixed
½ cup cream

sprays of parsley and watercress

Have your butcher make the rib lamp chops into a crown. He'll like to do it. It's a nice change from wrapping hamburg in cellophane. The fat should be towards the center, and it should be cut away from the ends of the bones, leaving 1½ inches bare.

Cut the sausages in two pieces. Make a slit in the cut end of each one and slip them over the ends of the chop bones. Light the oven: 300°. For a 3-pound crown roast allow 1¼ hours for medium rare, 1½ hours for well done. If you use a meat thermometer, insert it in lean meat. Be sure it does not touch the bone. For medium (slightly pink) it should register 160°, for well done 185°. It is so difficult to insert it properly in a crown roast that Mrs. Appleyard does not use one but depends on instinct.

While the roast is cooking, make the stuffing. Cook a cup of kasha for 5 minutes in 2 cups of boiling water. Mrs. Appleyard is lucky enough to have a neighbor who grinds wheat to just the right coarseness for kasha. You may also use groats or brown rice or wild rice.

After the first 5 minutes of cooking put the kasha over hot water and cook till it has absorbed all the water in which it was cooked. In the meantime wash the mushrooms. The best for this purpose are button mushrooms of medium size. Cut off the stems at the level of the caps and slice them vertically. Cook the onion in butter until onion is straw-colored. Add the sliced mushrooms. Sprinkle them with pepper, salt to taste, paprika, and thyme. Mix them with the kasha and keep hot. Twenty minutes before serving time fill the center of the roast with the stuffing. If there is any extra, serve it separately.

The tomatoes are a garnish for the roast. Cut them in halves. Cover them with crumbs mixed with crushed garlic and dotted with butter. Bake them in a shallow pan for 20 minutes. Just before serving time pour a little cream over each one. Slide them under the broiler till the crumbs are brown — 2 or 3 minutes.

Sprinkle the minced parsley over them. Arrange them around the roast. Put a sprig of parsley on top of the stuffing and a wreath of parsley and watercress around the platter. Cicely supplied one of Sheffield silver with a gadroon edge. Her mother polished up one with a border of grapes. Both wish the donors at the time of their weddings to know that the Viennese chef considered the effect worthy of his talents.

Paradise Jelly (H.J.P.)

Europeans are not supposed to like jelly with meat, but perhaps there were enough Americans present to account for its all vanishing. Anyway it was a Dane who asked for the rule and who said he would get his mother to try it next time quinces were ripe.

6 large apples	1 quart cranberries
9 large quinces	about 2 quarts water
	sugar

Wash apples and quinces. Remove blossom ends, stems and cores. Pick over and wash cranberries. Cut up quinces and apples, add water and cranberries. Boil till mushy. Put in a jelly bag and let juice drain off overnight. In the morning boil the juice twenty minutes. Skim it carefully. Measure. Add 1 cup of heated sugar for each cup of juice. Cook until it jells when tested on a chilled saucer. Cover with paraffin — first a very thin layer; when it hardens, another one. Put on sterilized covers.

Mrs. Appleyard hopes you know someone who has a quince tree and that they really grow in Denmark and that that nice young Dane has a cranberry bog. Or perhaps he'll get mountain cranberries from Sweden. He seemed a determined character: she's sure he'll manage all right.

Peas and Pearl Onions with Mustard Sauce (L.V.B.)

Allow one can of very small onions to 2 cans of tiny French peas. Drain vegetables and heat over hot water with 2 tablespoons of sweet butter. Pass the mustard sauce with them.

French Mustard Sauce

2 tablespoons butter	½ teaspoon crushed garlic
2 tablespoons flour	1 tablespoon grated Parmesan cheese
salt to taste	¾ cup light cream
a few grains of cayenne	1 egg yolk
1 tablespoon Dijon mustard au vin blanc	2 teaspoons butter (extra)

Melt 2 tablespoons of butter. As soon as it starts to foam, remove pan from fire and rub in flour mixed with salt and cayenne. Add mustard, crushed garlic, grated Parmesan and then the cream, slowly, stirring all the time until mixture is smooth. Return pan to low heat and add a tablespoon of the warm sauce to a beaten egg yolk, stir well add another tablespoon of sauce, mix thoroughly and stir mixture back into the sauce. Add the extra 2 teaspoons of butter, dot by dot, and cook till sauce begins to thicken. Remove pan from heat, cover it and set it aside where it will keep warm, not hot until serving time.

Scotch Oatcake (A.L.)

It was not possible to get real Scotch oats but A. L. turned out what seemed to Mrs. Appleyard like a very fine batch by putting regular oats, the kind she uses in oatmeal cookies, through the grinder.

2 cups regular oats, ground	1 cup flour
¼ cup sugar	½ cup butter
2 tablespoons butter (extra)	1 teaspoon baking powder
salt to taste	3½ tablespoons water

Mix the oats and the flour sifted with baking powder and salt together. Work in the butter, which should be at room temperature, with a pastry blending fork. Add the water. Pat out the oatcake into a well-buttered round tin. Crease it in wedge-shaped pieces. Dot with extra butter. Bake at 325° until delicately browned: 10 to 15 minutes. Serve hot or cold.

Artichokes Hollandaise

Cicely did these. She washed them and cooked them in a very large steamer for about half an hour while the soup and the roast were being eaten, and made the Hollandaise (p. 127) while the table was being cleared.

There is something restful about eating artichokes and it took a long time, so long that Mrs. Appleyard, never much of a dallier, excused herself and sneaked off into her kitchen to deal with the dessert.

Baked Alaska

The day before, Mrs. Appleyard had done the basic part or — to be quite accurate — Sara Lee in Chicago had done most of the work for her by baking pound cake with real butter and freezing it for Mrs. Appleyard's convenience.

(You may make your own, if you like, p. 272.)

She had sliced the pound cakes and lined the oblong pans the cakes came in first with wax paper, then with the slices. Then she had put in quart bricks of chocolate ice cream, which were by a happy coincidence the right size, topping them with the top slices of the cake. She had then returned the pans to the freezer so that the ice cream was good and hard.

Now she covered a cooky sheet with several thicknesses of heavy brown paper on it, lighted the oven: 450° and made the meringue.

Meringue (for two loaves)

whites of 6 large eggs	¾ cup sugar
¼ teaspoon cream of tartar	1 teaspoon vanilla

Beat whites until frothy with the cream of tartar, add the sugar a tablespoon at a time, beating after each addition. Beat till it sticks to the bowl and forms peaks. Add the vanilla. Remove loaves from pans, remove wax paper, set them on the cooky sheet. Cover sides and tops with meringue. Smooth it slightly along the sides but heap and swirl it lightly and casually on top. Bake it 3 to 5 minutes, in a preheated 450° oven until the top just starts to brown. Serve at once, so it will be warm outside and cold inside. One loaf is supposed to serve eight but Mrs. Appleyard says that's a little skimpy. For the sixteen internationalists she made three loaves. All vanished. She sometimes serves Hot Chocolate Sauce (p. 103) with it but not after a dinner like this one.

Cooking this meal and in betweentimes coasting or skiing on Cicely's hill, the one bordered with white birches, gave everyone a good appetite, including Mrs. Appleyard who got most of her exercise walking between her kitchen and Cicely's. Probably she walked about three miles, she thinks. She also went out into the zero air for a while and watched the skiers.

Their tracks, as they climbed the hill, made a pattern of pale blue featherstitching against the snow. The tracks downhill were deeper and bluer. Caps and jackets were spots of bright embroidery. Camilla had the dog sledge she got for Christmas out with Eric hitched to it. He pulled it amiably and curled his handsome black and silver tail until it touched his back but he did not make much headway. Eric is more interested in dreaming of chasing elk than in supplying motive power for a sledge with bright green cushions piped with scarlet. However, he added a picturesque touch to the landscape and though this year he had no icosahedral star to chew, he thoroughly enjoyed the bones from the crown roasts.

After the Baked Alaska was finished, the skiers went out to the hill again, by starlight this time. When they came back, Jean Gebhardt made cheese fondue for them. Luckily Cicely and her mother both have electric skillets. These are ideal for making the fondue.

Vermont Cheese Fondue
FOR EIGHT

1 bean garlic, peeled	2 pounds Vermont cheddar cheese
1½ cups white wine	cut in small cubes
½ teaspoon pepper	1 tablespoon kirsch
1 teaspoon Worcestershire	French bread sliced ½ inch thick
sauce	and toasted

Split the bean of garlic and rub the pan well with it. Pour in the wine and heat until it starts to bubble. Add seasonings except the kirsch. Add the cheese, lower the heat, stir until the cheese is melted and mixture is smooth. Add the kirsch. Stir well, reduce heat to below 200°. Give everyone a plate, a fork and a piece of toast and let them dip the toast into the fondue. Start the second skilletful as soon as the guests start dipping into the first one. Keep the fondue warm. The bottoms of the pans will ultimately be covered by a crisp golden crust. This is the best part of all. The more of it the customers get off with a spatula, the less trouble it will be to wash the pan.

How fortunate, Mrs. Appleyard thought, that she and Cicely had given each other an automatic dishwasher for Christmas. The kitchenmaids loved it and fed it several rounds of dishes. Orion, the canary, sang all the time to its pulsating swish. The mechanical Christmas tree joined in occasionally. The cats arranged themselves like gargoyles carved out of tortoise shell and listened politely. Eric thumped his tail in a rhythm of his own. Marie-Claire could play the piano besides being able to cook, ski and look like a porcelain angel, so till midnight carols in many languages rang through the house.

How nice to be able to go abroad without packing a suitcase, Mrs. Appleyard thought as she stepped over the sleeping bags on her way to bed. The occupants were already asleep in the light of her Christmas tree with its tinsel and starlight and white roses. What a brave old world that had such creatures in it! she thought and was asleep before she could remember what she was misquoting.

Furred and Feathered Friends

It took Mrs. Appleyard some time to recover from the international festivities. For nearly two weeks she spent most of the time reading her Christmas books. These however did not last her indefinitely. She received only fifteen and as she averaged about a book and a half a day, number of pages and density of ideas considered, the supply was soon exhausted. At one time her average was two a day but of late years she has made a conscientious effort to read more slowly. In fact the last time she reread *Gone With the Wind* it took her two days. Cicely tries to keep her mother supplied from the circulating library but she has to read the book first herself. There was a time when mothers read books to see if they were suitable for their daughters but times change and it is Cicely who carefully leaves a note tucked into some sturdy tall octavo saying: "Dear Mother, I forbid you to read this book."

This means that the book contains a larger proportion of obscenities than Mrs. Appleyard really enjoys. She goes back to Gibbon who did as he promised and, when he felt obliged to write anything improper, put it into a footnote where it was "veiled in the decent obscurity of a classic tongue." Mrs. Appleyard wishes modern authors would take up this practice which would, she thinks, encourage the study of Latin and Greek. She clings to an old-fashioned belief in the cultural value of these languages though she must admit, having glanced at some of Mr. Gibbon's footnotes, that it is possible to be as uncultured in Latin or Greek as in American.

During her reading period, as she supposes she would have called it if she had been an Oxford undergraduate, she lived chiefly on yogurt and Tiger's Milk (orange juice, brewer's yeast and delicious veal bones ground fine) with an occasional toasted cheese sandwich or a grapefruit sent to her by someone who knew exactly what she wanted. Occasionally she made a batch of candied grapefruit peel but after a time she became conscious of the fact that the peel, if placed end to end, would probably reach nearly to Florida so she gave up that sticky sport. She did however make a few candied cranberries while she was about it.

She also constructed a meat loaf, which seemed rather tasty the first six times she ate it. In fact at first she served it to herself under the flattering title of *pâté maison*. She always writes out the menu, of course, and inserts it in the rococo gilt frame she once had given to her for that purpose.

("Mrs. Appleyard," inquired her favorite editor at this point, "do you expect your readers to believe that?"

"No," said Mrs. Appleyard, "but I'm sure they'd like to.")

It was at this time that Mrs. Appleyard became so much more interested in feeding birds than in cooking for herself. At first she was embarrassed to find that her menus were no more interesting to the birds than her own were to her. Birds in Appleyard Center have so many feeders to choose among that they are pampered and blasé, she decided.

Naïvely she had expected that, like human beings, the birds would pass the word around that a charming little new restaurant, cafeteria service, had opened up back of the cedar hedge, near that sprangly old Golden Transparent apple tree; that the counter was protected from snow and rain; that sunflower seeds were exquisitely served in an emerald-green container and that all you had to do to get more was to jump on the handle. She had also supposed that possible customers would hear that the suet, handsomely set forth in silver dishes (formerly containing frozen pound cake) had a certain *je ne sais quoi* about it: pound cake crumbs in fact.

Obviously, she began to think sadly, what they were really saying was "No Cordon Bleu, she."

However one morning while she was still asleep, someone rapped sharply on her door.

"Come in!" Mrs. Appleyard said drowsily but politely.

No one came in and the rapping went on.

After a while she realized that it came not from her door but from the window near the bird feeder. She got up to look. The customer departed promptly in a great flashing of blue and white and West Point gray. He flew into the apple tree and screamed impatiently at Mrs. Appleyard who, being a woman, forgave him his bad manners because of his handsome appearance. Besides he was her first visitor. He and his fellow blue jays, sometimes there were five posing in the apple tree, had irritably snatched most of the suet by ten o'clock. They evidently re-

sented bird watchers though all Mrs. Appleyard was doing
was sitting at her desk writing a book, a quiet occupation,
she had always thought; nothing obviously menacing about it.
Still the blue jays may have known some other authors because
every time she moved her pen they would fly off announcing:
"The pen is mightier than the sword" or screams to that effect.

Perhaps they are Russian blue jays and think I am writing a
sequel to Dr. Zhivago, thought Mrs. Appleyard.

This seemed unlikely. She came to the conclusion that they
suspected her of being a capitalist. Little did they know how
near the purchase of sunflower seeds was bringing her to bank-
ruptcy.

However she was getting less nervous customers now so she
kept her smörgåsbord running. When the Christmas trees were
untrimmed, she set some of them up around the feeder and
decked them with holly. Sometimes on bright blue and white
mornings, the trees would be diamond-dusted with snow and
chickadees with their neatly tailored black velvet caps and bibs
would hop in and out among the branches before landing on
the feeder. They were more afraid of the jays than they were
of Mrs. Appleyard and her powerful pen, she noticed.

One morning as she sat writing, arrived a great flock of evening grosbeaks, splendidly caparisoned in yellow and white and
iridescent black. Their soft voices and fluttering wings made
a perpetual whispering as they found sunflower seeds and
cracked them. They seemed to regard Mrs. Appleyard simply
as part of the décor, a compliment of which she was humbly
appreciative. A downy woodpecker, stylish in black and white
with his scarlet cockade appeared. There was a pair of nut-
hatches, inquisitive and skeptical with their turned-up beaks;
red polls and pine grosbeaks came too. At last she had a visitor
well-known in Appleyard Center, a chickadee with cap and bib

mottled with white as if snow had been sprinkled on him. He had a pink bill instead of black and his eyes were surrounded by white instead of black so that he had an expression like no other chickadee. He had an excellent appetite, in fact he was so hungry that Mrs. Appleyard put out the rest of the meat loaf for him and some Yorkshire pudding with melted suet poured over it. He liked it so much that Mrs. Appleyard realized that she was now in ornithological society. He came every day and neither a moving pen nor rustled papers disturbed him at his lunch.

At last, thought Mrs. Appleyard, I have a feathered friend. And I, she reflected putting on her new platinum mink hat, am a furred friend. How nice we're so congenial.

Menu for Birds and Their Watchers

Meat Loaf* with Mushroom Sauce*
Broccoli with Garlic Croutons*
Yorkshire Pudding, giant-sized*
Candied Grapefruit Peel*   Candied Cranberries*
Mince Turnovers*

Meat Loaf

1 pound ground chuck	1 teaspoon minced onion
1 pound Vermont sausage meat	pinch of mixed herbs
6 slices of bread	pinch of celery flakes
½ cup milk	½ cup dried bread crumbs
2 eggs lightly beaten	6 strips of suet
¼ cup light cream	1 tablespoon melted butter

Have the butcher put the ground chuck and the sausage meat

together through the grinder. Soak bread in milk 5 minutes and squeeze it dry. Mix together the beaten eggs, light cream, onion, herbs and celery flakes and mix with the soaked bread, then work this mixture thoroughly into the ground meat with a pastry blending fork. Butter a bread tin and put in the meat mixture. Cover the top with the dry crumbs mixed with the melted butter. Lay over the top 6 very narrow strips of suet. Bake at 350° for one hour and 15 minutes.

Note: this time is for 2 pounds of meat. A smaller quantity will do in 45 to 50 minutes. In both cases reduce the heat to 300° if it browns too quickly. Before you put the loaf on the serving platter, pour off the melted fat. Save it.

As Mrs. Appleyard is frequently heard to remark at this season, "That's for the Birds."

Mushroom Sauce

1 pound mushrooms, peeled, caps only	salt to taste
	½ teaspoon paprika
1 teaspoon minced onion	¼ teaspoon pepper
2 tablespoons butter	¼ teaspoon nutmeg
2 tablespoons flour	piece of bay leaf
1 cup light cream	1 cup heavy cream
1 tablespoon sherry	

Save the mushroom skins and stems for soup. Slice the peeled caps vertically. Sauté onion in the butter until translucent, then add the mushrooms and cook till they are tender — about 5 minutes. Remove with skimmer to top of a double boiler. Now rub the flour into the butter. Add more butter if necessary. There should be at least 2 tablespoonfuls in the pan. Remove pan from heat while you are doing this. Return it to very low heat and cook the roux for 3 minutes. Now add the light cream slowly at first, stirring well to make a thin paste free from lumps. Add the dry seasonings, including the bay leaf. Add the heavy cream. Let the sauce simmer gently but not boil for 5 minutes. Pour it over the mushrooms in the double boiler. It will be all the better if it stands for an hour before you use it. At serving time fish out the bay leaf, heat sauce, add sherry.

Broccoli with Garlic Croutons

1 package chopped broccoli	¼ cup cream
1 tablespoon butter	garlic croutons (p. 56)

Follow cooking directions on a package of frozen broccoli. It will speed up cooking time and will not injure the flavor if you allow it to defrost at room temperature half an hour before you start to cook it. Cook uncovered after it is boiling hard. If the water has not all cooked away when broccoli is tender but not mushy, remove broccoli to a hot dish and cook the water down to 2 tablespoons. Add the butter and the cream, heat well and pour over the broccoli. Sprinkle over the garlic crumbs. Serves four, stingily.

Yorkshire Pudding
GIANT SIZED

If you have a 15-inch scarlet and ivory enameled iron frying pan or a plain 15-inch iron pan, now is the time to use it.

3 cups rich milk	3 cups flour, measured after sifting 3 times
salt to taste	tried out beef suet, half an inch deep in the
12 eggs	pan

Light oven: 400°. Try out suet over medium heat. Be sure the flour is warm and dry. Have a pitcher big enough to hold the entire mixture. Use an electric mixer or your blender. Mrs. Appleyard prefers the blender. Blend the ingredients in three lots, dumping in 4 eggs, a cup of milk and a cup of flour each time. Pour the blended mixture into your pitcher and repeat the process. You blend each batch only one minute so it does not take long. If you use an electric mixer or a hand beater it takes longer. Add the milk slowly to the flour, beating all the time, and then beat in the eggs one at a time. Do not let your suet overheat. It should be hot but cracklings should not be browned.

Pour in your batter. Stand back! The fat will spit, spatter and sizzle and come up around the batter on the edges of the pan. Set the pan in the oven. Bake it until the pudding has risen well and has started to brown — about 20 minutes. Don't keep looking at it. You will only be depressed by its sullen appearance and letting cold air in on it only delays the rising. Reduce the heat to 350°. It takes about an hour altogether for a 15-inch pudding to get crisp and brown. Leave it a little longer, reducing the heat to 300° if you have any doubts. You don't want any soft and soggy spots in it.

Mrs. Appleyard first made this for her friend Venetia Hopkins who was having ten people to dinner and who was afraid there would not be enough. There was. Fortunately one of them was a poet with strong wrists developed by tennis and skiing. It was he who maneuvered the pan in and out of the oven. In case Mrs. Appleyard forgot to thank him, she does so now.

For four people use a nine-inch pan and a third of this mixture. It should cook in 45 to 50 minutes.

Candied Grapefruit Peel

Cut the peel of two grapefruit lengthwise in ¼-inch sections. Soak overnight in 4 cups cold water with 1 tablespoon salt. Drain, cover with cold water, bring to boiling point and cook 20 minutes. Drain and repeat the process several times until peel has no bitter taste. Then cook until tender, an hour or more. Drain and cook slowly in syrup made of 1 cup sugar and ½ cup water. Use a candy thermometer and cook until it registers 238°. Or you can do it in the electric skillet with the control set at 238°. Put in the peel, cook till transparent. Remove peel with a spoon with holes. Spread on aluminum foil till cool. Roll in granulated sugar. Store in tightly covered tin box.

Candied Cranberries (J.B.)

When a former colonel in our armed forces turns his attention to cooking, he really makes something unusual and good.

1 cup sugar	1 cup cranberries, the largest and
1 cup water	best of a package

Make a syrup of the sugar and water in an electric skillet with the control set at 238° or in an iron skillet over the flame. It is hard to use a candy thermometer in a shallow pan, so test the syrup by dropping a little off the spoon until it spins a thread. With a good-sized needle make several holes in each cranberry. This is so that they will absorb the syrup and also it helps them keep their shape. When the syrup threads, drop in the cranberries and cook until they look translucent. Skim them out, place them on aluminum foil to dry overnight. The next morning roll them in granulated sugar, spiced if you like with a little cinnamon. Store in a tightly covered tin box.

Syrup left from either the grapefruit or the cranberries may be used in punch.

Mince Turnovers

If you have some of Mrs. Appleyard's 2000-Layer Pastry (p. 60) left in the refrigerator, it's an easy matter to make these: that is, if you also have a little mincemeat on hand.

Light oven: 450°.

Roll out the paste into a piece ⅛ inch thick and 8 inches square and cut it into sixteen 2-inch squares. Put a teaspoon of mincemeat on each one, moisten edges, fold the squares over into triangles and press edges together with the back of a fork lightly dipped in flour. Put into a shallow pan and bake for 15 minutes. Check to see if they are puffed and delicately browned. Bake 5 minutes longer if necessary. Don't worry if the mincemeat is oozing out at the edges here and there: it tastes all the better. Serve either hot or cold: very nourishing at 10° below zero.

Use packaged pastry if you must, though the turnovers will not be so delicate as these.

Snowbound

PERHAPS Icebound would be a better description but the snow came first. It fell steadily for two windless days and nights in tiny determined flakes that heaped themselves up so efficiently that even the slender gnarled branches of the Golden Transparent apple tree were piled six inches high. Maples, which had been fans of black coral against the sky, suddenly became white coral dusted with powdered rainbows. Elms were wineglasses holding bouquets of white leaves. Black twigs of white birches were whiter than the trunks. Only big pines a century old were still obviously pines, thrusting out their arms in their own pattern, carrying their burden with their old patience.

A storm like this would jam the streets of Boston or New York with crawling cars. In the District of Columbia it would occur to no one that the streets were for driving. Cars that had been freed from their owners' nerveless hands would rapidly get to look like igloos. It would be a time of peace. The only time that Mrs. Appleyard was ever offered champagne at ten o'clock in the morning was during a storm like this. She thinks there ought to be more of them. She likes to think of her Washington employees sitting at home quietly drinking champagne. No one would order nuclear tests in the atmosphere or think up any new "temporary" taxes (like the

income tax for instance) or raise the postal rates again.
Of course Mrs. Appleyard realizes that this is necessary. In
1912 it used to take a day for a letter to get from Boston to
Appleyard Center. Now that the Post Office has so much interesting automatic equipment, it sometimes takes four days. Naturally such service has to cost more than it did when letters were
sorted with a good deal of thumb-licking and carried in model T
Fords. Letters have to be kept somewhere all those days so
extra space is needed. Besides it is necessary to buy more automatic sorters so that the pace throughout the country will be
uniform. If it would only snow oftener in Washington, it would
save the taxpayer millions of dollars — or is it billions? Who
knows the difference? Or cares?

Not Mrs. Appleyard certainly.

She occupies herself with important distinctions such as
whether syrup is hot enough to spin a thread six inches long
(240° in case you have any spinning to do) or is merely at soft-
ball stage (238°). She also likes to try to tell a skunk spruce
from a fir balsam when both are pyramided with snow.

Snow can be enjoyed in Appleyard Center. It does not stop
traffic. This is not because the snow is essentially different from
Washington snow. Each crystal is unlike any other crystal but
the substance as a whole is the same. The attitude towards it is
where the difference lies. In Washington they figure that the
Lord sent it and will after a while take it away. In Appleyard
Center, Eric Vardon, the road commissioner, knows that if he
does not plow eighty miles of road, milk will not get to market,
mail will not leave, children will not get to school, their fathers
will not get to work. If snow is getting deep on the roads at
5.30 A.M., that's when he starts plowing. He keeps it up till
the roads are passable. And plows again the next day if necessary, adding sand and salt to taste.

In fact he is so efficient that Mrs. Appleyard heard one of her neighbors say: "Sometimes I wish I could be snowbound three-four days. I need a good rest."

So Mrs. Appleyard has not been snowbound since she became a winter Vermonter but she has been icebound. There were two clear blue and white days after the snowstorm. Then came the sleet, encasing everything in glass, every twig, every telephone wire, every pine needle. Maple trees were crystal fans instead of coral. The ski slope outside her window was a sheet of frosted glass banded with blue glass-shadows of birches. It was eerily beautiful — up to the time the electricity went off.

The first thing she missed was the lights but perhaps, she thought, I need a new fuse on that circuit. She went into the bathroom. From there the house usually sounds to her rather like the *SS Normandie* in the middle of the Atlantic. She can hear the purring of the oil burner, the throb of the pump, the swish and splash of washing machine and dishwasher, clothes being softly tumbled in the clothes dryer, the hum of her own refrigerator and freezer and of Cicely's too, and the whirring of electric clocks.

The TV, often unwatched, tries to convince an unseen and unseeing audience that one kind of toothpaste is different from some other kind. The record player plays the first half of Schubert's great *C Major Symphony*. No one turns the record over so it repeats the first half with all the thumps, conscientiously. Music more varied, interspersed with announcers'

voices, terribly cultured, that drop a minor third on the last phrase of each paragraph and mispronounce words interestingly in many languages including their own and the Scandinavian, drifts in over the FM radio. A kettle on her electric stove whistles excitedly.

Now this had all stopped. Fortunately, Cicely is ready for such an emergency. She has gas as well as electricity to cook with, candles to light, white birch logs to burn in the big fire-place. She drew what water was left in the taps and rationed it for drinking water.

"We could melt icicles if we need water for washing," Mrs. Appleyard announced. "There's one as big as my arm outside my window. I heard of someone who used them in martinis."

"How handy," said Cicely, "but why not pour the gin in the gutter and have it ready mixed."

"Because I don't care to have gin drop on my head while I am writing," her mother said firmly.

"I thought Roger fixed that place where the ice backs up," said her daughter.

"He did but that was at my left. Now that it's fixed, the water drops on my head unless I sit at one side and catch it in my silver mug. It takes more than an hour to fill it. Anyway it won't run in weather like this and he's going to take down the gutter tomorrow. I never expected to know so much about gutters," she added. "Or electricity — oh goodness, my freezer. Everything will melt in it. If you don't mind letting me use your gas, I think I'd better cook everything in it for dinner. Yours is so much bigger that if we cover it with newspapers and a rug it will probably keep till the power comes on but mine will soften up, I'm afraid. I'll start now while it's still light and we can eat stylishly by candlelight."

This was what she cooked.

Icebound Menu

Princess Pea Soup*   Seafood Casserole*
Green Beans with Sausages* (G.S.)   Kolacky*
Golden Bantam Corn, Baked*
Cream Puffs with Pistachio Ice Cream and Chocolate Sauce (p. 103)
or with Vanilla Ice Cream and Icebound Raspberry-Cranberry Sauce*

Princess Pea Soup

FOR SIX

4 tablespoons butter	¼ teaspoon mixed herbs
4 tablespoons flour	½ teaspoon parsley flakes
4 cups rich milk	1 cup chicken stock, jellied
1 cup frozen peas, cooked	1 small onion, cooked with stock
¼ teaspoon nutmeg	¾ cup light cream
½ teaspoon paprika	½ cup breast of chicken, cubed

Melt butter over low heat, rub in flour. Remove from heat.
Add slowly a cup of milk, stirring carefully until it is smooth.
Cook over low heat, stirring all the time until it thickens, about
3 minutes. Put it in the blender with half the cooked peas and
the seasonings. Blend 2 minutes. Put in top of double boiler.
Put the rest of the peas, the chicken stock into the blender,
blend 2 minutes and add to the contents of the double boiler.
Add the rest of the milk and cook over boiling water at least
20 minutes. At serving time add the cream and the chicken
cubes. Serve very hot with Kolacky.

Kolacky (Slovak Nut Bread) (E.J.C.)

This was already in Mrs. Appleyard's freezer. She had been
saving it for an emergency and was delighted that one had arisen.
The Kolacky and directions for making it were a present from
someone who had read one of Mrs. Appleyard's books and who
thought she might like it. How right she was!

It may be made either with a raised dough or with a baking
powder biscuit dough to which eggs are added. Given here are
the directions for the raised-dough method.

8 cups flour, sifted 3 times and
   measured after sifting. Use the
   extra flour for rolling out dough.
salt to taste, about 1½ teaspoons
⅔ cup sugar

2 cups lukewarm milk
¾ pound butter, melted
3 yeast cakes dissolved in ½ cup
   lukewarm water
4 eggs

Filling:

1 cup pecans or walnuts, chopped and
   mixed with 1 cup sugar
a little water

Mix flour, salt, sugar, milk, butter, yeast and beaten eggs.
Knead dough until it is smooth and elastic. Put it into a warm
bowl, cover and let rise until double its bulk in a warm place.
Turn onto a floured board, divide in 10 or 12 portions. Let rest
a few minutes.

Make the filling. Chop the nuts fine, add the sugar and a little
water, enough so it will stick together and spread easily.

Roll out each portion in oblong shape. Spread with filling,
roll up like jelly roll. Put in large iron dripping pan. Cover.

Let rise till double in bulk. Brush top of each roll with a little butter or with beaten egg if you prefer. Bake at 400° for 10 minutes. Reduce heat to 350° and bake until golden brown, about 20 minutes longer.

Other kinds of filling such as would be used in filled cookies may be substituted for the nuts but Mrs. Appleyard recommends the original kind.

In serving the Kolacky that had been in the freezer, she thawed it out about half an hour, then sliced it about half an inch thick, spread it with soft butter, ran the slices briefly under the broiler and served them very hot.

Seafood Casserole

¾ pound frozen lobster meat	2 egg yolks
½ pound frozen or canned crabmeat	extra butter, 2 tablespoons
½ pound frozen shrimp	1 teaspoon minced onion
1 pound flounder fillets frozen	1 small green pepper, seeded
4 tablespoons butter	and sliced thin
4 tablespoons flour	1 pimento, cut fine
¼ teaspoon nutmeg	8 mushroom caps, sliced vertically
½ teaspoon paprika	2 tablespoons sherry
½ teaspoon pepper; salt to taste	1 cup dry bread crumbs, rolled fine
3 cups rich milk	4 tablespoons grated cheese
1 cup cream	

The shellfish should be thawed at room temperature for at least an hour. Steam the flounder fillets over boiling water for 10 minutes, flake them into fair-sized pieces. Set aside. Now make a cream sauce, melt butter over low heat, work in flour mixed with dry seasonings carefully; it must not brown. Remove pan from heat, blend in milk carefully a little at a time. Return to heat and cook slowly for 3 to 5 minutes. Add cream. Beat egg yolks with a fork, pour some of the sauce over them in three lots, stirring well after each addition. Stir egg mixture into the sauce. Mix well and set sauce aside where it will be warm, not hot.

Now melt 2 tablespoons of butter and lightly cook the onion, green pepper strips, pimento and sliced mushrooms in it. When onion begins to turn straw-colored, add the seafood cut up, not too fine. Cook 3 minutes. Add the sherry. Cook 2 minutes more. Butter a 2-quart casserole. Put a layer of sauce in it, then a layer of the seafood mixture. Repeat. Finish with some of the sauce. Sprinkle the bread crumbs over it, dot with butter, sprinkle with grated cheese.

Bake at 375° until crumbs are lightly browned. As the fish is already cooked, 15 minutes will be long enough.

Green Beans with Sausages (G.S.)

This dish was the result of a fortunate accident. One of the most talented cooks of Mrs. Appleyard's acquaintance once baked enough sausages for 50 people. They were supposed to surround platters of nicely broiled chicken breasts but somehow the sausages stayed in the oven. Don't think for a moment that they were wasted. Cutting them in halves rapidly, she thrust them down into the big silver dishes of green beans and someone said, "What a clever new idea! And delectable! I *must* find out how she did it!"

For a family of eight, here's how:

2 packages French-cut green beans   ½ pound link sausages, baked in a
1 tablespoon butter   350° oven for 40 minutes

Cook the beans in the smallest possible amount of hot water. Watch them carefully and cook them until they are tender but not mushy and the water has all cooked away. Add the butter. Put beans into a hot vegetable dish. Cut sausages, drained of fat on paper towels, in halves and thrust the cut half down into the beans, leaving tops half an inch above.

Golden Bantam Corn, Baked

1 package frozen Golden Bantam corn
1 teaspoon sugar

½ stick butter
½ teaspoon paprika — salt to taste
¼ teaspoon pepper

Butter rather heavily a shallow iron enamel baking dish in which corn will be served. Mix seasonings with the corn, spread it out in the dish, dot all over with butter. Bake at 375° until golden brown around the edges — 20 to 30 minutes.

Cream Puffs

There is a blow-by-blow account of how to make cream puffs in *The Summer Kitchen* (p. 202). At the Icebound period she had some on hand, also some of Howard Johnson's Pistachio Ice Cream, also some of the Granite City Creamery's Real Ice Cream. She served a choice of Chocolate Sauce as made on (p. 103) or the Icebound Raspberry-Cranberry Sauce which she invented as the twilight waned.

Mrs. Appleyard's
Icebound Raspberry-Cranberry Sauce

½ package cranberries, cooked whole according to directions on the package

1 pint frozen raspberries
1 glass currant jelly

Thaw the raspberries by setting the package in warm, not hot water. Cook the cranberries until berries are all popped. Remove from heat, add the currant jelly, stir till it is melted. Cool slightly. Add the partly thawed raspberries. Stir well. Keep in a cool place till needed.

By this time — the electricity had now been off for four hours — there was no difficulty in finding a cool place to set something. In fact the only really warm place was by the fire. They moved the table in front of it and lighted a variety of candles — pale green ones in brass candlesticks, twisted red ones in silver, a giant white and gold one that Mrs. Appleyard had for Christmas, others in glass or pewter or tin.

Perhaps it was the light of the fire and the candles and the last reflection from a pink and gold sunset coming in the window or Cynthia playing Bach on the piano before dinner or the girls all setting the table or the scent of woodsmoke — but something made that Icebound meal taste especially good to Mrs. Appleyard. When it was over, no one seemed anxious to melt icicles and wash the dishes.

"The most practical thing for you to do is to go to bed and get the bed warmed up — no electricity for your blanket tonight," Cicely said.

"That is certainly one place where candles don't make much of a substitute," Mrs. Appleyard agreed. "I'll be in bed and think what I'll write tomorrow."

So she did — for almost five minutes.

Why, she thought sleepily, sun's in my eyes, must be morning.

Then a weary tenor voice said in her ear, "On Feb'uary 15th we will bring you . . ." And she was back in the electrical world where it is so easy to purée peas and so difficult to pronounce the name of the second month in the year.

Appliances began to purr and hum and thump all over the house. Pills for indigestion and headaches and colds were seductively mentioned. Gunmen started to shoot, horses cantered, Schubert began where he left off on what Mrs. Appleyard decided must be his second *Unfinished Symphony*. Radiators hissed — ah, happy sound! The button on the control of her electric blanket glowed a cheerful bright gold.

Blessing the name of Thomas A. Edison, Mrs. Appleyard began to do a Double Crostic by a good bright light.

Now what, she asked herself happily, is "pertaining to the muscle sense"?

(Kinesthetic, in case you're interested.)

February

Jingle Bells

IT IS DIFFICULT, Mrs. Appleyard says, to arrange about snow. It is often dumped on New York or Cairo, Illinois, where no one wants it and in the meantime the supply in Vermont is inadequate. Lack of it is resented by weekend visitors from the city who say gloomily, "There's better skiing on Broadway than there is here." They consider, rather naturally, that it is the duty of the natives, including of course Mrs. Appleyard, to get at least two feet of fine powder piled up during the week, to have the roads a good deal better plowed out than Fifth Avenue, right down to the black-top in fact, and at the same time to have the same roads with plenty of hard-packed snow on them so that they can go sleighing.

Mrs. Appleyard sympathizes with the wish to go sleighing. She wants her grandchildren to remember it half a century and more from now as she still does — a big sleigh packed with straw, with hot bricks in it, the creak of runners on crisp snow, the soft thud of horses' hoofs, fur coats and blankets and buffalo robes, trees dark against the moon, singing and laughing and — most important of all — sleigh bells.

It was not until February that enough snow was packed down on the roads so that she could telephone Hugh and say "If you come this weekend, I think there'll be sleighing. I'll ask Roger to be getting your house warmed up. Sam Flint has two big pungs ready and there are still four horses in town that are able to stand up and occasionally put one foot ahead of the other. Camilla and her friends in the 4-H Club are already making cookies so they can serve them here with hot chocolate afterwards."

"Fine," Hugh said, "and Erica says she wants the family at our house for supper beforehand. Just don't let the snow melt before we get there."

"I will preserve every flake," his mother said.

Mrs. Appleyard never did figure out just how many children were packed into the sleighs. She rode only from Hugh's house to her own, not a long distance but enough so that she had breathed all the 5-below-zero air she really needed and got plenty of straw in her fur boots and heard the silver sleigh bells under the silver moon. They were her own sleigh bells that usually hang in strategic places around her house. They sound — she noticed — quite differently on a cold night with the northern lights flickering in white and green and rosy streamers

across a green sky from the way they do when they call people
to supper on hot July evenings.

Supper tonight was served in two sections, the main course
at Hugh's before the sleigh ride, the dessert at Cicely's afterwards. The riders were stoked with the following menu:

Hamburg Strong-Enough* (E.R.K.)
Rice   Fresh Asparagus, Butter and Egg Sauce*
Mrs. Appleyard's Lemon Mint Chutney*
Garlic Bread*   Tossed Salad*

Later:

Hot Coffee Chocolate* with Whipped Cream
Coconut Cookies*   Flaming Angel Cake*

When Mrs. Appleyard asked Hugh's wife what she called
that tasty dish of meat balls in a hot zippy sauce, Erica replied
that Hugh had christened it. It was, she said, a sort of cousin of
Beef Stroganov only she hadn't used filet mignon so she asked
Hugh what she ought to call it.

He tasted the sauce and said "Call it Hamburg Strong-
Enough." So that was its family name. It was made that afternoon except for the final heating and the addition of the sour
cream.

Mrs. Appleyard promptly borrowed a not very co-operative
inkish pencil, a combination of pen and pencil with most of the
faults of both, and wrote down the formula.

Hamburg Strong-Enough
FOR TWELVE

4 pounds ground chuck	¼ teaspoon tarragon
4 tablespoons flour	½ teaspoon nutmeg
Wesson oil	¼ teaspoon curry powder
2 small onions, minced	1½ cups sour cream
1 pound button mushrooms	salt and pepper to taste
1½ cups beef stock	½ cup sherry
½ teaspoon thyme	½ cup vermouth

Make the meat into balls a little smaller than a ping-pong ball, pressing them firmly into shape. Put the flour into a bag and put the meat balls in and shake gently until they are well coated with flour. Put a little Wesson oil in an electric skillet over medium heat. Put in the meat balls, a few at a time and brown them all over. Pour off any surplus fat from time to time. Save it. (Such a substance is often just what you need.) Remove the meat balls as they are browned and in the same skillet sauté the onion and the sliced mushroom caps. Save the stems for soup. Now add the stock — it should be jellied — and about a cup of hot water. Stir it well and add the dry seasonings except the salt, the vermouth and the sherry. Add the meat balls. Simmer for 5 minutes. If the sauce seems too thin, thicken it with 2 tablespoons of flour, dissolved in cold water and rubbed through a fine strainer into the sauce. Turn off the heat. Cover the skillet and let the mixture stand for at least 2 hours. Just before serving time, bring it almost to the boiling point and let it simmer 2 or 3 minutes. Add a tablespoon of the sauce to the sour cream. Stir it in well. Add another and stir well, then stir the cream mixture into the sauce. Add the salt, vermouth and sherry. Taste it by dipping a crust of dry bread into it. Add more seasoning if you like. Don't let your assistants have too much dry bread or they will eat all the sauce before the dish ever gets to the table. After adding the cream, bring the mixture to the boiling point but do not let it boil. Serve it right in the skillet with a big bowl of freshly cooked rice beside it.

Garlic Bread
FOR TWELVE

If you have Italian or French neighbors they will tell you the name of the bakery where you can buy real crusty French or Italian bread, not the mushy crusted cottony stuff that masquerades under those honorable names.

> 2 loaves of crusty Italian   ½ pound whipped butter at room
>   or French bread   temperature
>   2 teaspoons garlic powder

Slice bread almost all the way through. Blend the butter and garlic powder. Spread the mixture between the slices of bread. This may be done ahead of time. Just before serving time put the loaves in a dripping pan and heat them 5 minutes in a 350° oven.

Mrs. Appleyard likes the primitive ferocity of real garlic put through the press and mixed with real butter, but she says a mixed group seemed to prefer this gentler version.

Tossed Salad
FOR TWELVE

The version on page 147 may be used. This is slightly different, chiefly because of the tomatoes. Do not use tomatoes at this season unless you can get real hothouse ones which have both color and flavor.

French Dressing

Erica mixed her dressing in a screw-type jar. She put into it:

⅛ cup olive oil	1 tablespoon chopped chives
3 tablespoons wine vinegar	⅓ cup Wesson oil
1 teaspoon sugar	1 teaspoon dry mustard
1 teaspoon salt	½ teaspoon pepper from the grinder
¼ teaspoon thyme	½ teaspoon paprika
1 bean garlic, crushed	¼ teaspoon orégano
1 tablespoon parsley, minced	

When this was well mixed she poured half of it into a big wooden salad bowl, crossed the spoon and fork and added the salad mixture.

1 head of iceberg torn into rather small pieces	half a carrot, shredded
	¼ pound Danish blue cheese
4 stalks of celery cut into ¼-inch cubes	1 cup cauliflower flowerets, raw
5 large hothouse tomatoes, cut in eighths	2 green peppers, freed from seeds and pith, one sliced, the other cut in rings

Mix all the vegetables together except the rings of green peppers. These are to decorate the top of the salad. Keep the bowl in a cold place for at least half an hour so the vegetables will be crisp. At serving time toss them gently but thoroughly in the dressing. Be sure not to crush the tomatoes. Add the cheese, crumbled not too fine. If salad seems too dry, shake up the jar of dressing and add a little more. The dressing should coat all the vegetables and not be in the bottom of the bowl. Just before serving lay on the pepper rings, pour over another table-spoon of dressing. For 12.

Asparagus, Country Style with Butter and Egg Sauce
FOR TWELVE

Some of the best asparagus of the year comes from California at this time; large stalks, tender, good flavor.

3 large bunches of asparagus	juice of one lemon
¼ pound butter	2 hardboiled eggs
salt and pepper to taste	

Cut off the ends of the asparagus stalks at the point where they break easily. Cut the stalks into inch pieces. Keep the tips in a separate dish. Cook the lower parts of the stalks in rapidly boiling water 15 minutes. Add the tips, cover and cook until tips and stalks are tender, about 5 minutes longer.

Have rounds of buttered toast ready on a big hot platter. Also have the sauce ready. It is made by heating the butter and lemon juice and then adding the hard-boiled eggs, cut up rather fine, and the seasonings. Drain off any water left in the asparagus. Cook it down to a tablespoonful and add it to the sauce. Heap the asparagus on the toast. Bring the sauce to a boil and spoon some over each heap of asparagus. This amount of asparagus will make 12 heaps — none extra.

Lemon Mint Chutney

In the life of everyone who has tomato plants in the garden the problem of what to do with the green ones arises. This was Mrs. Appleyard's solution for the summer of 1961.

6 large onions	2 cups cider vinegar
8 pounds small green tomatoes	2 pounds brown sugar
½ cup salt	3 pounds white sugar
7 lemons sliced thin and slices cut in eighths	1 cup mint leaves
	4 cups cubes of green early apples
1 pound sultana seedless raisins	2 tablespoons ginger
2 cups green seedless grapes	

Chop onions rather fine. Add the tomatoes, chop fine. Cover with salt and cold water. Let stand overnight. Next morning drain, wash thoroughly with cold water, then scald with boiling water. Put in a large kettle. Add the lemons and the raisins. Heat vinegar, dissolve sugar (brown and white) in it and pour it over the mixture. Cook 15 minutes. Next day reheat. Cook 10 minutes, stirring well. The third day pick your mint leaves (no stems). Your cupful should be solidly packed. Purée them in the blender with ¼ cup water. Add them, together with the cubes of apple (Golden Transparents in this case), the ginger and the green grapes. Bring mixture to the boil, cook 5 minutes. Put in jars and seal.

Until the last jar of this was used up, it never occurred to Mrs. Appleyard that she would ever wish she had some more green tomatoes. Well, the days are getting longer. Before she knows it she will be out in her garden, where passersby often confuse her with the scarecrow Roger Willard made for her. Even the indigo buntings, intelligent birds, can hardly tell them apart. Perhaps that is because the scarecrow is wearing some of Mrs. Appleyard's clothes so that both are suitably dressed for picking tomatoes.

As she thought happily of sunflowers in bloom with heavenly blue morning glories twining up their stems, of broccoli flowering like yellow butterflies because she forgot to pick it, of neglected zucchini the size of watermelons, of splendid stalks of grass ready and eager to be made into cake testers, Mrs. Appleyard suddenly heard something that brought her back to reality.

Yes, it was clear, it was crystal, it was silvery — as clear as zero air, as crystal as icicles, as silvery as moonlit snow — the sound of sleigh bells. She looked out the window. There they were, under the shimmer of the northern lights, coming down the hill, past the schoolhouse, past the white houses with their plumes of white woodsmoke, past the hidden brook, singing as they came.

> Jingle bells, jingle bells,
> Jingle all the way . . .

There was still singing after they came in and thumping of tunes that children already knew how to thump on the piano in 1897 and loud shrieks of delight when all the lights were put out and Erica brought in her flaming angel cake. There was even a moment of silence while it was being served and the scalding hot chocolate was being tasted.

Hot Coffee-Chocolate

There was plain hot chocolate or coffee or a mixture of both. Mrs. Appleyard likes coffee-chocolate. It should be rather a subtle blend, about half a teaspoon of instant coffee to a cup of chocolate is plenty and with whipped cream it is guaranteed to give the drinker a night with plenty of mental energy to think over the party.

Cicely had a good supply of miniature marshmallows on hand for putting into chocolate for those preferred them to cream. They disappeared rapidly and so did the coconut cookies made by the 4-H members.

Coconut Cookies (K.McK.)

1 cup softened butter	2 teaspoons baking powder
1 cup brown sugar	½ teaspoon salt
1 cup white sugar	2 cups quick oats
2 eggs, well beaten	2 cups Rice Krispies
2 cups sifted flour	1 cup coconut

1 teaspoon vanilla

Cream butter and sugar together. Add the eggs, the flour sifted with the baking powder and salt and the oats, Rice Krispies and coconut. Add vanilla. Mix well, make into small balls (about 1 teaspoon in each), put on a cooky sheet, press out with a fork. Bake until delicately browned, at 350° for 15 to 20 minutes.

Flaming Angel Cake
FOR TWELVE

Mrs. Appleyard leaves the acquiring of the angel cake to your judgment. Make it from your great great grandmother's treasured rule using 13 egg whites, or bake the packaged kind or buy it from the supermarket.

1 large angel cake	2 packages frozen strawberries,
1 quart vanilla ice cream	slightly thawed

7 lumps of sugar
2 tablespoons pure grain alcohol

Split angel cake into 3 layers. Spread ice cream between the layers. Set the cake on a large paper plate covered with chef's foil. Fill the center with ice cream and set cake into the freezer

for at least half an hour. At serving time, pour the thawed strawberries over it, spreading them around the sides of the cake with
a spatula. Soak the sugar lumps briefly in the alcohol. Fish them
out with sugar tongs and place them on top of the cake. Light
them. Turn off all the lights. Carry the cake in blazing blue.

There were two this time so they gave a fine magical illumina-
tion as Bruce and Polly carried them in, smelled delicious and
tasted good too.

It is hoped that a suitable combination of ingredients can be
arranged for another sleighride next year.

Family Favorites

THIS sounds as if some of Mrs. Appleyard's family were her
favorites and though of course they are, all of them in fact, what
she is talking about was their favorite things to eat. During the
sleighing weekend she rashly said that she would have a family
dinner and that they all could choose something they specially
liked and she would cook it. This statement was greeted by a
chorus of "Oatmeal lace cookies" and the subject had to be
approached differently in order to supply a somewhat more
balanced menu.

What she finally did was to write slips saying Soup, Meat,
Vegetable and so forth, and let each guest draw one. This

system resulted in Nicholas's (almost two) choosing the meat. "Chicken," he said firmly, leaving the method to his grandmother.

When the results of the lottery were published — on the slate near the front door — the menu was as follows:

Appetizers

Sardines on toast   Stuffed Eggs*
Peanut Butter and Bacon (p. 126)

Onion Soup with Custard*
Chicken Simmered in Cream*
Baked Potatoes†   Green Peas*
Orange Sherbert with Bananas*   Oatmeal Lace Cookies (p. 110)

Stuffed Eggs

Choose large eggs. Hard-boil them and remove the shells. Cut them in quarters. Mash the yolks with a fork.

For four eggs allow:

2 tablespoons mayonnaise   2 tablespoons deviled ham

Blend yolks, mayonnaise and ham and fill the whites with the mixture. Mrs. Appleyard finds it easier to quarter eggs neatly if they are first cut in halves lengthwise.

Onion Soup with Custard
FOR FOUR

Make the custard early in the day:

1 egg	4 tablespoons cream
yolk of another egg	1 teaspoon salt
2 tablespoons consommé	¼ teaspoon pepper

Beat all ingredients together. Have a small buttered mold ready: the kind of tin that walnut meats come in makes a good one. Fill it two-thirds full of custard, put it on a rack in a pan, with hot water under the rack. Bake at 350° until it is set — about 10 minutes. Test with a silver knife. It is done when the knife blade comes out clean. Keep in a cool place until serving time.

For the Soup, allow for each person:

1 large onion	a few drops of Kitchen Bouquet
1 tablespoon butter	1 tablespoon red wine
6 ounces jellied beefstock	4 slices of French bread, toasted
6 ounces water	2 tablespoons grated cheese

Mrs. Appleyard keeps her own strong, well-seasoned jellied beefstock on hand but it is no secret from her that practically everyone else uses canned consommé. She doesn't really expect to make the world over this afternoon so go right ahead. Whichever you use, allow an equal amount of beefstock and water. Don't worry about its being too weak — it will cook out again.

Slice the onions and fry them gently in the butter. They should not brown, a delicate straw color is the right tint. Stir them well so that they will cook evenly. Now add the stock and water and the Kitchen Bouquet and let the soup simmer for an hour. At serving time add the wine. Toast the bread lightly on both sides. Into each hot soup plate put a slice of toast. Remove custard from the mold, slice it and lay a slice on each piece of toast. Ladle soup over the toast. Be sure the onions are evenly distributed. Sprinkle grated cheese over the custard and pass extra cheese in a bowl. You may use real Parmesan if you like but a piece of aged, dry Vermont cheddar grated is good too.

Chicken in Cream
FOR FOUR

Allow half a chicken breast, wing removed, for each person to be served. Use an electric skillet or a large frying pan over low heat.

1 small onion, cut fine	2 cups hot chicken stock, made
4 tablespoons butter	from the wings
4 tablespoons flour	½ cup thick cream
pinch of basil	4 chicken breasts
salt to taste	½ pound mushroom caps, sliced
½ teaspoon paprika	2 pimentos
¼ teaspoon nutmeg	2 tablespoons sherry
	watercress

Cook the onion in the butter until it is yellow and transparent. Remove and set aside. Mix flour and dry seasonings in a paper bag. (Choose one without holes . . . Yes, of course you know enough to do that . . . Excuse it, please. Powdering the floor is just something that happens to Mrs. Appleyard.) Put the chicken breasts in the bag and swing it around until they are well coated with the seasoned flour. Put the breasts into the skillet, skin side down, and cook over medium heat until they are golden brown. Turn and brown the other sides. Add hot stock slowly. Cover and simmer till tender over very low heat, about an hour and a quarter. Add the cream slowly during the last 5 minutes. Remove breasts to a hot platter. Add onions and mushrooms and the pimentos cut in strips to the sauce. Stir well, add the sherry. Simmer a minute. Pour sauce over the chicken. Wreathe the platter with fresh watercress.

Green Peas

There are especially good frozen green peas on the market now. S. S. Pierce has them but there are also other brands where the peas are picked when they are young and tender. When you find them, buy a good supply and put them in your freezer. They cost more than ordinary peas and are worth the difference.

This is the way Mrs. Appleyard cooks them. She says the directions on the package call for so much water that it has to be drained off, taking most of the flavor, vitamins and minerals with it. Thaw the peas, remove from the package for half an hour at room temperature. Put ¼ cup of water for each package of peas in a pan. When it boils, add the peas. Cover, cook 3 minutes. Add more boiling water if necessary. Add 1 tablespoon of butter. Cover, cook 2 minutes. Uncover. By this time the peas should be done and the water almost gone. Season according to taste. Serve in a very hot dish.

Orange Sherbet with Bananas

Before Mrs. Appleyard ever visited Appleyard Center she was told by her husband that Vermont bananas were better than other bananas. He had also made the same statement about butter, apples, cheese, sausage, turkeys, dried beef, and maple syrup. The air was different too in Vermont, he said. Hills were greener than other hills — or bluer if they were blue. Maple leaves were especially brilliant in the fall. Gravel on the roads was of a superfine texture.

Cool nights in summer, fresh-caught trout, Montpelier crackers, granite for tombstones and triple-etched rainbows were also favorably compared with other people's rainbows, granite and so forth. Mrs. Appleyard accepted it all as gospel. Before she ever crossed the Connecticut River, she had practically become a Vermonter. However, she had a slight mental reservation about the bananas.

Weren't bananas after all a tropical fruit? Would they really be improved by being taken north? Did they ripen especially well in igloos? Was it bananas, not grapes, that Eric the Red found growing so luxuriantly? Was Vineland really Lake Champlain?

Fortunately Mrs. Appleyard did not ask these questions aloud because Vermont bananas, as she soon found out, *are* better than other bananas. Long before the days of radio commercials Vermonters knew enough never to put bananas in the refrigerator and for an excellent reason: in most houses and shops there weren't any refrigerators. There were cellarways and — when a really cold place was needed — cellar cupboards, neatly screened from bats and mice. Ice was something you cut on the pond in winter and kept in sawdust in summer in case you wanted to make some ice cream.

The Appleyards — they were pioneers in such matters — had the first icebox in town. It was made by the local carpenter out of native ash, nicely matchboarded and lined with zinc. It held a hundred pounds of ice, an amount which can make rather a large lake in case anyone forgets to empty the pan underneath. This box was a little younger than Mr. Appleyard and it was his duty to keep it filled with ice and the pan emptied. Perhaps that was why he decided to go to Boston and take up desk work. Mrs. Appleyard keeps her paints in the icebox now.

In Vermont in 1912 bananas were bought in enormous green bunches and hung wrong-side up in the shady part of the store. Mrs. Appleyard was much surprised when she saw some growing and found out that bananas point up. They seem to ripen quite happily pointing down, however, and they can be picked off when they reach the right stage. There should be no green on them at all, not even on the tips, and they should be streaked and spotted with dark brown. Of course there is a school of thought that upholds those ripened under a mattress as being especially delicious but Mrs. Appleyard has not tried that method. All she knows is that when they are ripened slowly at an even temperature they develop the right flavor and texture.

The way she served them on the day of the family favorites was sliced horizontally around a big mound of orange sherbet. There were also slices of preserved kumquats and scoops of vanilla ice cream dusted over with grated tangerine peel.

Mrs. Appleyard had milk toast for supper that night. She has no idea what anyone else had.

Swing Your Partner

Mrs. Appleyard and her daughter were sitting quietly reading by the fire. At least Cicely was reading. Mrs. Appleyard shut her book. She had finished it and five minutes had elapsed without her starting another one. She was thinking.

Cicely did not realize her mother was indulging in this dangerous pastime until she heard her say: "Isn't it lucky Valentine's Day comes in vacation this year? And just when the floor needs waxing."

Cicely realized at once by her mother's trancelike tone that, though the groundhog had seen his shadow and whisked back into his hole, Mrs. Appleyard was not in a retiring mood.

"What are you planning?" Cicely asked apprehensively.

Mrs. Appleyard said she thought a simple little Valentine dance would be nice. Just enough dancers for two squares and Robin Viereck to fiddle and a few people to look on. Everyone must wear something at least a hundred years old — she said. And she'd take down the Japanese prints and hang up her own collection of old Valentines instead.

"We'll have candlelight and firelight and just a very simple supper —"

"Please don't keep saying how simple everything is," her child pleaded. "It's simple to sit and read after eating cold roast beef. Anything else I regard as extremely complicated. We'd have to go down to your house and get all those tall hats and tail coats."

"And the dancing wax and those good Viennese waltz records so Robin can rest occasionally and a few extra Paisley shawls," said her mother, "and —"

At this point Camilla began to do handsprings around the room, announcing: "I'm going to wear the red velvet jacket."

"And I'll wear the plaid silk dress with the hoopskirt," said Jane, taking a few practice spins.

"This party is evidently going to take place," said Cicely. "I'll wear that scarlet burnous — it's the only thing that fits me. I thought we were going to diet while we were writing this cookbook. What did you say you were going to have for supper?"

"Well, I thought I'd make some Tomato Tulip and some dips and real chicken à la King for the dancers to have first and then we'll have dessert later for everyone else who comes. We'll have lots of hot spiced punch for the children and champagne punch for the grownups and something deadly and delicious for dessert besides an ice-cream bar. Supper can be at your long table and I'll serve the dessert in my apartment. It will be perfectly simp — I mean it will be great fun."

Cicely agreed that anyway it would be fun.

All went as planned — with a few exceptions. Mrs. Appleyard thought she would polish the Franklin stove in her apartment before the party. This was a worthy idea but she found that all her stove polish, an heirloom inherited with the stove, was used up. It was a shock to find that no one in outer space seems to need stove polish now so shops don't carry it. The label on the can said the heirloom polish had been made in a town across the mountains so Mrs. Appleyard wrote to a friend there to see if he could get some, or the formula for making it.

He replied: "Yes, stove polish was made here until about twenty-five years ago. The formula was — luckily for Appleyard Center perhaps — a secret. One day a batch of polish exploded and blew the factory to bits while the owner was out for lunch. He has not been back. Perhaps that's why everyone in town has stoves enameled in pastel shades."

"I hope you won't try to make any," Cicely said nervously.

"Well, I thought I might just try a little honey and vinegar," Mrs. Appleyard replied. "Vermont folk medicine says it's fine for whatever is wrong with cows and people. I should think it might be worth trying."

"Does Vermont folk medicine say stoves have arthritis?" inquired her daughter.

Mrs. Appleyard regarded this question as frivolous. By controlled experiment she found that honey and vinegar, even when darkened with carbonized beets (easily produced by turning on the wrong burner of her electric stove) is not a polish. Finally she made a decoction of dark blue Esquire Boot Polish (advt.), some vinegar and some carbon of which she had plenty. Aside from the fact that people would say "what's cooking?" with a certain air of skepticism, this first batch was fine. There has never been a second because her kind friend has sent her a can of a professional brew. It seems to be nonexplosive. However, Appleyard Center folk medicine says it is no good as hand cream or for the alleviation of cracked ribs or housemaid's knee.

Having brightened up the stove and having removed a good deal of the polish from her hands, Mrs. Appleyard began serious consideration of her menu. After consultation with her grandchildren she began work on this one:

Flounder Balls*   Pink Dip*   Green Dip*
Tomato Mint Tulip*
Real Chicken à la King*   Green Beans and Beets with Almonds*
Candied Yams with Orange Marmalade Sauce*
Valentine Cheesecake with Glazed Raspberries*
Hot spiced Fruit Punch*   Champagne Punch*
Ice Cream with Crushed Strawberries
Baked Fudge Brownies (p. 117)

Flounder Balls
FOR SIXTEEN

Mrs. Appleyard began the day before by making the flounder balls. First she made a court-bouillon by cooking the bones, heads and trimmings of the flounders in water with 2 sliced carrots, 2 onions, chopped, 1 teaspoon of mixed herbs, and a bay leaf. This was to cook the flounder balls in. If you use frozen flounder, you will need only a 12-ounce package. Make the broth with an extra piece of flounder instead of the bones and heads. Add a little white wine to the bouillon just before you use it.

For the mixture:

2 pounds flounder, filleted   2 eggs
1 small onion, ground   2 Montpelier crackers (crumbs,
½ teaspoon sugar   rolled fine and sifted)
¼ teaspoon pepper

While the court-bouillon is simmering, put the fish through the grinder unless you have the kind of blender that will do it for you. By all means use it if you have. Grind or blend the small onion with the fish. Add sugar, pepper and raw eggs, working them in thoroughly. Add the cracker crumbs. Do this with your hands and make the mixture into balls. Make them small, not over a teaspoon of the mixture because they will nearly double in size. The bouillon ought to be ready in about an hour. Add the white wine and strain the bouillon through a fine strainer into a saucepan big enough to hold your open-leaf steamer. Bring the bouillon to the boiling point, fill steamer with the flounder balls and lower it carefully into the boiling liquid. Cover tightly and cook 10 minutes.

Mrs. Appleyard cooked them in several batches without letting the bouillon dry out, an achievement of which she is quite proud, then laid them on a big platter and chilled them overnight. She served them impaled on scarlet toothpicks with the two dips.

Green Dip

½ cup mashed ripe avocado pear	bits of lemon rind
½ cup watercress, cut fine	1 tablespoon light cream
1 teaspoon onion cut fine	1 cup mayonnaise
2 tablespoons lemon juice	½ cup sour cream

Into the blender put the avocado, watercress, onion, lemon juice and rind. Blend 15 seconds. Add cream. Blend till smooth. Add this mixture to the mayonnaise. Add the sour cream. Chill.

Pink Dip

1 4-ounce tin of tomato paste	a few grains of cayenne
1 cup sour cream	2 tablespoons Worcestershire sauce
½ teaspoon garlic powder	4 ounces red caviar

Mix the tomato paste and the sour cream. Add the seasonings. Add the caviar. Chill.

Tomato Mint Tulip
SERVES SIXTEEN

2 lemons, sliced thin	3 drops peppermint extract
2 teaspoons garlic powder	ice cubes
1 teaspoon ginger	3 quarts tomato juice, chilled
sprigs of mint	1 quart pale dry ginger ale, chilled

Put the lemon slices into a large bowl. Crush them a little with a wooden pestle. Sprinkle in the garlic powder and the ginger. Add a few mint leaves and crush gently. Add the peppermint and the ice cubes and the tomato juice. Stir. Let it stand in a cool place 20 minutes. At serving time stir again. Add the ginger ale. Garnish with sprigs of fresh mint. Of course the easy way to get mint is to go out and pick it by your own pond when the hermit thrushes are calling in the woods and a deer is standing up to knock young apples off a tree on the hill and the click of croquet balls is heard from the lawn. However you can usually get it in winter by ordering it ahead of time.

Real Chicken à la King
FOR EIGHT

If you like the flour paste and ancient hen mixture that usually masquerades under an honorable name, do not read this receipt. If you persist in spite of this warning you will probably want to make it so start early on the day you are going to serve it.

2 3½-pound frying chickens	½ teaspoon paprika
1 carrot	salt and pepper to taste
1 small onion	2 cups light cream
1 teaspoon mixed herbs	1 cup heavy cream
3 tablespoons butter	½ cup jellied chicken stock
½ pound fresh mushrooms, caps only, sliced vertically	3 pimentos cut fine with sharp scissors
1 green pepper, seeded, sliced very thin	2 egg yolks
	juice of ½ lemon
3 tablespoons flour	½ cup dry white wine
¼ teaspoon nutmeg	1 tablespoon butter (extra)

triangles of toast or pastry

Have each chicken cut in 4 pieces. Cover with cold water. Add carrot, onion and herbs. Simmer slowly until meat falls from the bones. Remove meat from the bones. Return bones and skin to the broth and cook at least an hour longer. Strain and chill. When it has jellied, remove all fat from the top.

In the meantime cut up the chicken meat, not too fine. Do not use any very small pieces: save them for a casserole or pâté later. In a large frying pan, big enough to hold the whole mixture, or in an electric skillet, melt the butter and gently toss the sliced mushrooms and green pepper in it. Sprinkle on the flour, mixed with the dry seasonings. Cook one minute. Reduce heat to its lowest point. Stir in slowly first the light cream, then the heavy cream. Add stock. Cook over very low heat until the mixture begins to thicken — about 5 minutes. Add the sliced chicken. Cook a minute longer. Let stand at least one hour.

When serving time comes, reheat the mixture over low heat. Add the pimentos. In a pint bowl, beat the egg yolks lightly with a wire whisk. Add 1 tablespoon of the hot cream sauce to them. Keep beating. Add more sauce, beating all the time until you have about a cup. Add the lemon juice and the white wine. Stir them in well and stir the whole mixture into the chicken and cream mixture. Cook over very low heat until the mixture thickens. It will separate if you overheat it. Just before you serve it, slip in the extra tablespoon of butter. Have a hot platter ready. Serve the chicken on it. Garnish with triangles of toast or pastry. For the Valentine party Mrs. Appleyard baked pastry hearts. That is, they started as hearts but they puffed so enthusiastically that they were not anatomically recognizable. No one seemed to mind.

Green Beans and Beets
FOR EIGHT

2 packages frozen French-cut beans	1 tablespoon butter for beets
1 tablespoon butter for beans	½ cup blanched almonds
1 can S. S. Pierce's matchstick cut beets	2 tablespoons butter

Cook the beans till tender but not mushy in the smallest possible amount of water. Add 1 tablespoon of butter during the last few minutes of cooking. Heat the beets in their own juice with 1 tablespoon of butter. Watch them: they burn easily and suddenly. Toss the peeled, blanched almonds in 2 tablespoons of butter until they start to brown. On a hot circular dish, heap the beans, surround them with a ring of beets. Scatter the almonds over the beans. Serves 8.

Candied Yams, Orange Marmalade Sauce

The best yams available in Vermont come frozen in packages. Allow 2 packages for eight people. Follow directions on the package. They need only brief reheating.

Serve this sauce with them separately:

1 cup Seville orange marmalade	2 tablespoons lemon juice
2 tablespoons frozen orange juice, not diluted	1 teaspoon grated lemon rind

Mix all together. Simmer, stirring carefully, until marmalade melts. Bring to the boil but do not boil.

Valentine Cheese Cake
FOR EIGHT

Follow the rule for glazed strawberry cheese cake (p. 87) but bake it in a shallow circular glass dish. Chill thoroughly. For the glaze use:

2 packages frozen raspberries, defrosted	1 glass currant jelly
	1 tablespoon instant tapioca

Strain juice from defrosted berries. Add currant jelly and cook until jelly is melted. Add tapioca and cook until it is clear — about half an hour. Cool until it begins to thicken. Top the cheese cake with the drained whole berries. Spoon glaze over the berries. Chill. Serves 8.

Hot Spiced Punch
FOR TWENTY

1 quart water	12 whole cloves
2 tablespoons tea	1 can frozen lemonade
2 cups sugar	2 6-ounce cans frozen orange juice
2-inch stick cinnamon	3 quarts cider

Bring a quart of water to the boil. When it boils hard, throw in the tea. Let it boil exactly one minute. Strain over sugar, spices and fruit juice. Let it stand at least 10 minutes. Longer will do no harm. Add the cider. Heat. Serve hot in pottery mugs.

Champagne Punch
FOR EIGHT

For each quart of champagne:

1 quart club soda	2 ounces curaçao
1 tablespoon sugar	1 tablespoon lemon juice
1 tablespoon orange bitters	1 can frozen orange juice
2 ounces brandy	4 ounces Bristol Cream sherry
	large block of ice

Chill champagne and soda for several hours. Mix all the other ingredients and chill thoroughly. At serving time put the block of ice in a punch bowl. Pour the mixture over it. Add the soda. Last of all add the champagne.

Diced pineapple and whole strawberries may be added if you like. Mrs. Appleyard prefers it plain.

The ages of the guests at the dance covered a wide span. James Harrison Ford IV was the youngest. He came in a basket, which was placed on Mrs. Appleyard's bed among the fur coats. He greeted his hostess with a courteous smile that showed where his teeth would be before long and went sound asleep. Mrs. Appleyard of course was the oldest person present. She is getting accustomed to being venerable, even thinks there are some advantages in it. For instance as she watched this dance with Camilla, in her great-grandmother's red velvet basque and, her partner, in an ancient sailor suit, she saw not just the dancers who were whirling over the shining floor in this kaleidoscope of color. Patterns that went back into the last century drifted before her eyes. She two-stepped by gaslight in a high-ceilinged room on Beacon Hill where a great square of Holland linen was spread over the Brussels carpet to make the dancing floor. She went to a cotillion in a big ball room copied from a room in Versailles, a cotillion with "favors" — spangled fans, enameled and gilt boxes, bunches of violets. She waltzed at a Monday German in Baltimore where one of her partners was as old, perhaps as she is now and who seemed of course to her, something that one would expect to find in an Egyptian tomb. There was Cicely's coming-out dance and Sally's. There were dances on the lawn in Appleyard Center and one in a mountain camp where she played the accordion until her arms ached.

Perhaps best of all she remembered a dance in her father's house on Woodbrook Green before she was married. Mr. Appleyard came to help her put up the decorations. They were loops and swags and wreaths of laurel with real fruit fastened to them. Just as he came into the front hall, she fell off a stepladder and landed at his feet.

He picked her up, saying as he did so: "Why is it girls always manage to fall so gracefully?"

Why, she thought, he must be in love with me! and her various bruises stopped hurting.

Not long after this they were waltzing at their wedding and a few weeks later he was teaching her to dance "Hull's Victory" in Appleyard Center.

Now, comfortably draped in a Paisley shawl, the one with the white center, she was happy to look on and rest her feet.

"It was a nice party," Cicely said after everyone had gone home and they were loading the dishwasher for the fourth time.

"Yes," said Mrs. Appleyard, "and I've just thought of something. It was my Apartment Warming — now I've had it, only no one knew it. You don't think I ought to have another, do you?"

"I think," said her daughter, "that enough is sufficient."

March

Soup's On

Mrs. Appleyard does not really spend much of her time making champagne punch and cheese cake. She is much more likely to be preparing a little homemade soup and a lettuce leaf or two. It is by eating such menus that she is able to wear the same wardrobe year after year. There is that blue and brown tweed suit for instance. It is so faded on the left sleeve, where the light strikes it in her car, that the two sleeves seem to be made out of entirely different pieces of material. At one time she thought of having the suit turned the other side out — after all it is one of her more recent ones, barely nine years old. Then Cicely brought her an interesting book on hooking rugs and it seemed as if the suit might be useful in that craft in case she should take it up. In the meantime she still wears the suit, which is the right width anyway though a little long in the skirt.

Fortunately for cooking she has some smocks and they never go out of style. Properly be-smocked you can imagine you have just stepped out of *Trilby* or that you are an ancient of some British village still chatting in Shakespearean style. Thus costumed, Mrs. Appleyard finds it natural to make soup rather than to open a can in which a few weary noodles float in a bath of monosodium glutumate, a substance Mrs. Appleyard would not offer to any visiting blue jay, no, not even to a starling. There was a time when consommé in a can used to be made as you would make it yourself with beef and veal bones and meat and vegetables and spices. Now it is constructed on the principle of the famous horse and rabbit stew which contained both — one horse and one rabbit. Probably modern consommé, in order to conform with the label on the can, does come briefly into contact with a shin of beef but such flavor as it has is supplied by MSG. The consommé costs more than it used to before this substance for raising blood pressure and promoting coronary thrombosis was discovered, but it does not cost four times as much, as it would have to if it were made of substances suitable for human consumption. MSG however is not really inexpensive. The flavor it gives is chiefly that of salt. If you must have it, get it out of a shaker.

Mrs. Appleyard could say more — pages in fact — on this topic but she refrains. When she says that, if a friend comes to supper she gives her soup and salad or soup and a dessert, she means that she made the soup herself. Here are a few menus for cold evenings when soup is welcome in the star role.

MENU 1

Fish Chowder* or Lord Baltimore Soup*
Souffléd Montpelier Crackers*
Tomato Aspic with Blue Cheese Dressing*

As the Lord Baltimore soup is a by-product of Fish Chowder, Mrs. Appleyard will first reveal how she makes the chowder.

Fish Chowder (S.W.E.)

¼ pound beef suet or salt pork	¼ teaspoon black pepper
3 large onions, sliced thin	½ teaspoon mixed herbs
6 medium potatoes	salt to taste
4-pound haddock, head and all, cut for chowder	½ teaspoon paprika
	3 cups milk
Montpelier crackers	1 cup cream
butter for crackers	slices of lemon

Cut the suet or pork into very small dice. Try them out in a large kettle until they are a delicate straw color. Remove them with a skimmer and set aside. Add the sliced onions and cook them gently in the fat, stirring often, until they are yellow and transparent. Remove and set aside. Slice the potatoes very thin and lay them in with the pieces of haddock. If you use frozen haddock, cut the fillets in thirds. Cover fish and potatoes with hot water and cook until potatoes begin to soften, about 20 minutes. By this time it should be possible to separate the skin and bones from the fish and discard them. This is a nuisance, Mrs. Appleyard admits. It's much easier to use frozen fillets. The chowder does not taste quite so good, though, as when it is made with the whole fish.

This first stage may be done any time during the day. Return the onion and diced suet to the kettle. The chowder is all the better if it stands and ripens. Just before serving time split and butter Montpelier crackers. Put them in a pan and set it into a 350° oven for 10 or 12 minutes. They should not get too brown.

While they are heating, add the seasonings and the milk and cream to the chowder. Bring it to the boil but do not let it boil or your milk will curdle. It may just simmer a few minutes. Mrs. Appleyard likes to use the blue Canton tureen that her grandmother, who taught her how to make the chowder, used too. Any generous-sized bowl will do. Put in the chunks of fish, pour the rest of the chowder over them. Top the dish with some of the toasted crackers. Pass the sliced lemon and the rest of the crackers.

Lord Baltimore Soup (R.H.P. — G.S.)

The original version of this soup was made with that light-hearted disregard of the prices of food so characteristic of the nineteenth century. No housekeeper was so ill-bred as to mention the cost of things to eat. How could she tell you? — she didn't know. When she wanted a quart of oysters she ordered them from the fishman and he delivered them. At the end of the month her husband paid the bill. He also paid the cook the $4 a week she had earned by work every day, except every other Thursday and Sunday afternoons, from 6.30 A.M. to curfew, or thereabouts. When cooks began to demand $4.50 a week he grumbled a little but he never haggled over the price of a quart of Cape Cod oysters. He wanted the soup to taste the way it did when his mother's cook used to make it. This was the rule she followed.

Lord Baltimore Soup
19TH CENTURY VERSION (R.H.P.)

1 quart oysters	1 quart chicken stock
4 tablespoons butter	4 tablespoons flour
1 teaspoon Worcestershire sauce	1 teaspoon chopped parsley
1 cup heavy cream	a few grains of cayenne

"How many is a few grains?" Mrs. Appleyard once asked her grandmother, who replied unhesitatingly, "Nine."

Not being much of a counter of grains, Mrs. Appleyard usually leaves out the cayenne. If you like to put it in, that's the right number, she feels sure.

Pick over a quart of oysters, removing any pieces of shell. Parboil them 10 minutes in their own juice. Press them through cheesecloth. Add a quart of clear strong chicken stock. Make a roux of the butter and flour, blend in the oyster and stock mixture. Add seasonings and cook gently 5 minutes. Just before serving add a cup of heavy cream. Bring to the boil but do not let it boil.

A nice dish, Mrs. Appleyard thinks, in case royalty comes to visit you. She has just heard that in our great democratic country there is a society called the Illegitimate Descendants of Royalty in America. To become a member your papers have to be all in order just as if you were going to join the Mayflower Descendants or the Society of Colonial Wars. She would like it

clearly understood that when — if ever — she serves Lord Baltimore Soup (nineteenth century) none but legitimate royalty need apply. For the Queen Mother of England, a great favorite of hers, she will even include the cayenne, all nine grains.

Lord Baltimore Soup
20TH CENTURY – 1 (G.S.)

2 cups of leftover fish chowder	½ cup breast meat of fowl or
2 cups milk	chicken
2 cups of chicken stock, jellied	½ cup heavy cream

Put the fish chowder through your electric blender or chop fine and purée it by hand. If you use the blender, do it in two batches, adding a cup of the milk to each batch. Put the purée in the top of a large double boiler over hot, not boiling water. Add the chicken stock. Stock may be made from either fowl or chicken. Mrs. Appleyard uses a chicken breast cooked in water containing a slice of carrot, a sliced onion and half a teaspoon of mixed herbs. She chills the broth after it has cooked down to 2 cups and removes all fat from the top. While the soup is heating, cut the breast meat into neat cubes and add them to the soup. At serving time add the cream and bring the soup to the boil over direct heat. Put it into a hot tureen and serve it in well-heated plates. Serves four generously with second helpings.

Lord Baltimore Soup
20TH CENTURY – 2

When she has no chowder on hand as a basis, Mrs. Appleyard makes it this way.

½ cup breast meat of chicken,   3 potatoes, sliced very thin
    cubed   1 frozen haddock fillet (12 ounces)
1 carrot   2 cups chicken stock
½ teaspoon mixed herbs   2 teaspoons flour
½ teaspoon paprika   2 cups milk
¼ teaspoon pepper; salt to taste   1 cup heavy cream
3 medium onions, sliced   8 ounces oysters, frozen
2 tablespoons butter   sherry
           slices of lemon

Cook the chicken breast with a carrot, herbs and seasonings. Cook the stock down to 2 cups. Strain, chill, skim off fat. Sauté onions in butter until they are pale yellow and transparent. Do not let them brown. Add the sliced potato and the haddock. Cover with boiling water and cook till the potatoes are done: 15–20 minutes. Put mixture through the blender in two batches. Put the purée into a large pan over low heat. Add the 2 cups of chicken stock and the cubes of breast meat. Dilute the flour with a little cold water and rub it through a fine sieve into the soup. Stir well. Scald the milk and cream in another pan. Be careful not to scorch them. Bring the chicken and fish mixture to the boil. Drop in the oysters and cook until the edges curl, about 3 minutes. Add the scalded milk and cream and bring soup to the boil but do not let it boil. Put some sherry and sliced lemon into hot plates. Soup's on — come and get it! Now!

This Lord Baltimore soup was so elegant that Mrs. Appleyard thought of serving Lady Baltimore cake with it, a ghoulish suggestion whch she discarded in favor of

Souffléd Montpelier Crackers

After making these for twenty or thirty years Mrs. Appleyard noticed that the top halves of the crackers puff more mountainously than the bottoms. Slow to catch on but prompt to act, she decided henceforward to use the bottoms for ordinary toasting or to use for casserole topping or in meat loaf. Occasionally, when a moment of efficiency attacks her, she rolls out the crumbs ahead of time and keeps them in a jar in the refrigerator.

These then are the ingredients she now uses:

water with ice cubes in it
top halves of Montpelier crackers   butter

The amount of butter used will depend on how many crackers you use. Be generous with it. Quarter of a pound should do 12 or more crackers. Have it at room temperature.

Into a large pottery bowl put cold water and ice cubes. As the ice cubes melt, split the crackers and drop the top halves into the water, split sides up. Light the oven: 450°. Watch crackers all the time. Have ready a cooky sheet covered with a clean damask napkin. At the end of 3 minutes — or sooner if they seemed to be softening too fast — remove crackers from water. Use a pancake turner with holes in it to do this. The crackers will be wider than when you put them in. Put them on the cooky sheet and set the sheet in the refrigerator for 5 minutes. Butter iron dripping pans and transfer crackers to the pans, working as quickly as possible. Dot them thickly with butter. Bake them until they are puffed, crisp and golden brown. This will take at least 35 minutes, longer if you have more than one panful. Check them at the end of half an hour. Add more butter if they look thirsty. Allow at least an hour for the whole process. If you try to hurry them, you may end with something resembling a moist blotter. What you want is something as dry and light as a dandelion ball. It is the sudden exposure of the soaked, chilled buttered cracker to intense heat that produces this effect. Customers must wait for them rather than the other way. If you put a second batch into the oven, to be ready when the salad is served, Mrs. Appleyard thinks you will not have much trouble in disposing of them.

Tomato Aspic

Make this the day before you plan to serve it.

4 envelopes (tablespoons) of plain gelatin	2 teaspoons sugar
	4 cloves
1 cup cold water	salt to taste
2 large onions, chopped fine	2 large cans of tomato
1 teaspoon grated lemon rind	juice (7 cups)
1½ teaspoons pepper	4 tablespoons lemon juice
1 tablespoon Worcestershire sauce	

Soften the gelatin in cold water. Simmer the onion, lemon rind and the seasonings with the tomato juice for half hour. Strain some of the juice over the soaked gelatin and stir well. Strain the rest of it into another kettle. Add the gelatin, lemon juice and Worcestershire sauce. Rinse a 2-quart ring mold with cold water. Pour in the tomato mixture. Set the mold into the refrigerator.

Ah, how steady the hands must be! How vital to see that a large enough space in the refrigerator is clear! How fatal if the corner of a rug is turned up!

Perhaps it is only Mrs. Appleyard who has to think of these things. Let us turn to the moment of unmolding, also a perilous time. You are — she suddenly recalls — supposed to stir the aspic twice before it sets. This however is a minor moment of danger. Even Mrs. Appleyard can usually manage the stirring without calamity; but the unmolding — that is really crucial.

Have ready a round chop plate, charger or silver tray. Put a little water on it, less than a teaspoonful, and spread it around evenly with a pastry brush. In case you do not center the mold exactly on the plate, the moisture will make it possible to tease the aspic into position without dislocating its personality. Now summon your courage, your judgment, your philosophy. Set the mold in warm (not hot) water for 5 or 6 seconds. Don't leave it too long. Loosen the aspic around the edges with a silver dinner knife.

Put your platter over the mold. Reverse the whole thing. Did you hear a gentle plop? Rather like the noise made by a ripe apple falling on sun-warmed grass? Good! Sink gracefully into a Chippendale chair, heave a sigh of relief, mop your brow. Mrs. Appleyard does so hope you won't have to mop the floor too. Perhaps you prefer to collapse into some other type of chair. Mrs. Appleyard's winter kitchen is also her living room so she has to use what is at hand.

When you are sufficiently rested, put the aspic back into the refrigerator. Before you serve it, make this filling to go in the center, if you used a ring mold, or to put in heaps around the edge if you used some other shape.

1 cucumber	lemon rind
1 small onion, thinly sliced	¼ cup French Dressing
green pepper	lettuce or watercress
2 tablespoons chives cut fine	½ cup sour cream
1 tablespoon fresh parsley, minced	½ cup Mayonnaise (p. 265)

Peel the cucumber. Engrave the edges by drawing the tines of a fork down the outside of it. Slice it thin. Add the onion slices. Slice the green pepper in very thin rings. Remove seeds and pith and add rings to cucumber mixture. Sprinkle with the chives, parsley and lemon rind. Add the French dressing and toss until the vegetables are well coated with it. When serving time comes, put sprays of watercress or leaves of Boston lettuce around the aspic. Put the cucumber mixture into the center of the ring. Mix the sour cream and the mayonnaise and mask the cucumber mixture with this dressing.

Pass Danish Blue or Roquefort cheese with the aspic. If the souffléd crackers have vanished, sesame crackers are good to put it on or homemade whole wheat bread or Melba toast. In fact Mrs. Appleyard likes it on pretty nearly everything. There is however no law that says you shouldn't use cream or cottage cheese if you prefer.

MENU 2

Beef chowder*   Popovers (p. 13)
Tossed Salad (p. 147)

A chowder is, of course, anything made in a kettle. Probably you knew that already. Mrs. Appleyard did not until she began to write a book about Champlain and noticed that one of the dangerous whirlpools he and his Indian guides had to portage around was called the Kettle — La Chaudière. For the first time chowder and chaudière struck together in her mind. Up to that moment she had always thought that chowder had to be made of fish. Laying down her pen and getting out her electric chaudière, she promptly invented

Beef Chowder Appleyard

¼ pound beef suet, diced	½ teaspoon mixed herbs
2 large onions, sliced thin	4 cups beef stock
3 carrots, sliced	1 tablespoon lemon juice
½ teaspoon cinnamon	1 teaspoon instant coffee
¼ teaspoon nutmeg	2 tablespoons sugar, caramelized

Dice the beet suet and try it out in the skillet over medium heat. Skim out the cracklings and set them aside. Spoon out 3 tablespoons of fat and set aside. Add the sliced onion and sauté until it is straw-colored. Add carrots and sauté 2 minutes. Add cinnamon, nutmeg and herbs. Add the beef stock, the onions, the instant coffee and the caramelized sugar. Rinse out the pan in which you caramelize it with a little stock so you will get all the brown color and flavor. Cook over low heat until carrots are done — about half an hour. Add the lemon juice.

In the meantime make some meat balls, using:

1 cup homemade bread crumbs	1 bean garlic or ¼ teaspoon garlic powder
½ cup milk	1 minced onion (small)
½ pound Vermont sausage	2 tablespoons butter
1½ pounds ground chuck	3 tablespoons flour
1 egg, lightly beaten	2 tablespoons minced parsley

3 tablespoons beef fat (from skillet)

The sausage Mrs. Appleyard uses may be Colburn's in Montpelier or Harrington's in Richmond, Vermont. Both are made of excellent materials, finely ground and lightly seasoned. Jones Brothers and MacKenzie are also brands she likes.

Soak the bread crumbs in the milk 5 minutes and squeeze them dry. Mix sausage and ground beef thoroughly together. Add the egg and the bread crumbs. Put the garlic through the press and add it or sprinkle the garlic powder over the mixture. Sauté the minced onion in the butter until it is yellow and transparent and mix it in. Make the mixture into small balls, pressing them firmly. Put them into a paper bag with the flour. Shake the bag gently until the balls are well coated with flour. In the pan in which you sautéd the onion put the tried-out beef fat. Put in some of the meat balls and brown them on all sides over low heat. Repeat until all are done. Add more butter if necessary.

By this time the vegetables should be done. Add the meat balls, simmer 5 minutes. The chowder should now stand at least an hour barely simmering or until you are ready to serve it. At serving time if the gravy does not seem thick enough, add 2 tablespoons flour, diluted with cold water and strained through a fine sieve into the chowder. Let the mixture simmer a few minutes then bring it to the boil and serve it very hot with the diced cracklings and the parsley sprinkled over the top.

This is the basic rule for making it. Mrs. Appleyard varies it slightly according to materials on hand. If she has no stock on hand she substitutes tomato juice. Sometimes she adds mushroom caps sautéed in butter and broth made from mushroom stems to the kettle. A dozen small radishes may be sautéed with the carrots and added. They taste like very mild young turnips. If she has a few stalks of celery, she cuts them fine and adds when she starts the carrots.

Sometimes she adds

Dumplings

1 cup flour 2 teaspoons baking powder
½ teaspoon salt 2 tablespoons butter
½ cup milk

Sift dry ingredients. Cut in butter with pastry blending fork, add milk. Pat out about ½ inch thick, cut with biscuit cutter. Butter top of steamer. Have water boiling hard in bottom part. Place biscuits in the top. Cover tightly. Steam until raised and light — 10–12 minutes. Put on top of the chowder.

If you *must* salt the chowder, do so just before you serve it. It only toughens the meat if it is added earlier. Another thing that Mrs. Appleyard found out while writing about Champlain was that the Huron Indians, the handsomest and healthiest people Champlain had ever seen, never ate salt. The Indians never had scurvy either until they ate the white men's salt meat and fish. Eating salt, Mrs. Appleyard concluded, is just a nervous habit. So, perhaps you may think, is having stock on hand. Skip this if the habit annoys you.

Stock

The ideal place to make stock is the top of an old-fashioned coal or wood stove. The invention of gas and electric ranges for a long time made the stock kettle a thing of the past. Even Mrs. Appleyard did not make stock. However, modern gas burners thermostatically controlled, deep-well electric cookers and electric skillets, electric burners with well-controlled low heat all make producing stock easy and practical.

Into the stockpot, whatever you use for one, should go bones from roasts, leftover vegetables, tomato juice, mushroom stems, celery tops, and any water left over from cooking vegetables. This is perhaps the most valuable thing in the stock since it contains vitamins and minerals, which otherwise would be lost. Mrs. Appleyard makes a practice of cooking vegetables in very little water and she usually comes out even — except of course when the telephone rings and she finds on her return some carbonized beans and an hour's work of saucepan scouring. With certain kinds of vegetables — asparagus and potatoes, for instance — even she has cooking water left over. That water goes into the stockpot instead of down the drain. Calcium, another substance valuable in your diet, gets into the stock from bones, which otherwise would be thrown away.

A stockpot also helps keep the refrigerator in order. Instead of serving small dabs of things, which you ultimately throw away because you are so tired of seeing them, put them in the stockpot. It is not necessary to keep stock cooking all the time. Make a kettleful two or three times a week, letting it simmer a few hours. Then strain it and cook it down until you have about a quart. It will take up much less room than all those saucers. You will be surprised by how often you use it.

Menu 3

Cream of Pea and Shrimp Soup*
Fruit Salad*

Cream of Pea and Shrimp Soup

Make cream of green pea soup. Use the rule for the Princess Soup (p. 178) but omit the breast meat of chicken. For four people make a quart of soup. Allow one 6-ounce package of flash-frozen cleaned shrimp to each quart of soup. Put the soup into the top of a double boiler over hot, not boiling water. Cook the shrimp, tightly covered, in a very small amount of water until tender — about 5 minutes. Add them and any liquid remaining to the soup. Bring to the boil but do not boil. Serve at once.

Fruit Salad with Cream Cheese Balls

Mrs. Appleyard uses the fruit that comes frozen in glass jars, drains it, saves the juice to drink. She adds a sliced ripe banana, 4 canned pears, halved, and some whole fresh strawberries to the fruit. She marinates it in the following:

Fruit Salad Dressing

1 tablespoon lemon juice	1 tablespoon honey
3 tablespoons Wesson oil	¼ teaspoon mustard
½ teaspoon paprika	½ teaspoon white pepper
salt to taste	1 teaspoon lemon extract
2 drops peppermint extract	

While the salad is marinating make

Cream Cheese Balls

2 tablespoons powdered sugar	1 teaspoon thick cream
3-ounce package cream cheese	2 tablespoons candied ginger, cut fine
1 tablespoon chopped blanched almonds	

Sprinkle a small cutting board with the powdered sugar. Mix cream cheese, cream and candied ginger. Sugar your fingers slightly and make the mixture into balls. Sprinkle chopped almonds on the sugared board and roll the balls in the mixture.

Line the salad bowl with watercress or Boston lettuce. Toss the fruit gently a few times in the dressing and heap it in the bowl. Put the cheese balls around the edge. Serve.

This is what Mr. Appleyard used to call feminine food. He was not unkind about it. He just wanted to make it clear that he would rather have a thick steak or tripe or hash or, in fact, pretty nearly anything else. Mrs. Appleyard feels it her duty to let it be known that when a man says: "How did you make this?" he is not necessarily paying you a compliment. He may just want to be sure that his wife never makes it.

More masculine is

MENU 4

Onion Soup in Casserole*
Deep-Dish Apple Pie (p. 102)
Vermont Cheese

Onion Soup in Casserole
FOR FOUR

4 large onions, sliced thin	8 slices French bread, ½ inch
4 tablespoons butter	thick
1 quart stock	butter for toast
½ teaspoon Kitchen Bouquet	4 tablespoons red wine
8 tablespoons grated cheese	

Slice the onions and fry them in the butter until they are straw-colored. Do not let them brown. Add the stock and 2 cups of water. This will cook out again, leaving the stock as strong as before. Add the Kitchen Bouquet and let the soup simmer for half an hour. Toast the bread on both sides. Spread lightly with butter. Put the soup into a large casserole, add the wine, put the slices of toast on top of the soup. Cover them thickly with the grated cheese. Set the casserole in the oven at 350° and cook until the cheese is well browned — about half an hour.

With sophisticated elegance Mrs. Appleyard serves Tuscarora Beaujolais with this meal. When she asked the wine expert at the Golden Dome Market if there were any difference between Tuscarora Beaujolais Claret and Burgundy, he replied: "Sure there's a difference. You make the Burgundy by pouring half a gallon of Beaujolais and half a gallon of Claret into a gallon jug . . . No, it won't spoil — it's pasteurized."

Mrs. Appleyard hopes no one in France will hear about this.

Quiet Please

HER FRIENDS in Boston find it hard to understand why Mrs. Appleyard has buried herself — that's what they call it — in the country. They realize that in the summer it is possible that someone might drop in but in the winter — ?!

"It must be so *quiet!*" they say.

Mrs. Appleyard's idea of a quiet place is the corner of Fifth Avenue and Forty-second Street. Some of her most peaceful moments have been spent outside the New York Public Library watching for a bus. There is also something relaxing about standing at the corner of Tremont Street and Temple Place in Boston. Things about it have changed since she was a girl but not so much as in most places. The spire of Park Street Church still thrusts itself into the sky as decoratively as it used to when it was the seventh tallest building in the world. The dome of the State House is still a golden bubble. The Masonic Temple where her grandmother went to school, where Bronson Alcott used to teach, is still on Temple Place. It is on top of Stearns's store. Mrs. Appleyard can remember when it was discovered, in the process of adding several stories to the store, that legally the Masonic Temple, part of the old building, must remain on the site forever. So, instead of being pulled down, it was pulled up. Watching the process was one of Mrs. Appleyard's favorite occupations. She liked to think that if it had happened when Alcott taught there that he might easily have been pulled up into the sky and never have noticed it.

The Common is a peaceful place. If Mrs. Appleyard's apartment were in Boston instead of in Appleyard Center, she could sit on a bench on the Common and no one would speak to her. An occasional squirrel might look at her skeptically. Pigeons would waddle around her feet but otherwise her reveries would be undisturbed. Yet the Common is not always completely impersonal. Nor is Fifth Avenue. Once, as she crossed the Common near the Frog Pond she smiled at a particularly attractive little Boston bambino. His Italian grandmother promptly snatched him up and made the sign of the evil eye at Mrs. Appleyard. Once at Forty second Street J. P. Morgan, Jr., crossed Fifth Avenue to the library beside her. He removed his flat-topped pale gray hat and said "Good Morning" but not to her. On the whole social life in these centers of culture is limited.

Not so in Appleyard Center. Cicely's house is central and she has that nice big room. In it may be found at intervals the 4-H Club, the Bible Study group, the Development Council and other organizations too numerous to mention. Music lessons take place there and ballet dancing and parcheesi. Pictures cut into a thousand pieces are put together again. Mozart, Vivaldi, the sound of the typewriter and highbrow jazz echo through it, accompanied by descants from the canary's cage. He loves music whether by piano, dishwasher, washing machine or TV.

Kittens bat balls across the floor of the big room. Elkhounds drop in to call on their brother Eric and to play with the kittens. Each dog has his favorite kitten, which he carries around by the scruff of its neck. Nils, an especially amiable elkhound, drops in from time to time to get Cicely to pull the latest batch of porcupine quills out of his nose.

Then outside the house there is always something going on. Nils is tracking another porcupine. Eric is baying at the moon. A deer hears him and makes a great curve of bounding tracks across the snow. Blue jays frighten a flock of evening grosbeaks away from the sunflower seeds. Mrs. Appleyard frightens the blue jays, not on purpose, just by knocking over the inkbottle. She uses jet-black.

When snow falls deep, Sam Flint brings his ivory and scarlet jeep and plows out the garage, so Cicely can get out, and the drive, so that the oil truck and the gas truck can get in. In zero weather they are frequent and welcome visitors. The town plow and the sander often go up and down the hill. The drivers wave as they pass. The cars that make their cautious way to the store all belong to someone you know. They are not so numerous as the cars on Fifth Avenue but they have more personality.

Every now and then there is an out-of-state car. Above the roof, skis thrust their noses condescendingly into the air. Inside, summer residents clutch the steering wheels and peer out nervously upon the landscape as if — Mrs. Appleyard thinks — they are afraid the Vermont panther is going to pounce upon them for lunch.

A good many of these visitors stop at Cicely's to get news of the roads to their houses. Hearing statistics about the height of snow above the ground and the depth of frost below it, they often decide it would be simpler just to put their sleeping bags down on the floor of Cicely's living room and sleep there. Most of them eat at Cicely's house between visits to the top of Mount Mansfield.

Perhaps Mrs. Appleyard's favorite among these adventurers is one who carries an electric blanket with him. He and his bride just plug it in anywhere. Once, at Christmas time, they unplugged a community Christmas tree, plugged in the blanket, slept cozily till dawn, detached the blanket, plugged in the Christmas tree and drove on.

Usually Cicely's visitors are less efficient than these tourists. They seem to have thought chiefly about providing themselves and their hosts with good things to eat. Mrs. Appleyard is delighted to get involved in menus based on what they happened to bring from the city. Not being obliged to ski, she is able to experiment while they are away at work. It's lucky she has two kitchens available.

Skiers, she notices, are not interested in light nutritious snacks. Perhaps it is no endorsement of the following menus to say that they were eaten with enthusiasm. Probably TV dinners, about four apiece, would have done just as well. At least Mrs. Appleyard is able to report that the guests, after having washed the dishes, slept soundly. Soothed by the purr of the dishwasher, she slept all right too.

One of the guests brought a goose for roasting with him so this menu was constructed with the goose as the special feature.

Menu 1

Celery   Carrot sticks   Radishes
Goose Liver Pâté with Truffles*
Zippy Tomato Juice*   Sesame Seed Melba Toast
Roast Goose* with Chestnut Stuffing (p. 65)
Apple Sauce   Baked Potatoes with Sour Cream*
Cauliflower and Broccoli, Garlic Crumbs*
Peaches Cardinal with Orange Water Ice*
Red Wine   Pastry Pinwheels*   Coffee

Goose Liver Pâté with Truffles

There being only one goose liver and several sleeping bags full of guests, Mrs. Appleyard decided to combine goose and chicken liver.

2 tablespoons butter	½ teaspoon burnt onion powder
1 large goose liver	¼ cup bread crumbs,
1 package frozen chicken livers	dried and rolled very fine
¼ cup jellied chicken stock	2 tablespoons soft butter (extra)
½ teaspoon sugar	2 ounces truffles

Melt 2 tablespoons butter over meduim heat. Put in the livers — the goose liver cut in 6 pieces, the chicken livers, slightly thawed, in halves. Cover. Cook 3 minutes. Turn them over. Cover. Cook 2 minutes longer. Into the blender put the livers. Rinse the pan out with the chicken stock and add it. Add sugar, onion powder, bread crumbs and the soft butter. Blend until the mixture is smooth and of the consistency of thick cream. Part of the fun is dipping a piece of bread in it and sampling the mixture to see if it is smooth enough. Mrs. Appleyard's blender, an aged veteran, does it in about a minute. Stir some of the truffles, sliced thin, into the mixture. Do this with a small rubber scraper, which is also good for getting the pâté out of the blender. Pack the pâté into the dish in which you plan to serve it. Chill several hours.

Please, just as a special favor to Mrs. Appleyard, do not pronounce truffles to rhyme with ruffles or scuffles. She knows that American dictionaries, operating on the principle that if enough people do something wrong, it makes it right, have accepted this pronounciation but she has not. Tru as in true, please, when mentioning this fragrant delicacy.

Zippy Tomato Juice
FOR EIGHT

1 cucumber, peeled and diced	2 teaspoons sugar
4 tablespoons chopped green onions and tops	2 tablespoons Worcestershire sauce
thin peel of 2 lemons	3 drops tabasco
1 tablespoon prepared horseradish	salt and pepper to taste
5 cups Hunt's Tomato Juice	juice of 2 lemons
	lemon slices

Put the cucumber, onions and tops, lemon peel and horseradish through the blender into a cup of the tomato juice. Pour into a tall glass pitcher, add the seasonings, lemon juice and the rest of the tomato juice. Chill thoroughly. Add ice cubes and the sliced lemon. Serve.

Roast Goose

Mrs. Appleyard had never cooked a goose before. Someone else had always cooked the ones her family used to have at Christmas time. She approached the bird with respect and a certain amount of nervousness. She is glad to report that it yielded amiably to the slow method, being spied upon by a meat thermometer in Cicely's electric roaster.

She began by stuffing it with chestnut stuffing and then brushed it all over with Wesson oil and sprinkled it lightly with flour seasoned with pinches of sage, thyme and marjoram. She allowed 25 minutes to the pound at 300° and cooked it to 185° on the meat thermometer. It weighed a little over 12 pounds so she allowed 5 hours. It actually reached 185° in 4 hours and 20 minutes so she removed it from the roaster and set it in a warm place. It carved all the better for being taken out ahead of time.

Baked Potatoes with Sour Cream

Bake good-sized potatoes for 15 minutes in a preheated oven at 450°. Reduce heat to 350° and bake 35 minutes longer. Cut a slice from the side of each and remove contents to a heated bowl. To each potato allow ½ tablespoon of butter, 2 tablespoons soured cream, ¼ teaspoon paprika, salt and pepper to taste, and finely scissored fresh parsley.

Mash the potato with butter, seasonings and half the sour cream. Beat until light and pile into the potato shells. Use the rest of the cream to top each potato. Set the potatoes on a baking sheet and run them briefly under the broiler until the cream just starts to brown. Sprinkle with parsley and serve.

Cauliflower and Broccoli, Garlic Crumbs

1 large head of cauliflower   4 tablespoons butter
2 bunches fresh broccoli   ½ teaspoon garlic powder
1 cup bread crumbs   salt and pepper to taste
yolks of 2 hard-boiled eggs

Remove the stalk and leaves from a head of cauliflower, soak it in salted water 10 minutes. Use flowers of the broccoli, not the stems, and put flowers also in salted water. Drain and rinse well. Have water boiling hard in a large saucepan. Set your unfolding steamer into it. Place the cauliflower in the center of the steamer and surround it with the broccoli. Cover closely and cook until the vegetables are tender but not mushy — about 20 minutes.

Toss the crumbs in the butter until golden brown. Add the garlic powder and other seasonings. Mix well. Make the cooked egg yolks into rather coarse powder. Sprinkle the crumbs over the cauliflower and the broccoli and the powdered egg yolks over the broccoli. Mrs. Appleyard serves this combination on a rather shallow old yellow pottery dish that she thinks is rather becoming to it.

Peaches Cardinal with Orange Ice
FOR EIGHT

The day before she made this dessert, Mrs. Appleyard had rinsed out a melon mold with cold water, packed it with orange water ice and set it in the freezer.

2 packages frozen raspberries   2 packages frozen peaches
¾ cup sugar   1½ quarts orange water ice
½ cup blanched, shredded almonds

Boil the raspberries with the sugar, strain them through a fine sieve to remove the seeds and boil the syrup until it is quite thick. Chill. Leave the peaches in the refrigerator for several hours so they will be partly thawed. At serving time unmold the orange ice in a large rather shallow bowl. Arrange the peaches around the ice. Springle almonds over the peaches. Pour raspberry sauce over ice and fruit and serve.

Pastry Pinwheels
ABOUT TWO DOZEN

These are sometimes called Pastry Leaves — taste good under either name.

Roll out pastry into an oblong 8 × 12 inches. It should be rather less than half an inch thick. Mrs. Appleyard uses her own pastry (p. 60) but she thinks the packaged kind ought to work all right. Dredge your molding board or pastry cloth well with sugar mixed with a pinch of cinnamon and a pinch of nutmeg. Allow at least ½ cup of sugar. Lay your sheet of rolled pastry on the sugared surface. Dredge it with another ½ cup of sugar and spice. Roll up the pastry like a jelly roll. Do it the long way so your roll will be 12 inches long. Dredge more sugar on any bare spots. Slice it as you would jelly roll only much thinner, about ⅜ of an inch. Lightly grease baking pans or heavy cooky sheets. Lay the pinwheels on them, not too close together. Bake at 450° for 5 minutes. Turn the pinwheels, using a pancake turner and a spatula. Reduce heat to 350°. Bake 10 minutes longer or until the sugar starts to turn to caramel. Do not overbake as they may burn suddenly. Keep them in a tightly covered tin box with wax paper between layers.

On another night of deep snow a guest arrived bringing a leg of lamb with him. This tactful gesture resulted in

Menu 2

Mushroom and Bacon Canapés*   Cheese and Chutney Appetizers†
Roast Lamb*
Mashed Potatoes   Spinach Ring with Peas*
Tossed Salad (p. 147)   Currant Jelly
Apricot Crossbar Pie*   Vanilla Ice Cream

Mushroom and Bacon Canapés

Mrs. Appleyard uses her own mushroom sauce (p. 169), made from mushrooms she picked in her own pasture for these. There is plenty of it in her freezer except in non-mushroom years.

In using it for the canapés, Mrs. Appleyard cooks the sauce down for an extra 3 or 4 minutes so that when it has cooled for about half an hour it will be a good consistency for spreading. In the meantime she cuts out small circles of thinly sliced bread and toasts them on one side. She cooks bacon until not quite crisp, drains it on a paper towel, cuts it into small squares. Then she spreads the untoasted side of the bread with the mushroom sauce, tops the sauce with squares of bacon. At serving time she runs a pan or baking sheet of the circles under the broiler just long enough to heat them thoroughly and crisp the bacon.

Roast Lamb

Let the lamb stand in a cool, not cold place for 24 hours before you roast it. A covered roaster with the vents open is a good thing to keep it in. For a 5-pound leg (trimmed) allow 30 minutes to the pound —2½ hours at 300°. Insert a meat thermometer. Be sure it does not touch the bone. Rub the lamb all over with Wesson oil and then with seasoned flour: 4 tablespoons of flour, ½ teaspoon mixed herbs, pepper from the grinder, ¼ teaspoon nutmeg, 1 teaspoon garlic powder.

Start it in a cold oven. Mrs. Appleyard likes to use an electric roaster for lamb. She and her family like it slightly pink so she considers it ready at 155°. Let it reach 160° or 165° if you like it well done. This will take perhaps half an hour longer. If it is not brown enough to please you, run the roast under the broiler for a few minutes.

On this hungry evening the family left only enough lamb to make soup for supper the next night. Perhaps this is the moment to tell how.

Lamb Soup

Leave the lamb right in the roaster. Cover it with hot water. Add 2 carrots, sliced, a large onion, also sliced, pinches of herbs — rosemary, basil, tarragon — a cup of thick tomato juice, ½ teaspoon of Worcestershire sauce, ½ teaspoon of instant coffee, a pinch of curry powder. Let the lamb simmer until the meat falls from the bones — about 3 hours. Remove and discard the bones. Pour the soup, meat, carrots and all, into a large bowl and set in a cold place.

At this point you may wash your roaster. Mrs. Appleyard calls it to your attention that you have roasted meat and made soup, and washed only one receptacle, also that it is practically washed already.

When you make the soup, skim all the fat from the broth. Sauté, in 2 tablespoons of the fat, 2 large onions sliced thin. Sprinkle in 2 tablespoons of flour seasoned with pinches of cinnamon, cloves, pepper and garlic powder. Blend it in well. Remove pan from the heat. Spoon in the cold broth, stirring well until you have a smooth mixture. Add the rest of the broth, the meat and the carrots. Taste it. Add more tomato juice and some lemon juice if you like. Serve with Montpelier crackers, split, buttered, sprinkled with sesame seeds and toasted until lightly browned. With a dessert this is a whole meal.

Spinach Ring with Peas
FOR EIGHT

2 bags washed spinach	1 teaspoon nutmeg
1 tablespoon chopped onion	¼ teaspoon pepper;
¼ cup water	salt to taste
1 cup milk	½ cup cream
3 tablespoons butter	4 eggs, not separated
3 tablespoons flour	1 package frozen peas

croutons from 2 slices homemade bread (lightly browned in
2 tablespoons of butter — do this while the spinach is baking)

Chop spinach and onion with the water until the spinach is limp. Keep chopping. It takes about 4 minutes. Now put ⅓ of the milk, water from the spinach and half the spinach into the blender and purée it. Add the rest of the spinach in two more lots. Now melt the butter, work in the flour and seasonings slowly. Remove from heat and stir in the rest of the milk. Be sure there are no lumps. Stir in the cream. Cook over low heat till it thickens. Remove from heat. Add the spinach purée. Mix well. Add eggs one at a time. Beat well after each addition. Put the mixture into a well-buttered 1½ quart ring mold. Have oven at 325° with a pan containing hot water on the lowest shelf. Set the ring on a shelf close above it. What you are baking is a little like a soufflé, rather more like a custard. Bake it until a knife blade comes out clean — about 35 minutes. Cook the peas during the last 6 or 7 minutes. Do not overbake the spinach or it will separate.

To get it neatly out of the mold, let it stand a minute. Run a spatula around the outside edge of the ring and a small dinner knife around the inner edge. Invert on a circular dish. Fill the center with the peas, cooked in as little water as possible and for the shortest possible time. After you have put the peas in the ring, cook the liquid remaining in the pan down to the last half teaspoonful. Add a tablespoon of butter and one of thick cream. Season to taste. Pour it over the peas. Scatter the croutons over the spinach.

Apricot Crossbar Pie

The apricots must be cooked at least 24 hours before you make this pie. They are really even better if they stand several days. This is how Mrs. Appleyard cooks them after experimenting with several different methods.

Conserved Apricots

2 cups water   2 packages dried apricots
1¼ cups sugar

Start water boiling. Put apricots into a folding steamer. Have the legs of the steamer long enough so that they hold apricots above the water. Cover tightly and steam till apricots are tender and have increased in bulk — 12 to 15 minutes. Be sure water does not cook away. You should have about 1¼ cups left in the pan. Pack the apricots into a quart jar. Press them down if necessary. Some of their flavor will be left in the water in the pan. Add the sugar to it and cook until the syrup just starts to color. Pour it over the packed apricots.

If you like apricots pallid, ragged, sour and watery, don't do them this way.

Now back to the pie. You will need:

2 eggs, well beaten	1 tablespoon Cointreau
2 tablespoons syrup from apricots	(optional)
2 tablespoons lemon juice	1 pint conserved apricots
grated lemon rind	½ cup blanched, shredded
1 tablespoon frozen orange	almonds
juice, not diluted	1 teaspoon butter, melted

Enough of Mrs. Appleyard's pastry for one pie (half the rule on p. 60). Line a 9-inch pie plate with the crust, fluting it neatly around the edge.

Mix the beaten eggs, syrup from the apricots, lemon juice and rind, orange juice and Cointreau together. Add the apricots. Put the mixture in the pie shell. Sprinkle over it the blanched and shredded almonds, brushed with the melted butter.

Light oven: 450°.

Now make the crossbars. Roll the pastry into a piece 9 inches long and cut it into strips. Moisten the places to which you fasten them slightly with a pastry brush dipped in cold water. Lay them across, the first strip north and south, the next one east and west and so on, until the pie is latticed. Do not put them too close together because they are going to expand. Chill the pie for a few minutes, then bake it at 450° for 15 minutes. Reduce heat to 350° and bake until pastry is well puffed and delicately browned — about 35 minutes longer. Turn it in the oven if it browns on one side more quickly than on the other.

Serve it warm with vanilla ice cream, thick Vermont cream in a pitcher or, for Mrs. Appleyard, some Vermont cheddar cheese.

Menu 3

The next pair of guests had prudently and generously equipped themselves for the rigors of a New England winter with an enormous ham, all cooked and sugary brown and bristling with cloves like an amiable porcupine. They told Mrs. Appleyard how they cooked it. They read the label, they said.

This already shows that they were promising cooks. The label tells you whether the ham has been precooked or not and this is something you had better know. This ham had been precooked and it weighed about 15 pounds. They estimated it would take 10 minutes per pound to bake it, and they used a meat thermometer and baked it at 300° until the internal temperature was 155°. First they scored it in diamonds and rubbed into it a mixture of brown sugar, a little mustard, a pinch of ginger, and finely rolled bread crumbs, and then stuck it with cloves. For a sauce with which to baste it they used ½ cup of ginger ale, ½ cup of dry white wine, one cup of light brown sugar, one teaspoon of mustard and one of ginger. They basted it every 20 minutes and when the ham was done they poured the sauce left in the pan over it.

It sliced beautifully. You could read *Paradise Regained* through a slice in case you had an early edition and were in the mood. The guests also endeared themselves by bringing half a bushel of oysters in the shell, beautifully packed in ice, the cold being reinforced by dry ice and Vermont weather.

This menu was easy to plan:

Oysters on the Half-Shell
Oyster Bar Sauce*
Brown Bread and Cream Cheese Sandwiches*
Baked Ham (cold) with Minted Pears*
Cheese Croquettes*   Cole Slaw
Mocha Angel Cake*

Mrs. Appleyard had not seen so many oysters in one spot since she was last in an oyster bar on Broadway. She and Venetia Hopkins were going to the theater together. They had managed to get two tickets, one for *My Fair Lady* and the other for something depressing by Tennessee Williams. Mrs. Appleyard had already received a slight dose of melancholia from this in Boston and Venetia had already seen *My Fair Lady* so the only problem was where to eat. Luckily Venetia chose the Oyster Bar and fortunately Mrs. Appleyard told the barman she thought the cocktail sauce was the best she had ever eaten.

He recognized a kindred soul and said, "I have to make another batch before I go off duty. Wanta see me do it? Take notes if you like."

Mrs. Appleyard's notes were on the edges of a piece of paper which contained something she had found in the New York Public Library about John Paul Jones. She happened to be writing a book about him at the time. Using her own filing system (Pat. Applied For) she had filed it under two headings: J.P.J., watch, lost under interesting circumstances and Cocktail Sauce, Oyster Bar, Broadway. What is more she found it just now when she needed it.

Oyster Bar Sauce

Mrs. Appleyard's original manuscript calls for a gallon of Heinz Tomato Ketchup and a pint of horseradish among other things.

Using the set of Napier's Bones her grandson made her for Christmas she reduced the quantities to more homelike proportions.

1 cup Heinz Tomato Ketchup	1 cup Heinz Cocktail Sauce
1 cup Heinz Tomato Juice	1 tablespoon Lee & Perrin's
2 tablespoons prepared horseradish	Worcestershire Sauce
2 drops tabasco sauce	1 sliced onion, minced fine

thin peel and juice of ½ lemon

Mix everything together. Chill.

This turned out so well that her guests said they would get her a job on Broadway. She thinks however that she had better stick to off-Broadway (approximately 278 miles off) production. Drop in any time, bring your oysters and one of those twisty knives. She will supply the sauce.

Mrs. Appleyard usually makes her own brown bread but on this occasion no one wanted to wait three hours so it came out of a can. She says Friend's Brown Bread and Yellow-Eye Baked Beans are as much a part of New England as Plymouth Rock — more nourishing too.

Brown Bread Sandwiches

Slice brown bread about ⅜ inch thick. Have butter and cream cheese at room temperature. Into a 3-ounce cream cheese mash

1 tablespoon of thick cream. Spread rounds of bread thinly with the butter, more thickly with the cream cheese. Cut the circles in halves. Allow 3 halves for each person to be served.

Minted Pears

These were a garnish for the ham.

½ cup juice from can	1 tablespoon lemon juice
½ cup sugar	grated rind of 1 lemon
¼ teaspoon green coloring	5 drops peppermint extract
8 halves of canned pears	

Boil the pear juice and sugar till thick and syrupy. Add the green coloring, lemon juice and rind and the peppermint extract. Add the pears, 2 or 3 at a time. Turn them gently in the syrup until they are evenly colored. Remove with a slotted pancake turner and a perforated spoon. Hold the pear over the pan and let all the syrup drain back into the pan then place the pear on a cold plate and cook the others in the syrup till all are done. Use as a garnish for ham with watercress and half circles of sliced canned cranberry sauce.

Pears done this way may also be used as a dessert with lime or pineapple sherbet.

Cheese Croquettes

Mrs. Appleyard has never been down into the Grand Canyon on a mule, flown in a plane or fried anything in deep fat. All three ideas terrify her. Cicely, however, is made of sterner stuff and besides she has an electric fryer. Mrs. Appleyard marvels at her child's skill but she supposes it is natural to each generation to enjoy its own dangers. In her time she took being nearly drowned when a canoe upset or being missed by inches by a steamer in a thick fog with a certain amount of aplomb. For her grandmother a kettle of hot fat had no terrors. This was how she inspired her cook to make cheese croquettes, often frying the first ones herself, just as a form of sport. This rule served eight hungry ski maniacs generously.

6 tablespoons butter	1 teaspoon Worcestershire sauce
½ cup flour	few grains of cayenne
1⅓ cups milk	yolks of 6 eggs
salt and pepper to taste	1 cup dry cheese, grated
½ teaspoon paprika	1 cup mild cheese, cubed
1 teaspoon dry mustard	2 egg yolks (extra)
1 cup fine dry bread crumbs	

Make a thick white sauce of the butter, flour, milk and seasonings. When it is smooth, add the egg yolks, unbeaten. Add the dry cheese — Parmesan if you like but aged dry cheddar is all right — and stir well. Add the mild cheese. Do all this over rather low heat and take the pan off the fire as the cubes begin to melt. Cheese gets stringy and tough if overcooked.

Pour the mixture into a 9 × 13 pan. Spread it out. Cool. Mark in oblongs. Beat with a fork the extra 2 egg yolks and 2 tablespoons of water together. Roll each oblong of the cheese mixture into a cylinder. Dip them first into the dried crumbs, then into the egg mixture, then into crumbs again. Chill briefly. Fry in deep fat (Crisco) at 380°–390° till golden brown — about a minute. Do a few at a time. They should be crisp outside, a little like Welsh rabbit inside.

Mocha Angel Cake
FOR TWELVE

Making this was an adventure needing no special daring. Mrs. Appleyard gladly undertook the task. As the angel cake was handed to her in a neat carton the project seemed pretty well suited to her capabilities.

½ cup strong hot coffee
2 tablespoons Chocolate Sauce
   (p. 103)
24 marshmallows

1 large angel cake, sliced
   in 4 layers
1 cup thick cream
1 square bitter chocolate, shaved

Make the coffee with 1 tablespoon of instant coffee to half a cup of water. Make it in a pan big enough to hold the marshmallows and chocolate too. If you do not have chocolate sauce on hand, use 4 tablespoons of chocolate bits and melt them in the coffee. Add either sauce or bits to the coffee and then the marshmallows. Keep stirring until they melt. Cool until mixture begins to thicken. Spread it between the layers of cake, placing them on top of each other. Do this on the plate on which you plan to serve the cake. Cover it with four triangles of wax paper so that any spots will be on the paper instead of on the plate.

Mrs. Appleyard learned this example of culinary neatness by watching TV. If there were more cooking and fewer singers who cannot sing on it, she would probably never have any time to cook.

Chill the cake till serving time. Whip the cream and swirl it around on top. Sprinkle on the bitter-chocolate shavings. Pull out the paper triangles.

After the ham and the mocha cake and their donors had disappeared a strange era of peace descended upon Appleyard Center. Eric ran away, chasing an elk presumably. Nils, having had all his porcupine quills extracted, went off on a round of visits. One of the cats ate the canary. The TV stopped working, Cynthia stopped sandwiching Bach with Israeli folksongs and took up experiments in ESP, Mrs. Appleyard was presented with a new book of Double-Crostics, Jane taught Camilla how to set her new Italian haircut so it would be crooked in the right places. Cicely brought home six books from the library and censored them with a view to her mother's Victorian attitudes towards literature. She forbade Mrs. Appleyard to drive.

Since the roads were glare ice, and since Mrs. Appleyard had seen her former adversary zooming down the hill in a series of skids at 60 m.p.h. she agreed to stay indoors.

She sat in her suntrap. She wrote up her diary. She looked out at the hillside with its brocaded surface of blue and silver. She prepared delectable meals for the birds. The Escoffier of Appleyard Center, they called her. Or did she dream that? It's quite possible: she slept a good deal of the time.

One morning, we are a little embarrassed to report this, she woke up thinking, Peace — it's wonderful! But isn't anything going to *happen?*

Yes, it had been quiet enough even for Mrs. Appleyard.

Democratic Progress

I sometimes think," Mrs. Appleyard said to her daughter Cicely, "that it would be easier to get this book written if I went to prison. You know Cervantes was a prisoner for a while and he got a lot of writing done. And Bunyan — he wrote nine books in prison. One of them was a best seller."

"What kind of crime would you commit to get in?" Cicely inquired.

Mrs. Appleyard considered a few she had seen on TV lately and crossed them off.

"Something clean and neat," she said, "and that really wouldn't bother anyone much. I guess perhaps embezzling some money from a bank might be the best."

"You would have to be working in a bank," her child pointed out. "Does that seem likely?"

"My checkbook balances," Mrs. Appleyard asserted with natural pride.

"Oh, that's what you were groaning about before supper. I was afraid you were having sciatica. Besides didn't you tell me you have a list of forty-five different kinds of errors you've made at some time?"

"Yes," said her mother. "The list is very useful. I just glance it over and see if I forgot to write a stub or copied the balance wrong or subtracted a deposit instead of adding it or — well, there are ever so many kinds of mistakes, some I haven't made yet, I daresay."

"You could learn to make the others if you worked in a bank," Cicely said encouragingly. "Besides you're practically a prisoner here at this season anyway."

Mrs. Appleyard admitted that this was true. The drive was a sheet of glare ice. The mercury was at 20° below zero, and a March gale was howling around the house.

"The trouble is the company is too good. It would be different in jail," she said.

"It's been very quiet lately," Cicely said. "I think your trouble lies there."

She was right of course. Fortunately the quiet was temporary.

The next afternoon while Mrs. Appleyard was sifting flour for a pound cake, just to calm her nerves, the telephone rang. Since she has never outgrown the belief that something mystic and magical lies behind each ring, she snatched up the receiver with a floury hand.

"I'd like to speak to Cora Maxwell," said a man's voice.

Mrs. Appleyard knew how he had got her number instead of the Maxwells. It's quite simple. You just dial the first three figures of the exchange instead of the first two. She explained this fact of life patiently and politely. The caller thanked her and hung up. The telephone rang again. The young man — his slight Southern accent sounded very attractive to Mrs. Appleyard — still wanted the Maxwells.

No wonder, Mrs. Appleyard thought. Cora is a lovely girl.

She told the caller so and gave him a refresher course in how to dial Cora's number.

"I think you're mighty nice," said the young man. "Why don't you go out with me instead of Cora?"

"Because I think you're crazy," Mrs. Appleyard told him frankly and returned to her pastry.

It would have served him right if I had, she thought as she sifted the flour again, and I could have worn my black velvet and my new pretty nearly ermine cape.

Again the telephone, imperative, ingratiating.

"This must stop," Mrs. Appleyard said.

She floured the receiver once more and spoke in what her children call her dragon's voice, a combination of chill and fire, terrifying because so seldom used by the owner.

"My good young man," she began, but it was not her young man — good or otherwise.

This voice said:

"Mother, this is Anne?"

"Who?" Mrs. Appleyard asked.

"Your oldest daughter. The one whose house is where you are a prisoner — mother of Cynthia, Tommy, Jane and Camilla."

"I thought your name was Cicely," Mrs. Appleyard said. All conversation seemed peculiar this afternoon, so she added, "The voice is familiar but I don't remember the name."

Her daughter said patiently, "Don't you remember I was christened Cicely Anne so I would have a pretty name when I was a débutante. And Anne in case I grew up and turned out sensible. I've decided I'm going to be from now on."

"Did you call me to tell me that?" her mother inquired.

"No," Cicely said. "I am at the Hoyts and I called to tell you what we are planning. The Hoyts have some visitors, students from Brazil and two charming ladies from Portugal; one of them came from Brazil in the first place. We thought we'd have a progressive supper. It will be a chance for you to get out. Pamela Hoyt says to tell you it will be a Royal Progress and we want you to help us plan it."

"Fine," said her mother, "only if I have anything to do with it, we'll have a Democratic Progress. At a royal one they used to serve roasted peacocks with their tails on and enormous game pies and haunches of venison and whole salmon in jelly. I think we'll have to simplify it a little. Anyway, I'll have a pound cake — if the telephone doesn't ring again."

"We thought perhaps you and I would do the salads. Pamela will have the main course and we are going to ask Venetia to have the drinks and appetizers so we just have to find someone to have the dessert."

"I'll contribute my pound cake," said Mrs. Appleyard. "I mean it's only Half-a-Pound Cake but it might help."

"Pamela wants suggestions for the main course."

"All right. I will brood while I bake."

This process and several conferences resulted in the following menu.

Appetizers
Bacon Dip*   Marinated Haddock*   Sardine Dip*
Potato Chips   Melba Toast   Corn Crisps
Stuffed Celery

Main Course
Roast Capon*   Celery and oyster stuffing*
Green Beans with mushrooms (p. 67)   Mashed potatoes

Salad
Tossed Salad, French dressing*
Sea Food Salad*   Homemade Mayonnaise*
Curried Bread*   Deviled Biscuit*
Hot Coffee Chocolate (p. 193)

Dessert

Apricot Parfait*   Hot Mince Pie (p. 68)   Pound Cake*
Cheese   Coffee

"I think I'll ask the Maxwells to have the dessert," Cicely said.

"That's a fine idea," said Mrs. Appleyard. "Cora knows the nicest young man."

"Have you seen him?"

"No," said Mrs. Appleyard, "but I have private sources of information."

The night of the Progress was the night spring began. There was a full moon, the snowbanks were high along the roads so that no one slid off anywhere. Pussywillows were encased in ice. Plumes of smoke and steam rushed up from the Maxwells' sugar house and dimmed the moon. It had a rainbow of snow crystals around it. Maple sugar crystals perhaps, Mrs. Appleyard thought. How nice for astronauts!

On their way to Venetia's they passed Mrs. Appleyard's own house. It looked about as hospitable as an Egyptian pyramid would if it were made of ice and had two feet of snow on it. Mrs. Appleyard knows just how such a structure feels inside in winter and, as she shivered, she thought gratefully of her apartment. It had never needed an official warming. It had its own warmth, not just the sunshine of the southwest corner but companionship and happiness.

Voltaire, thought Mrs. Appleyard, said that happiness is a good that nature sells to us. But I never supposed it could be bought. After all, you can buy a prism but not a rainbow.

Then they came to Venetia's where Orion sparkled above the twisting branches of the big elm and Minet, the white cat, sat on the gatepost as if he were a snow angel among cats. Vermont hostesses can always tell when winter guests arrive because they hear them stamping snow off their boots on the porch. It is etiquette for the hostess to say, politely but insincerely, "Don't mind the snow. Come right in," and for the guest to reply, hopping on one foot: "No, no: I'll leave them here."

Perhaps the most remarkable thing about the Democratic Progress was that at the end of the evening sixteen people all had the same overshoes they started with.

There were big maple logs burning in Venetia's fireplace, their light shining on curtains of faded cherry-colored brocade and on walls the color of a chocolate ice-cream soda and picking out the gold on the backs of books. Here Mrs. Appleyard drank orange juice while other people drank whatever people do drink on such occasions and took note of the delicious things that people ate.

Bacon Dip

6 slices of bacon, cooked slowly till crisp, drained, cooled and crumbled	2 teaspoons onion, crushed through a garlic press
	1½ cups thick soured cream
2 tablespoons lemon juice	½ teaspoon grated lemon rind
1 tablespoon minced parsley	1 tablespoon chopped chives

Mix all together in a pottery bowl. In summer the flavor may be varied by the addition of a little fresh tarragon or dill, very finely minced. Serve well chilled.

Marinated Haddock

1 12-ounce frozen fillet of haddock	containing tarragon, basil, marjoram, dill seed, parsley
1 tablespoon white wine vinegar	and a pinch of garlic powder
½ teaspoon each of dry mustard, sugar, paprika	2 tablespoons lemon juice
1 tablespoon of mixed herbs	6 tablespoons olive oil
	1 tablespoon piccalilli
1 small onion, put through garlic press	

Cut the fillet in 4 pieces. Place them in a folding steamer in rapidly boiling water. Insert a meat thermometer in one of the pieces. Cover the pan and cook until temperature of the fish reaches 150°. This will take only 4 to 5 minutes. Longer cooking only toughens and dries the fish.

Place the pieces of fish in a shallow pan. Mix all the other ingredients in a small saucepan and heat them to the boiling point. Pour the mixture over the fish and let it stand in a cool place for at least 12 hours. When serving, drain the fish and cut it up into small cubes. Pass sesame crackers or melba toast with them.

Sardine Dip

12 ounces sardines	1 cup thick soured cream
2 tablespoons olive butter	1 tablespoon Oyster Bar Sauce
½ cup Mayonnaise (p. 265)	(p. 248)
1 teaspoon lemon juice and a little grated rind	

Mash the sardines and mix all the ingredients together. If it seems too thick for dipping, add a little more mayonnaise.

During this pleasant interval Mrs. Appleyard had an opportunity to use her seven words of Portuguese, learned from two of her grandchildren, Cariocans in their youth. Luckily the guests had many times seven words of English so communication was not difficult. When the fire had safely burned down, they set off for the Hoyts' house. The caravan now consisted of one Mercedes-Benz, one Saab, two Volkswagens, one Citroën and — just to show that there are American cars that can drive Vermont roads in winter — one Falcon. All arrived safely at the Hoyts' long, low, gray house where every window sent light across the snow.

Here the guests sat at small tables in several rooms. Magically, the roasted capons came out of the big oven cooked just right. There were two of them, weighing about 8 pounds apiece. They were set on a rack in an open roasting pan, brushed all over with softened butter, sprinkled with flour which was seasoned with mixed herbs and roasted at 300° until the meat thermometer read 185°. Pamela said she allowed 30 minutes to the pound, a little over four hours. She figured that one bird alone would have cooked in less time.

One of the great improvements of modern times, Mrs. Appleyard thinks, is the cooking of meat at a constant low temperature watched, not by you but by a meat thermometer. She supposes the result may be a little like the slow even cooking of the old brick ovens but use of the thermometer is really something new. However, cooks who depended on coal or wood stoves were often wonderfully skillful at estimating and controlling heat. Mrs. Appleyard can remember seeing a family cook put first the back of her hand, then the palm, then her cheek in the heat from the opened oven door and then hear her regulate the heat according to her diagnosis. She would clank the dampers, shake down the fire, add soft or hard wood, talking to the fire all the time in a sort of incantation of encouragement. The results were of memorable excellence.

Oyster Stuffing

For an 8-pound capon allow:

¼ cup juice from oysters	4 cups stale homemade bread
⅔ cup butter	cut into ¼-inch cubes
1 onion, minced	2 Montpelier crackers, rolled fine
1 cup oysters, cut in small pieces	pinch of thyme
1 cup celery, cut fine	pinch of nutmeg

In a saucepan big enough to hold the mixture, heat the oyster juice; add the butter, and as it melts, the onion, oysters and celery. Cook until butter froths up well. Remove from heat. Using a pastry-blending fork, stir in the bread and cracker crumbs, the seasonings and the beaten egg. Mix thoroughly and lightly. If you like a very moist dressing, add a little thick cream.

The Progress now overshod itself and moved on to Appleyard Center. If this had been a Royal Progress — in Queen Elizabeth's time, for instance — there would have been beeves roasted whole for the common people. This is no longer true and for an interesting reason: there are, in the United States, plenty of beeves, which is after all merely the plural of beef. The trouble is there are no common people. So the Star-Spangled Banner, long may it wave o'er the land where everyone has two cars in the garage and half a Black Angus critter in the freeze locker. Even Mrs. Appleyard has two pounds of ground chuck.

At the moment she will give her attention to salad and salad dressings.

Seafood Salad
FOR EIGHT

2 12-ounce frozen haddock fillets
1½ pounds frozen lobster meat
2 pounds fresh crabmeat
2 pounds flash-frozen cooked
    shrimp
½ cup diced celery

French Dressing (see below)
Boston lettuce
watercress
2 hard-boiled eggs
6 large stuffed olives
mayonnaise

Cut frozen haddock fillets into quarters and cook them in a folding steamer until they flake easily. Time of cooking will depend on how much they have thawed: 4–6 minutes should be enough. Break into flakes and chill. Mix lobster and crabmeat, both cut up, not too fine; shrimp, left whole; celery and flaked haddock. Marinate in French dressing for several hours. When serving the salad, Mrs. Appleyard arranges it on a large platter. She mixes some of her own mayonnaise (see page 265) with the fish and makes it into individual mounds, each resting on lettuce, surrounded by watercress, masked with more mayonnaise and decorated with sliced hard-boiled eggs and olives.

Mr. Appleyard's French Dressing

Mrs. Appleyard has never eaten any that she prefers to Mr. Appleyard's. It was made with French red wine vinegar, with two beans of peeled garlic in the bottle, and the best olive oil. For a bowl of native lettuce, enough for four people, he used:

½ teaspoon salt
¼ teaspoon pepper from the grinder
1 teaspoon dry mustard
½ teaspoon paprika

a few grains of cayenne
1 tablespoon garlic red wine
    vinegar
3 tablespoons olive oil

He put all the dry ingredients into a big wooden salad spoon and mixed them well together with the fork. (He did this over a soup plate.) When they were well mixed, he first poured the vinegar into the spoon, mixing it well in with the fork, and then added the olive oil a tablespoon at a time, always pouring it first into the salad spoon, then into the soup plate. He gave the dressing a final thorough mixing in the plate, then poured it over the bowl of salad greens and tossed them gently and carefully until every leaf was coated with the dressing.

For a marinade:

If you are making a marinade, it is easier to put the ingredients into a jar with a screw top and shake them well. Use double the amounts suggested for the Tossed Salad (p. 147) and keep it on hand to use when needed.

Now that Mrs. Appleyard has to get things ready without much help she sometimes uses the method described on page 149 in which the dressing is poured into the salad bowl, the spoon and fork laid on top of it, crossed, and the greens put in on top of the spoon and fork. If you can find a conscientious guest to toss it for you at the last minute this is an excellent method. In either case one of the most important points of a tossed salad is to be sure the lettuce is dry. Oil and water don't mix. If there's water on the leaves there won't be oil. You want the dressing on the leaves and not in the bottom of the bowl.

Mrs. Appleyard prefers pure olive oil in salad dressing. If you are going to use something else she suggests that, rather than corn or peanut oil — both of which have very definite flavors different from olive oil — you should try either Wesson (cotton-seed) oil or safflower oil. Both of these are more delicately flavored.

Here are a few winter salad combinations that she likes with French dressing.

Cooked shrimp, hothouse tomatoes, torn romaine and Boston lettuce, ripe olives.

Crabmeat, sliced avocado, celery, watercress. Make the dressing for this with lemon juice instead of vinegar.

Iceberg lettuce sliced in thin rounds, red onion rings, watercress.

Jerusalem artichokes, cooked, peeled and chilled, marinated in French dressing to which 2 beans of garlic crushed through the press have been added. Serve with a mixture of salad greens — romaine, endive, watercress — and toss well in the marinade.

Frozen tiny peas and French-cut green beans. Cook the vegetables *al dente*. Pour on French dressing while they are hot. Chill. Serve with watercress, red onion rings and garlic croutons.

Cauliflower flowerets, sliced avocado, hothouse tomatoes, Boston lettuce, French dressing to which 1 tablespoon of Roquefort cheese, crumbled, is added for each 4 tablespoons of dressing.

Avocado, sliced, with Bermuda onion rings, orange and grapefruit sections, watercress.

When no watercress or romaine or Boston lettuce are available, slice iceberg in rings and sharpen it up with one of these dressings:

Mix Mrs. Appleyard's Lemon Mint Chutney (p. 191) with French dressing — 1 tablespoon of chutney to 4 tablespoons dressing.

Add: 1 tablespoon Parmesan cheese to the dressing and sprinkle the lettuce rings with garlic croutons.

Or: 1 tablespoon olive butter, 1 tablespoon minced green pepper, 1 tablespoon onion, put through garlic press.

Or: 1 hardboiled egg, minced, thin rings of green pepper, anchovy fillets.

The dressing may also be varied by the addition of garlic

powder, mixed herbs for salad, finely scissored chives or parsley or aged Vermont cheddar cheese.

For "feminine" fruit salads omit garlic and onion and make the dressing with lime or lemon juice instead of vinegar.

Homemade Mayonnaise (M.W.)

Mayonnaise originated when the Duc de Richelieu was besieging the Fortress of St. Philip at Mahon on Minorca. The siege was going slowly. The Duc's chef was in despair. No milk, no cream, no butter — how was he going to make a sauce to sustain his master through the battle! But ah! — he said — even in this barbarous place we have eggs, we have olive oil. I will think of something . . . so he did.

Naturally the Duc led his men up a cliff never climbed before and took the fortress. Now try saying Mahonnaise fast three times and see how it sounds. Right! This is not exactly how the chef made it because he did not have a blender. If you have one and sixty seconds to spare you can have mayonnaise too.

1 whole egg unbeaten	1 teaspoon powdered sugar
1 tablespoon vinegar	¼ teaspoon pepper
salt to taste	1 teaspoon dry mustard
1 tablespoon salad oil — olive, Wesson, safflower	extra salad oil, at least 1 cup

Put everything in the blender except the cup of oil. Run the blender 10 seconds. Now in four batches add the rest of the oil, running the blender 10 seconds after each batch. After the last of the oil is added, run the blender an extra 10 seconds to be sure the oil has all been absorbed.

Your mayonnaise is now ready. You can of course also make it by hand with an eggbeater or with an electric mixer.

In case you are feeling restless, you can vary the mayonnaise in several ways.

For fruit salads make it with lemon juice instead of vinegar and add some thin lemon peel.

For Russian dressing add to 1 cup of mayonnaise, 1 minced green pepper, 1 tablespoon grated onion, 4 tablespoons chili sauce.

For iceberg lettuce cut lettuce in eighths or thin rounds and serve it with 1 cup mayonnaise, 1 tablespoon chopped stuffed olives, 1 bean of garlic, put through the press, 1 chopped hard-boiled egg, 1 tablespoon minced green pepper, 1 tablespoon finely cut parsley.

For Potato Salad: mix half sour cream and half mayonnaise, add celery and dill seeds.

Boiled Dressing

1 tablespoon sugar	2 eggs
½ teaspoon mustard	½ cup cider vinegar
½ teaspoon salt	2 tablespoons sweet butter
¼ teaspoon pepper	½ cup cream

Mix dry ingredients. Add eggs well beaten. Add vinegar and cook over hot water, beating all the time with a wire whisk until the mixture is thick and light. Add butter. Remove from heat. Chill. When ready to use it, whip the cream and add it (or add sour cream). Especially good for potato salad or cole slaw. The cooked dressing may be added hot to either and the mixture chilled. At serving time add sour cream.

Sour Cream Dressing

1 cup sour cream	1 teaspoon prepared horseradish
½ teaspoon curry powder	½ teaspoon sugar
2 tablespoons mayonnaise	

This is good on cucumbers, Jerusalem artichokes or avocados. For fruit try adding to ½ cup sour cream 1 tablespoon mayonnaise, 1 tablespoon crushed mint mixed with 1 tablespoon lemon juice, ½ teaspoon lime juice, and 1 teaspoon sugar.

As she makes these notes, Mrs. Appleyard begins to see a giant kaleidoscope of salads whirling around in front of her eyes. It makes her dizzy. Perhaps it does you too. She will cease and return to the Progress.

Curried Bread

Make this like garlic bread. Soften the butter. To ½ pound of butter allow 1 teaspoon curry powder, ½ teaspoon garlic powder. (Use half these amounts of seasoning if you do not like it pretty powerful.) Blend seasonings and butter. Cut a loaf of French or Italian bread in ½-inch slices almost all the way through. Spread slices with the softened seasoned butter. This may be done ahead of time. Just before you serve it put the bread in a pan into a 400° oven and heat until it starts to brown — about 10 minutes. Or you may cut slices all the way through, spread them with the mixture, lay them flat in a pan and bake them until they start to brown. Do not overbake in either case: the centers of the slices should be rather soft.

Deviled Biscuit

Make tiny baking powder biscuits. Use your favorite rule, or a packaged mix will do for these. Roll the dough rather thin. Brush half of it with melted butter. Lay the other half on top of it. Cut the dough into small squares. Bake until lightly browned at 450°, about 12 minutes.

Make this filling:

1 4-ounce tin Underwood's Deviled Ham	1 egg
1 cup grated mild cheese	1 teaspoon onion, put through garlic press
1 tablespoon mayonnaise	softened butter

Mix ham, cheese, mayonnaise, beaten egg and onion well together. While biscuits are still warm, split them and spread the insides of the top halves with the softened butter, then the lower halves with the filling. Put halves together again. At serving time put them into a 400° oven just long enough to heat through. Serve hot.

At Cicely's the long table was in front of a fire of birch logs. Her daughters joined some of the guests there. Others sat at a smaller table in Mrs. Appleyard's apartment. This table had Copenhagen onion-pattern cups, plates and napkins on it. The big one was set with blue willow ware. Both patterns had a characteristic much appreciated by the family dishwashers: they could be burned in the fireplace afterwards.

"So in your country you destroy the porcelain after a meal! This I have always wished to do. To go to college, I wash dishes," said one of the guests.

"You shall be the one to burn them," said Cicely.

The Maxwells, the next hosts, left while the sacrificial pyre was still burning. When it was safely out, the rest of the party, which now included Cicely's daughters, drove on towards the Maxwells'. The guests had now been in three houses — a brick one, a weathered gray one, a yellow one. All followed a basic Vermont pattern — a story and a half house with a long ell. Yet no two were really alike. Outside dormers and porches had changed the original roof lines. Inside you might find a wall-paper a hundred and forty years old with Spanish castles on it or silvery gray boards from the outside of an old sheep barn, or walls painted by the family with birds and flowers or — as in the Maxwells' big living room — panels from pines that were young when their ancestors came to Vermont from Massachusetts, walking beside an ox team. The house is white. That night even the roof was white, its thick meringue of snow sparkling in the moonlight. The pillar of white smoke still rose from the sugar house.

Inside, in the big kitchen, a coal fire burned in the old-fashioned iron stove, which somehow gives warmer heat than anything else. There was a delicious smell of maple syrup. In the pine-paneled room, apple wood scented the room and dropped pale pink coals among white ashes. Stereo jazz resounded. Alma's hooked rugs were rolled up in a corner. The floor was crowded with dancers from Brazil, Montpelier and other points south of Appleyard Center.

The Maxwells have only one child but luckily that one is Cora, who has enough charm for six, so there is always something going on in their house. Mrs. Appleyard enjoyed sitting and watching the dancing. After a while a young man brought her a small folding table and something delicious to put on it. He called her ma'am and treated her with so much gentle consideration that she began to feel fragile, exquisite and a hundred years old.

The Maxwell house is on the brow of a hill from which you can look down on the lights of Montpelier, stars dropped into a bowl of clouded marble, the pattern of trees and houses blurred against the snow. Mrs. Appleyard was glad to sit quietly and look down on the view and listen to half a dozen conversations at once and not talk herself. The young man who had brought her the apricot parfait (so good, she must get the rule from Alma) was entertaining a group that included two of her granddaughters.

"And I said to this girl — well actually I reckon I ought to say lady — she had not been a girl for quite a while, I imagine, I said, 'You seem mighty nice. Why don't you go out with me instead of Cora?' and she said, 'Because I think you're crazy,' and hung up. And you know I'd have gone through with it. That is the kind I am. I'll always keep my word to a girl."

"How old do you think she was?" asked Jane in the tone of one awed by daring and chivalry.

"Well, it's hard to be sure — maybe twenty-four or five. But I'd have taken her out," he said gallantly, "even if she was thirty."

The girls gazed at him in admiration. Mrs. Appleyard did not dare to. She sat looking, she hoped, a little under one hundred in her black velvet and her almost-ermine cape and turned her smiles down upon star-spangled Montpelier.

She well remembered how, when she was eighteen, anyone over twenty-one seemed to her to be staring over a desert scattered with granite tombstones, mummies and a few ill-arranged skeletons.

I'll send him an autographed copy of my book with that picture of me that doesn't look a day over sixty-seven, she thought. That will teach him.

Of course she really did not expect to teach him anything. When he is a grandfather he will learn for himself how perplexing it is for a young man to have such old grandchildren.

At this moment he brought Mrs. Appleyard some of her own pound cake. She thanked him for his thoughtfulness. Did he start slightly? He certainly looked puzzled as he asked: "Have we met before, ma'am?"

"No," said Mrs. Appleyard, "but I hope we shall again."

She finished the pound cake (not bad really) collected her black lace mantilla, one of her best-known fur coats, her black velvet and fur boots and went out into the night.

"You look as if you'd been up to something, like a cat that's eaten a canary," Cicely said.

Her mother said: "Of course you are an expert in such matters but I would say offhand more like a benevolent owl who caught a kitten but decided to let it go. I have seldom," she added, "enjoyed an evening more."

Apricot Parfait
FOR SIX

1 large can apricots	2 egg whites, beaten stiff
½ tablespoon gelatin	2 tablespoons lemon juice
⅓ cup sugar	½ pint heavy cream, whipped

Drain the apricots. Soak the gelatin in 2 tablespoons of the syrup and cook the rest of it with the sugar till it threads. Pour it on the beaten egg whites. Stir the mixture all the time with a wire whisk. Stir in the gelatin. Cool. Put the lemon juice and apricots into the blender and blend until smooth. Add this mixture to the beaten whites. Chill thoroughly. Whip the cream and fold it into the apricot mixture. Put the parfait into a refrigerator tray or into a covered aluminum dish and set it into the freezer. Freeze 3 hours, stirring thoroughly to break up crystals three times during the first hour.

Unmold it on a circular dish. Surround it with vanilla ice cream and raspberries or with Conserved Apricots (p. 244).

Half-a-Pound Cake

Perhaps you are not in the mood this morning to use a dozen eggs and a pound of butter. That is what you'd have to do if you made a pound cake. Well, how about half-a-pound cake?

extra butter, melted
½ pound (1 cup) butter at room temperature
½ pound (1 cup) granulated sugar, sifted

6 eggs, separated
1 tablespoon brandy
½ pound (2 cups) cake flour, sifted 3 times with ¼ teaspoon nutmeg

¼ cup powdered sugar

· Light the oven: 300°.

Oil a Pyrex loaf pan and line it with wax paper, brushed lightly with the melted butter.

Cream the butter, beat in the sugar, using a pastry-blending fork. Beat the egg yolks and stir them well into the mixture. Stir in the brandy. Add the flour gradually, beating smooth after each addition. Beat the egg whites stiff, but not dry, and fold them into the mixture.

Bake until a testing straw comes out clean from the center of the cake — about one hour. Check it after half an hour's baking and reduce heat if cake seems to be browning too fast. Let it stand a few minutes after you take it out of the pan. Peel off the paper carefully. Turn it topside up. Cool. Sprinkle with powdered sugar.

There is a tradition in Mrs. Appleyard's family that pound cake will fall if anyone walks heavily past the stove during the first half hour of baking, or if the oven door is slammed shut. Apparently these offenses were never committed in her grandmother's kitchen, for the cake was always light, yet firm and it sliced beautifully. Mrs. Appleyard is not going to slam any doors to test this tradition scientifically. Let someone else try. She rather thinks that if you accept the superstition blindly, you will have a pretty nice loaf of pound cake at the end of an hour or an hour and a quarter. If you have self-control enough to keep it in a tightly covered tin box for three days, the texture will be especially good.

Maple Butternut Fudge

Cracking the butternuts is the really hard part of this job. You have to have a man in the family and he has to have a patient disposition. Mrs. Appleyard does not like to sound cynical but she will suggest that walnuts or pecans may be substituted for the butternuts.

Butter two plates lightly. Cover the plates with nuts. Using a candy thermometer cook 2 cups of maple syrup to 232°. Remove from the fire, stir until it just starts to thicken and pour it over the nuts, mark in squares before it hardens.

The batch the Maxwells served was especially good because it was made with butternuts and with syrup that had been sap, rising in century-old maples, only three days before.

You may add some thick cream during the last part of the cooking if you like. Mrs. Appleyard likes it better without.

For those who do not happen to have a sugar house handy, here is a palatable substitute.

Brown Sugar Pecan Fudge

1 cup pecans	4 cups golden brown sugar
1 cup thin cream	1 tablespoon butter
1 teaspoon vanilla	

Butter plates and lay nuts on them, not chopped but as they come from a vacuum-packed can. Cook the cream and sugar to 238° (soft ball). Remove from fire. Add the butter. Beat hard until it is creamy and begins to thicken. Add vanilla. Pour over nuts. Mark in squares while it is still soft.

April

Ventilation Tour

Mrs. Appleyard said to her daughter — not entirely, we are afraid, without a slight air of complacency — that their book was practically finished.

"I've done March," she said, "and that's the last winter month. Now all I need to do is to put in the symbolism. You know — the way modern teachers of writing show their students how to do: a pinch of Freud here, a snip off a Jungian archetype there. Or perhaps I'd better put in philosophy, the way you do when you put sherry into Newburg Sauce, just at the end. Add philosophy, bring to the boil but do not boil. Or perhaps I'd better add symbolism and philosophy to taste and serve. For as many as will. What do you think?"

Cicely looked at her mother with indulgent pity.

"I think," she said, "that you have forgotten that in Vermont April is a winter month. So is most of May. You need not only philosophy but hearty sustaining food in both of them. After all, Vermonters have to build themselves up for the summer. Symbolism does not cure chilblains."

It was this remark, a truth as solid as a granite doorstep, that made Mrs. Appleyard decide to go south for the winter. She realized, of course, that she was lucky to have some winter left to go south in. A singularly grim cold spring prevailed as far south as Washington, where the cherry blossoms were late. In Philadelphia there were a few reluctant red buds on the maples but the country still looked bleak. In New York State the robins had come. There were hundreds of them beside the road with their wings so iced up in a sleet storm that they could not fly. Cold winds blew everywhere. In Boston it was the east wind right off a few icebergs.

"This," Mrs. Appleyard wrote to Cicely, "is my ventilation tour. My hat blew off in Washington and was picked up by a very pleasant-looking poodle. He looked it over carefully and decided he would wait for a more seasonable model, a fur one probably. Mine had violets on it. They are the only ones I have seen. However," she concluded, "nourishing and delightful menus have been thought up for me. I was brought up to think it a virtue to eat what was set before you. I'm afraid in my present circumstances it is not."

Here are some of the menus she encountered.

Menu 1

Clam and Chicken Soup*
Planked Porterhouse Steak with Broiled Stuffed Mushrooms
Mashed Potato   Asparagus — Butter and Egg Sauce (p. 191)
Tossed Salad (p. 147)
Sponge Cake*   Grapefruit*

Clam and Chicken Soup
FOR FOUR

2 cups strong chicken stock	salt and pepper to taste
1 tablespoon butter	2 tablespoons white wine
1 tablespoon flour	½ cup milk
8 ounces minced clams	½ cup heavy cream

Make the chicken stock by cooking a fowl with a carrot, a large onion, celery tops, a teaspoon of mixed herbs. Remove meat from the bones, use it as you wish — salad, creamed chicken, sandwiches. Return the bones to the broth and cook them at least an hour. Strain. Stock should jelly when chilled. Skim all fat from the top. In a frying pan melt the butter, blend in the flour, remove pan from heat and stir in a cup of the stock slowly. Cook until it starts to thicken, about 3 minutes. Put it into the blender with the clams and blend until you have a smooth purée, about half a minute. Put it into the top of a double boiler with the rest of the stock, then cook about 20 minutes over hot water. Add salt and pepper. When you are ready to serve it add the wine, the milk and the cream. Bring it to the boil but do not boil. Serve at once in hot soup plates.

Sponge Cake

grated rind of one lemon	1 cup flour, measured after
1 tablespoon lemon juice	sifting
¼ cup frozen orange juice,	1 cup sugar
not diluted	7 eggs separated
sugar, extra, about ¼ cup	

Grate lemon and mix it with the lemon juice and thawed orange juice. Sift flour 3 times and measure. Sift sugar twice and measure.

Light oven: 325°.

The cake may be baked in either a 9-inch tube pan or a 14 × 10 dripping pan, or in muffin tins. It will fill about 18. In any case the pan or pans must be lightly floured.

Beat the egg whites to soft peaks. Beat 4 tablespoons of sugar into them, one at a time. Beat egg yolks until thick and lemon-colored. Beat in the rest of the sugar alternately with the fruit juices and rind. Fold the whites gently into the yolks, alternating with the flour. Mrs. Appleyard used a wire whisk for this. It is important not to break up the air bubbles you have beaten in, as their expansion is what makes the cake rise. Put the batter into the pan or pans. If you use muffin tins oven should be at 350°.

Bake until well risen, about 10 minutes; then sift the extra sugar over the top. It is done when it springs back lightly when pressed with the finger. It will take almost an hour in the tube pan, 35–40 minutes in the dripping pan, 25–30 minutes in muffin tins according to their size.

Grapefruit

Mrs. Appleyard loves grapefruit. It is really her favorite dessert. It is farther around a grapefruit than you think but she does it pretty fast. The result however is not very much like those she encountered in Boston.

They were enormous Indian River Reds. Every single seed had vanished. They were perfectly cut, with all the divisions between the sections and the centers removed. Some epicure had mixed half honey and half Cointreau and dribbled a tablespoon of the mixture over each half. Try it, she says.

MENU 2

Shrimp, Crabmeat and Avocado Cocktail*
Roast Duckling*   Wild Rice and Mushrooms*
Currant-Orange sauce (p. 54)
Braised Celery*   Corn Dodgers†
Crème Brûlée†

Shrimp, Crabmeat and Avocado Cocktail

For each person to be served have half a ripe avocado brushed with lemon juice. Mix shrimp and fresh crabmeat, cut in rather small pieces, with mayonnaise, minced green pepper, finely minced onion and tomato cocktail sauce, 2 tablespoons of the sauce to half a cup of mayonnaise. Heap the mixture lightly into the avocado halves. Garnish with a little watercress.

Roast Duckling

People vary so much about how they like ducklings cooked that it is hard to please everyone. There is the idea of treating them like a wild duck, simply whisking them into a 450° oven and out again 18 minutes or you may go to the other extreme and cook them at 300° to 185° on the meat thermometer. In this case allow 25–30 minutes to the pound. It is not necessary to stuff ducks, either wild or tame — an apple quartered and with the seeds removed, a small whole onion and a few celery tops will help keep a duckling from drying out. A good deal of fat runs into the pan and that should be poured off twice at least during the roasting.

Wild Rice with Mushrooms

Directions for cooking wild rice better than Mrs. Appleyard can give you are on the package. Half a pound of mushroom caps, sliced and sautéd with a little finely minced onion, are often mixed with it. Crumbled crisp bacon is also sometimes added.

Brown rice may be treated in the same way and is an acceptable substitute to many people.

Braised Celery
FOR EIGHT

4 bunches, best parts only, of
  crisp celery
¼ pound butter
1 cup jellied chicken or beef
  stock, well seasoned with
  herbs and spices

½ cup coarse bread crumbs
grated cheese
minced chives
parsley

Cut the celery in pieces 4 inches long. Wash well. In a shallow enameled iron pan in which the celery can be served, melt the butter and toss the celery in it so that all sides are exposed to the heat. Cover and cook over very low heat 7 or 8 minutes. Add the stock and simmer over medium heat until celery is tender — about 20 minutes. If more convenient it may be baked in the oven at 375°. Just before serving time, brown the crumbs in the extra butter. Sprinkle them and the grated cheese over the celery. Run the pan under the broiler until the cheese melts. Sprinkle with chives and parsley.

It was a great pleasure to Mrs. Appleyard to get back into fish-eating country. Vermonters like to catch fish but except for trout they are not much interested in eating them. Along the eastern seaboard people take the matter more seriously. On a Friday night she was happy to encounter:

MENU 3

Celery   Eggs Stuffed with Crabmeat*   Radish Roses   Carrot Sticks
Shrimp Soup*   Planked Shad*
Baked Corn and Cheese*   Tossed Salad (p. 147)
Deep-Dish Apple Pie (p. 102)

Eggs Stuffed with Crabmeat
FOR FOUR

4 hard-boiled eggs
3 tablespoons mayonnaise
1 tablespoon finely minced green
  pepper

¼ pound crabmeat
4 stuffed olives
parsley

Hard-boil 4 eggs. They will peel better if you have them at room temperature when you start them and cover them with water at 70°. You can acquire this by running some lukewarm water from the tap and letting it stand while the eggs are warming. Such is the magic of the law of thermodynamics — or something — that if the water is too cool it will get warm enough and if it is too warm it will get cool enough while time saunters on. Put the eggs in the water. Cover and bring rapidly to the boil. As soon as water boils, remove pan from heat and let eggs stand for 20 minutes. Then plunge them at once into running cold water. Crack shells under water and roll eggs in hands to loosen shells but do not peel them until they have cooled. Begin peeling them at the large end. This method produces eggs as smooth as Parian marble, not the kind that look as if they had been pecked by predacious blue jays. Perhaps you never shelled any like that. Congratulations from Mrs. Appleyard, who has only recently learned that it was not just a matter of luck.

Cut the eggs lengthwise. Mash the yolks with the mayonnaise and mix in the green peppers. Add more mayonnaise if necessary. The mixture should be easy to spread. Flake the crabmeat and fill the whites of the eggs with it. Top with the mashed yolk mixture, swirling it a little with a fork. Decorate with sliced stuffed olives. Serve with fresh parsley around them.

Shrimp Soup

3 tablespoons butter	1 tablespoon onion
3 tablespoons flour	6 tablespoons sauterne
1 teaspoon paprika	1 pimento, cut rather fine
½ teaspoon pepper from the	2 cups heavy cream
grinder	1 tablespoon butter (extra)
¼ teaspoon nutmeg	1 tablespoon finely scissored
¼ teaspoon garlic powder	parsley
2 cups milk	1 tablespoon chopped chives
1 pound flash-frozen shrimp	lemon slices

This was prepared in an electric skillet but could of course be done in a skillet over the fire and a double boiler.

Melt the butter over medium heat. Blend in the flour mixed with dry seasonings. Reduce heat to its lowest point and pour on the milk slowly, stirring all the time till the mixture is smooth. Leave it over very low heat while in the blender you purée the shrimp and onion with the sauterne. Add this mixture and the pimento to the skillet mixture. Cook covered over very low heat 20 minutes, stirring several times. At serving time add the cream. Bring to the boil but do not boil. At the last minute slip in the extra butter. Pour the soup into hot bowls, sprinkle with parsley and chives. Add lemon slices. This serves four generously. In cups it could serve six. A few whole cooked shrimp may be added to each bowl.

Planked Shad
FOR SIX

This was done not on a plank but on a large heatproof platter, but the effect was splendid. Mrs. Appleyard is delighted to be in a world where roe shad still exist, and also that geniuses have arisen who know how to bone a shad. Even under their skill, shad is not usually completely boneless — there always seem to be a few bones left. It is, however, very superior to the fishy pincushions of Mrs. Appleyard's youth.

4 large potatoes, mashed with hot milk and butter
2 or 3 large hothouse tomatoes
8 slices of bacon
matchstick carrots
extra butter
brown sugar
tiny frozen peas
6 boned serving pieces of shad

shad roe
¼ cup butter
juice of 2 lemons
½ teaspoon pepper from the grinder
1 teaspoon paprika
½ cup bread crumbs, browned in butter
watercress

If you have a plank by all means use it, but you can get a very good planked effect by beginning with aluminum foil and using a fireproof glass, aluminum or fireproof enamel platter.

Begin by making plenty of good creamy mashed potato. Mrs. Appleyard prefers real potatoes but if you use the packaged kind, this is a handy place for it. Slice tomatoes into 6 slices. Cook the bacon till it is translucent but not crisp. Cook the carrots, glazing them with butter and a little brown sugar. Cook the peas till they are not quite done, in a very little water. Do not overcook the vegetables as they will get more cooking under the broiler.

Now lay the shad, skin side down, and the roe on a large piece of heavy aluminum foil. Turn the edges of the foil up carefully around it to make a box that will keep the juices in. Put the box on a cooky sheet. Melt the ¼ cup of butter with the lemon juice, add pepper and paprika and pour the mixture over the shad and roe. Broil 8–10 minutes. If you use gas and can turn flames down to pinpoints, have fish one inch from flame. Do not turn the shad but at the end of 5 minutes turn the roe and baste both shad and roe with the lemon and butter. Test fish for flakiness. Do not overcook it. Put the aluminum foil on your broiling platter. Spread out the edges. Make a wall of mashed potato around the outside edge, score the potato lightly with a fork, dot it with butter. Inside the potato make a ring of tomato slices, covered with the browned crumbs, partly cooked bacon, heaps of peas and carrots brushed with melted butter. Put the platter under the broiler and broil until the potatoes are brown — about 3 minutes.

A strong man, not only an excellent cook, but a painter of some of Mrs. Appleyard's favorite pictures, presided over this dish. He decorated it with watercress and carried into the dining room without slipping, tripping or spilling this artwork. Mrs. Appleyard wished she had a picture of it. Perhaps it's just as well she has none. She's already ravenous just writing about it.

It seems to Mrs. Appleyard that her host must be a man of rashness as well as courage to cook what is practically a soufflé at the same time he was dealing with the shad, but he did and it came out perfectly. She was allowed to toss the salad that went with it, a mixture of romaine, French endive, chicory, and Boston lettuce (which you can always buy in New York). She felt that great tribute was being paid to her reliability and conscientiousness and did her best to coat every leaf as neatly as if she had been using one of the painter's best sable hair brushes.

Baked Corn and Cheese Puff
FOR SIX

3 tablespoons butter	½ teaspoon paprika
½ teaspoon onion, minced	salt to taste
2 slices green pepper, minced	1 cup rich milk
1 pimento, cut fine	1½ cups cream style corn
2 tablespoons flour	½ cup grated mild cheese
¼ teaspoon pepper	3 eggs, separated

In a fireproof enamel dish put the butter over medium heat. Add the onion, green pepper and pimento and sauté till the onion is straw-colored. Sprinkle in the flour, mixed with the seasonings, and blend thoroughly. Remove pan from heat, pour in the milk and stir till smooth. Cook 3 minutes over low heat. Cool for a few minutes. Add the corn, grated cheese and egg yolks, beaten light, and mix well. Light oven: 350°. Beat the whites of the eggs to stiff peaks. Fold them gently into the corn-cheese mixture. Set the dish in the oven and bake until it has risen well and is nicely browned — about 35 minutes.

Mrs. Appleyard learned several things about cooking while she was on her ventilation tour. One of them was the use of aluminum foil in cooking fish. Here is an example of how to use it with halibut as the fish used. The same method may be applied to other kinds and of course the seasonings varied.

Halibut Steaks
FOR FOUR

4 tablespoons butter
½ pound mushroom caps, sliced
2 tablespoons finely cut celery
1 tablespoon onion, put through
    garlic press
1 pimento cut in strips

2 tablespoons lemon juice
grated rind of 1 lemon
½ teaspoon mixed herbs
4 small halibut steaks, 1 inch thick
2 hothouse tomatoes, sliced
1 tablespoon butter, extra

Light oven: 450°.

In the butter toss gently the mushrooms, celery and onion until onion is straw-colored. Add the pimento, lemon juice and rind and the mixed herbs.

Place each halibut steak on an oblong of aluminum foil and fold up edges to make a box. Put some of the mixture on each steak. Add tomato slices and dot with extra butter. Lay another piece of foil over the fish and fold the edges of the box up over it so that it is in a bag from which the juice will not escape. Put the bags on a rack in a dripping pan. Put a meat thermometer into one of the steaks. Cook to 145°: 10–12 minutes.

Have hot platter ready. Remove top pieces of foil. Lay the aluminum boxes right on the platter. Turn down the edges, overlapping them. Garnish the platter with lemon slices and heaps of asparagus, country style with Butter and Egg Sauce (p. 191).

With this dish were served:

Cheese and Chutney Crumpets
FOR FOUR

4 crumpets, split, buttered and
   lightly toasted
2 tablespoons butter (extra)
1 cup mild cheddar, grated

½ teaspoon paprika
1 teaspoon dry mustard
4 tablespoons Major Grey's
   chutney, chopped fine

1 tablespoon syrup from chutney

Melt the 2 tablespoons of butter, remove pan from the fire, mix in the grated cheese and stir till it just melts. Stir in seasonings and the chutney and syrup. Spread on the buttered crumpets. Mixture will spread, so keep it away from the edges. Put them on a baking sheet. Run them under the broiler till the cheese starts to bubble — about 2 minutes.

Mrs. Appleyard sometimes uses her own Lemon Mint Chutney (p. 191) in this way. Some people prefer it because it's milder. She rather likes the determined heat of Major Grey's herself.

Cheese has an affinity for fish, she thinks, and with another foil-cooked dish — frozen haddock fillets cut into serving portions and done in the same way as the halibut steaks — she served

Baked Cheese Balls

These are something that valiant characters might fry in deep fat but she does them by this peaceful method and finds them quite satisfactory.

½ cup grated Vermont cheese
½ cup grated Roquefort or
   blue cheese
1 egg, beaten
½ cup soft crumbs of Anadama
   white bread
1 teaspoon Worcestershire sauce
1 teaspoon mustard
1 cup dry crumbs, rolled very
   fine
½ teaspoon paprika
¼ teaspoon pepper

1 egg beaten light with 1 teaspoon of water

Mix both kinds of cheese with the beaten egg, soft bread crumbs, Worcestershire and mustard. Roll the mixture into balls about an inch in diameter. Then roll them in the fine crumbs, mixed with seasoning, next into the beaten egg and water mixture, then into the crumbs again.

Light oven: 450°.

While it is heating — about 5 minutes — chill the balls in the refrigerator. Put them on a lightly buttered iron frying pan. Do not let them touch each other. Bake until they are brown. Turn them, using a small pancake turner and a spatula, at the end of 5 minutes. The whole process, including turning, should take about 12 minutes. If you like them browner, run the pan under the broiler for a minute. Do not overcook them.

Luckily for Mrs. Appleyard it was still oyster season and she encountered them cooked in various ways, one of the most welcome of which was a de luxe version of scalloped oysters.

Oysters with Croutons

4 cups of cubes of homemade
   bread
extra butter
1 pint of fresh oysters
¼ pound butter
¼ teaspoon nutmeg
¼ teaspoon pepper from the
   grinder
¼ teaspoon garlic powder
½ teaspoon paprika
½ cup heavy cream
extra paprika

Slice homemade bread in ¼-inch slices. Trim off crusts, spread slices with soft butter. Cut into ¼-inch cubes. Pick over oysters, removing any bits of shell and of course saving any pearls you find to make earrings for your granddaughters. Drain oysters, mix the liquor with the ¼ pound of butter and heat the mixture. Sprinkle in the seasonings. Toss the bread cubes in the mixture. Do this a cup at a time, adding more butter if necessary. Light oven: 450°. Butter lightly a 9 × 12 Pyrex dish and cover the bottom with the bread cubes. Add half the oysters. Cover with more bread cubes. Add the rest of the oysters and the rest of the cubes. Pour the cream over all. Sprinkle with paprika. Put in the oven and bake until well browned — about 20 minutes.

More flattered than she can possibly say was Mrs. Appleyard when she went to dinner with one of her favorite composers and found that he had composed in her honor not a symphony, not a ballet, not a sonata, but something he called

Chicken Appleyard
FOR FOUR

For once — this is really an extraordinary compliment — she was so overcome that she forgot to ask for the rule but this is the way she has made it since and it is at least reminiscent of this happy occasion.

chicken breasts, wings removed
butter, about ¼ pound
2 cups chicken stock, made from
　wings and neck
4 tablespoons white wine

2 cups soft bread crumbs, not
　too fine, browned in butter
4 ounces liver pâté (French) or
　your own (p. 124)
watercress

Bread Sauce

Butter each chicken breast well. Put on a rack in a large skillet, put in chicken stock and wine, cover and simmer until tender — about one hour. Brush breasts again with butter. Slide pan under the broiler and brown the breasts. Sprinkle the breasts with browned crumbs. Top each breast with a small mound of pâté. Serve wreathed in watercress. Pass bread sauce with them.

If you have time to make gravy from the juices in the pan, you will find it good. Just take 2 teaspoons of flour, season it as you wish, dilute it with cold water, strain it into the pan, stir until it thickens and cook over medium heat for 3 minutes. Strain, add a little more white wine if you like, sprinkle it with minced fresh parsley.

An artistic triumph served with the chicken was a

Symphony in Green Vegetables

A large circular yellow dish had a mound of small tender green peas in the middle of it. Radiating out from the peas were thick stalks of asparagus. Between these were green beans and Brussels Sprouts and around the edge was a wreath of broccoli flowers. Lemon butter was passed with this.

The dessert for this meal was vanilla ice cream with a sauce made of

Marrons Glacés

What used to be practically a lifetime project, Mrs. Appleyard learned, is now a few minutes' work because chestnuts can now be bought shelled, cooked and cleaned of tough skin. You just open a can, drain and dry thoroughly 2 cups of chestnuts and fix this syrup:

2 cups sugar   1 cup water
1 teaspoon vanilla

Boil sugar and water without stirring until the syrup just starts to discolor. Watch it. The change can take place suddenly. You want thick syrup, not caramel. Remove from fire, put over warm (not hot) water. Put drained chestnuts into the syrup. Leave them exactly 5 minutes. Remove them with 2 silver forks to a warm steamer. The kind that opens out flat is good. Put it on a plate and leave the chestnuts on it overnight. Allow the syrup to cool to room temperature. Do not chill it. Next morning reheat it. Put the chestnuts in for another 5 minutes. Take them out again and put them back to drain again on the steamer, which has been washed in very hot water and thoroughly dried. If they are to be used that day or the next put them, when they have drained, into paper cases. (The easy way to get these is to save them from a candy box. In fact, to tell the truth, Mrs. Appleyard does not know how else you would get them. Stealing seems impractical and why should some rarely visited candy shop help set you up in business?)

If you are not going to use the marrons at once, put them, still handling them delicately with those silver forks, into a wide-necked jar or jars, bring the syrup to a boil and pour it over them. Add another teaspoon of vanilla. Cover tightly. Keep in the refrigerator till you need them. Mrs. Appleyard guarantees that they will not take up space long.

She remembers poignantly an occasion on which a dish, containing many different kinds of delicious candy including one — only one — marron glacé, was passed around a rather large table. The guests, that is the first eight, were all too polite to take the marron, but at last someone did take it. There was a general, an almost imperceptible sigh during which the lady next to the fortunate one said gently but sadly: "Ah! My favorite piece!"

It was every lady's favorite piece including Mrs. Appleyard's, alas. She believes however that she was probably the only one whose husband followed up his first meeting with her by sending her five pounds of marrons glacés. It occurred to her almost at once that this was no ordinary gesture. When he continued with the *Encyclopedia Britannica* (Eleventh Edition) she was sure she was right.

Luckily she was.

What Am I Offered?

REPORTS from Vermont were very cheering to everyone south of it. Snow, sleet, rain, mud, frost, glare ice and hail were reported with the gloomy pride Vermonters take in their weather. Mrs. Appleyard, admitting to Cicely that April was indeed a winter month, decided to stay in tropical Massachusetts for the Business Meeting and Auction of the Pinball and Scissors Club.

It is hard for Mrs. Appleyard to tell which she enjoys most

— the Business Meeting or the Auction. When the girls — they have been meeting for more than half a century — get together for a bout of parliamentary law, they sound like a murmuration of starlings in a high wind. Motions, sometimes three at once, are discussed and amended with bounce, brightness and benevolence. All except those who have a touch of laryngitis express their opinions but only to their next door neighbors, who agree or disagree with resonant enthusiasm. Every now and then the president remembers that remarks are supposed to be addressed to the chair and says so but of course no one hears her.

There is however a magic tranquilizer that always works. The hostess suddenly announces, "Lunch in five minutes, girls."

It is extraordinary how swiftly peace, order and agreement fall upon the assembly. From the eighteen organizations suggested as possible targets for their generosity, they quickly choose one to be endowed with the proceeds of the auction. Someone says, "Oh well, I'll be treasurer if you like," and the secretary casts one ballot for her amid applause before she has time to change her mind. They decide, as they have been doing ever since 1929, that the hostesses must keep the luncheons very simple. "Why don't we," someone asks, "just each bring a sandwich?"

"Splendid idea," everyone agrees and they all go into the dining room where under the family portraits, among Chippendale and Lowestoft, gilded glass and damask, they do full justice to the following menu.

Consommé with Rings of Green Pepper
Sesame Seed Sticks*
Lobster Newburg* with Pastry Diamonds   Cold Roast Turkey
Green Beans with Sausages (p. 181)   Parker House Rolls†
Ice Cream Bombes   Orange Ice with Vanilla Parfait

Chocolate Ice Cream with Marron Parfait
Scotch Shortbread*   Fruitcake (p. 116)   Madeleines†
Coffee   Hot Chocolate

Sesame Seed Sticks
FOR EIGHT

Use your favorite pastry mix for this if you do not feel like making your own pastry (p. 60).

1 package of pastry mix   1 tablespoon butter
½ cup sesame seed

Roll out the pastry into an oblong about ¼ inch thick. Dot with butter, fold, turn, and roll out again. Sprinkle with sesame seed. Cut in 24 strips. Bake at 350° until delicately brown, 15–20 minutes. Reduce heat to 325° after the first 5 minutes.

Lobster Newburg

Of course the Lobster Newburg at the Pinball and Scissors Club was made of fresh lobster and the pastry diamonds were light puffs of real pastry. Mrs. Appleyard heartily and enviously endorses the freshest possible lobster. In her far-off childhood, she spent her summers on an island off the coast of Maine. It was a habit, in that country of pointed firs, of mountains thrusting out of the sea, of screaming eagles pouncing on ospreys and stealing their fish, to keep, in the cove near the wharf, a lobster car full of live lobsters. They used to be brought up to the house, snapping and fighting, in a large basket. Their sudden change from bronze-green to coral-scarlet was a daily miracle.

Monotony was avoided by serving them plain boiled with melted butter, as soup, stew or salad, broiled or as Lobster Newburg.

Mrs. Appleyard seldom sees as much as a lobster feeler any longer. She assumes that you probably don't have a lobster car in the front yard either and that, like her, you are grateful to gaze upon frozen lobster in a neat plastic-topped container, especially on winter evenings when it wouldn't be very convenient to row out to the lobster car in a northeaster. On the island the Newburg was made in a chafing dish. There was something charming about the chafing dish with its bright silver reflecting a flickering blue flame, only there was always the question whether you put in enough alcohol to finish the cooking. When you needed more, the bottle was often empty. The nearest shop was four miles across Frenchman's Bay, which was often blanketed in thick fog or else produced something called a short chop (pronounced shawt chawp) by the tide running against the wind.

Seen against this background an electric skillet looks reasonably attractive.

Lobster Newburg
FOR SIX

¼ cup butter	a few grains of cayenne
1½ pounds frozen lobster cut up, not too small	½ teaspoon paprika
	¼ teaspoon nutmeg
3 tablespoons good sherry (*not* "cooking" sherry)	1½ cups light cream
	3 egg yolks, lightly beaten

Melt the butter over low heat. Toss the lobster meat in it 2 minutes. Add sherry, mixed with the seasonings. Cook 2 minutes. Mix cream and beaten egg yolks in a small bowl. Add a tablespoon of juice from the pan and stir well. Add another tablespoon of juice. Stir again. Then pour cream and egg mixture over the lobster. Cook gently, without letting it boil, until the sauce is thick and smooth. Add the cognac. Stir. Serve at once with triangles of buttered toast.

This same method can be applied to shrimp, oysters, crab or scallops with excellent results.

Scotch Shortbread

½ pound butter   ½ cup sugar
3½ cups flour

All should be at room temperature.

Cream the butter until it stands in soft peaks. Use a pastry-blending fork. Work in the sugar, a little at a time. Work in a cup of the flour a tablespoon at a time. Use some of the remaining flour to flour a board. Put the mixture on it and knead in the rest of the flour. Light oven: 325°.

The more you knead it the "shorter" it will be, so add the flour in very small amounts. Turn the dough over and turn it around from time to time. When all the flour is used — get every bit on the board into it — press the dough into a 9 × 13 aluminum pan, not greased. Dough should be less than ½ inch thick. Mark dough in squares. This size pan will make 48 squares about 1¼ inches square, or 32 larger ones, but as the shortbread is very rich the small size may be what you prefer. Prick it all over with a fork. Bake 20 minutes. By that time the squares around the edge will be delicately brown. Remove them. Shove others against the edge of the pan. Bake 10 minutes longer. Remove those that show any brown and give the remaining ones an extra 10 minutes. They will be browner on the bottom than on top. It is important that they should not be browned too much. Their goodness lies in the rather sandy texture and the cooked but not scorched flavor of what advertisers coyly describe as "the more expensive spread."

Yes, it is more expensive than substitutes and for an excellent reason: it produces better flavor and texture than they do. Don't try to make shortbread with anything but the best butter.

Whose voice could it possibly be making this remark?

After lunch the girls were much relaxed, but the auction began before anyone went to sleep so they soon became mentally alert. The billiard room was the scene of the auction and the green table was covered with interesting lumpy packages. It seems miraculous, after all these years, that attics should still be producing treasures. Perhaps they are simply rotated from one attic to another and are brought down for some other auction. Ellen Pryor, who gave up her attic when she built her contemporary house, is still a generous contributor. She often buys things to present to the P. and S.C. auction. Not having become very familiar with these objects, she is apt to bid on them absent-mindedly and has been known to take them home again at a price rather higher than she originally paid.

She is that auctioneer's dream, a constant bidder. She even bids on hats. The part of the auction Mrs. Appleyard likes best is when the girls start trying on hats, all telling each other how becoming they are. Sometimes they model negligees too and hold up dresses on each other to get an idea of the probable cubic contents. In this way, last year, Mrs. Appleyard acquired her best black velvet dress, graduate of many Theater Guild openings with dinner beforehand. If it could only tell the menus at which it has presided! However, for $7.50 one could hardly expect the costume would have built-in clairvoyance.

The club is lucky in its auctioneer, Pauline French. She would, Mrs. Appleyard feels sure, make her fortune if she would take up auctioneering professionally. She is genial, skeptical, quizzical, relentless in getting the last penny. She has wit and friendliness and a repertoire of stories not learned from one of those auctioneering schools where men are taught to apply the mother-in-law joke to anything from a cracked plate to a photograph frame that won't stand up. ("Nice to keep your mother-in-law's picture in.")

Pauline's jokes are her own, told in her own way and in a voice which, Mrs. Appleyard thinks, must be the echo of an ancestral voice, as much a part of the family inheritance as the portraits by Copley and the silver by Paul Revere. Just as firm, sensible, cheerful and stronghearted must the Frenches have sounded as they hurried past the old elm on Boston Common dressed as Indians on their way to the Boston Tea Party.

No wonder everything in the billiard room changes hands. No wonder Erica Pryor goes home more heavily laden than she came and with three billiard balls (later returned by her chauffeur with suitable apologies) in her new Andalusian satchel. No wonder Mrs. Appleyard goes back to Vermont with a collection of real necessities such as a bronze bowl full of ivy, seven mystery stories (she needs some to lend), a cracked Lowestoft bowl (she's heard it can be made as good as new by boiling in milk and garlic), and a hat from Stella LaRose's intimidating little salon.

Stella will not sell hats to just anyone. Is it quite honorable for Mrs. Appleyard to have a Stella LaRose model? There is a terrifying story about a Boston woman on a train for New York. Realizing that of course there was no use in trying to look as if she belonged in New York, she decided to look as Bostonian as possible so she wore her LaRose hat, given to her by a cousin, Helen St. John, who had passed it on after only two years.

She was sitting quietly on the Merchant's Limited, reading

the *Saturday Review* and feeling liberal yet conservatively elegant, when Stella LaRose walked through towards the dining car. (The lady in the hat had a packet of sandwiches.)

Stella stopped in front of her and said, in a voice that would go through a wall of Roxbury puddingstone insulated with peacock feathers: "I see you are wearing one of my hats. Please tip it slightly forward over your right eye. It does not belong on the back of the head. Remember me to Mrs. St. John."

Would she be safe, Mrs. Appleyard wondered, if she wore her LaRose hat in public? She would hardly wear it in private, would she? In her apartment suntrap with only the chickadees at the feeder to enjoy it?

I might give it away, she thought. Why, of course! I'll take it to the auction next year. Now what am I offered?

May

The Right Mix

Iᴛ ᴡᴀꜱ spring when Mrs. Appleyard left Boston. It was a
wonderful hot day. There were as many tulips as people in the
Public Garden. In the country flowering crabs, forsythia and
daffodils had all rushed into bloom at once. Willows were rain-
ing green gold. Leaves smaller than a chipmunk's ear were quivering on white birches. She stopped to see some friends. When
they saw her coming they rushed out and picked their own asparagus and made her stay to lunch. It was not difficult to persuade her. Probably it is gratifying to have a red carpet spread
down for you but not, Mrs. Appleyard thinks, nearly so pleasant

as being passed a platter of fresh asparagus with a delicious sauce
of butter and thick cream.

She stayed to dinner. She stayed for the night. She saw a
dogwood tree, loaded with greenish ivory flowers the day before, turn overnight to a shining white cloud. She saw the tight
dark buds of lilacs change to waving plumes of fragrance with
orioles flashing in and out of them. She saw elms cloud into
green fountains and red knobs on the apple trees burst into pink
and white stars. White candles started to open on the horse
chestnuts. Evidently it was safe to pack up the Appleyard
papers and go and tell Vermonters it was spring.

This was a project noble in purpose but a little hard to execute
because, as she crossed the Connecticut River, it began to snow.
It rather improved the looks of the hills, which were bare and
bleak and gray close by and a sullen inky blue in the distance.
The snow quickly capped them with white. This was no frivolous flurry, melting as it fell. It meant business. It frosted the
chocolate of plowed fields and the dark green steeples of firs.
It made red-winged blackbirds wish they had stayed south and
cowslips wish they had not opened their shining gold flowers.
Bloodroot was happy that its white petals were wrapped in
cocoons of silver-green leaves. It made farmers glad that cows
were still in the barn, and road commissioners groan. At Appleyard Center children were joyfully snowballing each other
among the crocuses and a car that had skidded on the hill was
being hauled out of the birch wood.

Cicely was so accustomed to the weather that she never even
mentioned it. It was her mother who introduced the topic.

"Won't it even be spring for the christening?" she asked. "I
was planning to open my house and have the party there. I
might as well entertain on an ice floe."

Her child soothed her with an optimistic remark.

"Snow never lasts long in May and June," she said.

She was right. The next morning the fields were full of blue-eyed ponds. Cowslips were bright gold along darkly rushing brooks, spring peepers rang sleigh bell chimes. Ferns uncurled like the tops of cellos. Roger Willard opened the shutters of Mrs. Appleyard's house and let the sunshine in. She went into the front hall. She inhaled happily the smell of woodsmoke and potpourri, with faint overtones of pedigreed mice, descendants of those for whom the Appleyards have been keeping the house in good order since 1822. The house sheltered chimney swifts too. Mrs. Appleyard could hear their wings whirring. No doubt there were bats hanging upside down in the shed chamber. A weasel popped up in the woodshed, looked cynically at her and returned to his furnished apartment.

Human beings, Mrs. Appleyard reflected, are a great convenience to animals.

She began to make plans for the christening. It would be in the old church after the service on the Sunday nearest to Camilla's birthday, which was also her own birthday. They had meant to have Tim christened at this time last year, but he had the measles so it had been postponed. This year it could be his christening and Nick's too. Afterwards she would have a buffet lunch for everyone. The children could take their plates out on the grass — if it just didn't snow. She began to make lists.

Cicely picked one up off the pantry floor. "Silver polish, almonds, plastic plates, etc., Willow pattern, Mouse seed, Balloons, Flowers, Kaleidoscopes, Brandy snaps, Find stove polish, Telephone connected, Oatmeal cookies," she read.

"Is this the menu?" she asked.

"Just a rough sketch," her mother told her. "I haven't quite worked it out yet."

In its final form the menu was:

Chicken and Spaghetti with Sausages*   Veal Loaf, with Truffles*
Cold Sliced Ham   Shrimp Mold*
Tossed Salad (p. 147)   Homemade Whole-Wheat Bread*
Real Strawberry Ice Cream*   Oatmeal Cookies (p. 110)
Brandy Snaps*   Almond Cake*
White Grape Juice Punch*   Coffee

On the Friday before the party Mrs. Appleyard and Patience Barlow were already at work making almond cake and oatmeal cookies. It was a wonderful bright day, with bobolinks singing as they soared over the cowslips. Bluebirds were building a nest in Patience Barlow's mailbox. She told Frank Flint just to wrap the letters in the newspaper and throw it on the grass. Phoebes were announcing their name, a scarlet tanager was an instant of bright flame in a young maple and then burned away north. Forget-me-nots winked up at the sky.

It was, the experts decided, a perfect day to make oatmeal cookies. Patience worked on them and then on brandy snaps while Mrs. Appleyard made almond cake and polished silver. She went out occasionally to check up on the landscape. She was beside the pond helping Nicholas tickle the head of a very green frog with a piece of last year's witch grass when Cicely, Jane and Camilla arrived. Until she saw the Delft Posset Cup, the big bunch of roses and the carton of goldfish, she had forgotten it was her birthday.

"The goldfish," Cicely told her, "are for your pond. They will grow into carp and you can simmer them in red wine."

"I can't imagine doing anything so mean," Mrs. Appleyard said.

She slid the fish carefully into the pond. All promptly swam off except one which struggled in a tangle of forget-me-nots.

"Poor little thing — it doesn't seem to be able to swim!" Mrs.

Appleyard exclaimed bending over to help it, and falling into the pond with a rather loud splash.

"Luckily I can," she added as her descendants helped her out. She changed her swimming costume for something less moist. "From now on," she announced, "I'll attend to my cooking." Nothing else happened to interfere with the menu.

Chicken and Spaghetti with Sausages
FOR SIXTEEN

2 fowls weighing at least 5 pounds apiece	¼ teaspoon each of cinnamon, clove, allspice, pepper
3 tablespoons butter	2 large cans of tomatoes
2 large onions, sliced thin and minced	3 beans of garlic, put through the press
3 green peppers, seeded, sliced thin, minced	2 pounds small link sausages
1 pound mushrooms	1 pound spaghetti (2 packages)
3 tablespoons flour	4 pimentos, finely cut
2 teaspoons sugar	1 cup dry Vermont cheddar cheese, grated
bit of bay leaf	1 teaspoon paprika
2 tablespoons minced parsley	

The day before you are going to serve this dish, cook the fowls. Simmer them in water in which you have put 2 sliced carrots, 2 sliced onions, celery tops and a teaspoon of mixed herbs. Cook until meat slips easily from the bones — 4–5 hours. Remove skin. Cut meat into serving pieces, wrap in wax paper and keep in the refrigerator till needed. Return the bones to the broth and cook until the broth is thick enough to jelly. Strain into a bowl. Add any small pieces of meat. Keep it in a cool place till needed. (Mrs. Appleyard wishes a warm one were as easy for her to find.)

The next day melt the butter in a large iron skillet. Sauté the onion, peppers and mushrooms — caps and the tender part of the stems — in it until onions are yellow. Skim the chicken fat from the broth. Add a tablespoon of it to the contents of the pan. Sprinkle in the flour mixed with the dry seasonings, except paprika. Blend it well with the fat over low heat. Add the tomatoes and garlic. Stir well, let the mixture simmer for an hour. Watch it. Add chicken stock occasionally. Stir mixture well from the bottom so it will not stick.

Half an hour before you plan to serve the spaghetti, start to cook it and the sausages. Put the chicken stock on to heat in a large kettle. Put the sausages into a frying pan. Pour warm water around them so that they are almost covered and let them simmer. The water should cook away in about 20 minutes. Turn them at the end of 10 minutes. Do not prick them. After the water has cooked away leave them in the pan until they brown. At the end of 5 minutes, drain off the fat and turn them. Cook 5 minutes more.

When the chicken stock boils hard — there should be 3 quarts — slip spaghetti into it slowly so that it curls up and the water never stops boiling. Coil it around in the water. Cook till it is tender but not mushy, about 7–8 minutes. Drain it and put it on a hot heatproof platter. Save the stock and reheat the cooked chicken in it for a few minutes. Skim it out and arrange the large pieces on top of the spaghetti. Add small ones to the tomato sauce. Add pimentos. Arrange sausages around the spaghetti and chicken. Pour the sauce over the whole thing. Set the platter in the oven for a few minutes. Sprinkle with grated cheese. Sprinkle the cheese with paprika and parsley. Serve.

Veal Loaf

½ pound calves' liver
1 tablespoon butter
½ pound baked ham, cubed
2 large onions
2 pounds of veal cutlet and
   1 pound of lean pork put twice
   through the grinder together
6 Montpelier crackers

salt to taste
pinch of nutmeg
1 teaspoon pepper
1 teaspoon poultry seasoning
2 truffles, sliced and quartered
2 eggs, well beaten
1 tablespoon flour
4 slices of bacon

extra butter

Your market man will grind the veal and the pork together for you. Cook the liver in the butter over low heat, covered, until it is tender — about 5 minutes. Chop it very fine. Dice the ham. Mrs. Appleyard used part of her baked ham for this but a slice of boiled ham cut ½ inch thick will do.

Chop onions very fine, chop liver into them, then the veal and pork until everything is well mixed. Roll crackers (Boston Commons will do if you can't get Montpelier crackers) into fine crumbs, add seasonings and mix them in. Next add the ham cubes and the sliced truffles. Their nutty fragrance is delicious with the veal and pork.

Butter a bread tin and put in the mixture. Press it well into the corners of the tin. Dredge the top with flour and a few very fine crumbs. Cover it with bacon cut into narrow strips. Set the pan on a rack in a covered roaster. Surround the pan with hot water. Bake at 350° for 2 hours.

When it is thoroughly chilled, it will slice beautifully.

Mrs. Appleyard sometimes serves it as a main dish with mushroom sauce. She had this plan the last time she made it, three loaves in Pyrex glass pans. She had intended them for the Pinball and Scissors Club. Unfortunately she dropped the roaster and contents, thus adding an extra ingredient, ground glass, to the mixture. She felt she was very lucky at such short notice to be able to get chicken breasts for twenty-four people. They were simmered in cream with mushrooms (p. 198) and were not unpalatable, but she advises baking veal loaf in tin pans.

Shrimp Mold

2 tablespoons plain gelatin soaked in ½ cup ginger ale	2 teaspoons onion, put through garlic press
2½ cups hot ginger ale	2 pounds flash-frozen cooked shrimp, thawed slowly
4 tablespoons lemon juice	
1 tablespoon lime juice	a little olive oil
1 cup celery, cut fine	watercress
1 green pepper, minced	tiny green peas
	Stuffed Eggs (p. 196)
mayonnaise	

Soak the gelatin in cold ginger ale. Dissolve it in hot ginger ale. Stir in lemon juice and lime, celery, pepper, onion and the shrimp. Brush a mold with olive oil. Add the mixture. Chill. Unmold on a platter. Surround with watercress, tiny green peas, cooked and chilled, and Stuffed Eggs.

When they are in season in her garden, Mrs. Appleyard surrounds the mold with cucumber and tomatoes, sliced, and sliced stuffed olives. Serve mayonnaise with it.

Homemade Whole-Wheat Bread (E. and H.B.)

Mrs. Appleyard is lucky enough to have a neighbor who grinds whole-wheat flour and he is lucky enough to have a wife who makes this bread.

Mix in a large bowl:

2 cups warm (not hot) water or milk
2 tablespoons (pkgs) dry baker's yeast
¼ cup honey, molasses or brown sugar

Stir in 3½ cups whole-wheat flour. Beat 300 strokes by hand
(or about 8 minutes at low speed in the electric mixer). Work
in another 3 to 3½ cups whole-wheat flour. Use your hands
when necessary. Turn out on well-floured board and knead
well. If it seems sticky, knead in more flour. When dough is
smooth and elastic, return it to the bowl, cover, let stand in a
warm place until double in bulk (about 2 hours). Punch down,
turn out on a floured board, divide in half, shape in 2 loaves,
place in oiled bread pans, cover, let double in bulk again (about
1 hour). Bake at 350° for 45 minutes. Turn out on wire rack
to cool.

This flour is not "enriched." Enriching used to mean adding
something extra to something rich already. It now means taking
all the vitamins out of flour and putting some of them back in
synthetic form. This is about as enriching as it would be if
someone picked your pocket and then took pity on you and
handed you back enough for carfare. Real home-ground whole-
wheat flour has the wheat germ in it and will spoil if it is not
kept under refrigeration. It is not enriched; it doesn't have to be.

Real Strawberry Ice Cream or Mousse

Mrs. Appleyard makes this in her electric freezer and it is
like ice cream frozen by hand with ice and salt around it. It
contains nothing but strawberries, cream and sugar. No isinglass, for instance. This is a substance used like gelatin. It
comes out of a sturgeon. If you were growing your own caviar

you could probably have isinglass too. It would not be any good to put in the windows of an old-fashioned cast-iron stove. They look like isinglass and are called isinglass but they are really mica. Neither should ice cream contain cornstarch or powdered eggs or artificial vanilla or any form of glue.

If you do not have an electric freezer you can make it quite satisfactorily in your deep-freeze or in the freezer section of your refrigerator. Put the mixture into a pan at least 3 inches deep. Stir it thoroughly to break up ice crystals three times during the first hour of freezing. Once during the second hour. Freezers vary so much in temperature that it's hard to be accurate about the length of time needed but three hours ought to be enough.

Of course if cream and fruit are not beaten continuously during freezing you are making mousse rather than ice cream. Its texture will not be quite so smooth but if you use only crushed and puréed fruit, sugar and whipped cream, the flavor will be delicious.

Strawberry Ice Cream

2 cups crushed strawberries	½ cup sugar
1 pint heavy cream, not beaten

Put strawberries and sugar through the blender. Mix with the cream. Put into electric freezer. Freeze until dash will no longer move. Mrs. Appleyard makes this ahead of time, several batches of it, and stores it in her deep-freeze. A quart of ice cream is supposed to serve six. It is Mrs. Appleyard's duty to tell you that this will not do so unless your guests are on a diet. Make plenty.

Strawberry Mousse

2 cups crushed strawberries   ½ cup sugar
1 pint heavy cream, whipped

Put strawberries and sugar into the blender and blend until smooth. Chill. Whip cream until it stands in soft peaks. Fold it into the strawberry mixture until the mixture is a beautiful even color, like snow at sunset. Freeze according to the directions above.

Brandy Snaps

½ cup butter   ½ cup flour
½ cup sugar   ½ teaspoon mixed spices —
½ cup molasses   nutmeg, cinnamon, ginger
½ cup coconut   2 tablespoons brandy

Melt butter over low heat. Stir in sugar, molasses and coconut. Heat to boiling point. Sift flour and spices. Add brandy to the molasses mixture. Stir in the flour and spice. Drop by half teaspoonfuls, well spaced to take care of spreading, on a lightly greased dripping pan. Bake at 325° for about 7 to 10 minutes. Have a second pan ready as the first one comes out. To get them off the pans is the problem. You need patience, a flexible spatula, a small pancake turner and a large spoon with a wooden handle. This spoon is so you can roll the snaps around the handle when you have removed them from the pan. Let them cool first. After a minute, test the edges with the spatula till you find the snaps are ready to leave the pan. Then you must work quickly, bending each one you detach around the spoon handle, or you may swiftly curve them over the edge of the mixing bowl. You may be skillful enough so you can roll them into cornucopias and serve them filled with whipped cream. (Mrs. Appleyard has never reached this adept level. She humbly admires those who have.) Don't try to make them on a sticky day with the barometer falling. Store them in a tin box with a tight cover, between layers of wax paper.

Almond Cake (S.H.L.)

1 pound butter	20 egg whites
½ pound almonds, blanched and skinned	4 cups flour, measured after sifting
2 cups sugar	1 teaspoon almond extract

Let butter warm to room temperature. Chop almonds. Cream butter, add sugar gradually, cream till light and fluffy. Add almonds, lightly floured. Beat whites to soft peaks. Add them alternately with the flour. Add the almond extract. Grease a large tube pan and line it with wax paper. The oven should be at 300°–325°. The cake requires long and uniform baking, about 2 hours. Test with straw, which should come out clean.

Boiled Frosting

2 cups sifted sugar	2 egg whites
1 cup cold water	1 teaspoon almond extract

Put sugar and water together in saucepan. Stir until sugar dissolves to keep crystals from forming, then boil without stirring. Use a candy thermometer. Cook till syrup will spin a thread that will turn up at the end — 238°. Remove syrup from the fire and let it cool a little while you are beating the egg whites stiff. Add the flavoring. Pour it over the egg whites in a thin stream, beating steadily. You need either an electric mixer or a co-operative friend for this process. Mrs. Appleyard much prefers the latter.

White Grape Juice Punch
FOR TWENTY

16 lemons	2 cans orange juice
2 cups sugar	(frozen)
1 gallon boiling water	2 gallons pale dry ginger ale ⎫ chilled
3 tablespoons tea	2 quarts white grape juice ⎭

Slice lemons thin. Add the sugar and crush it into the lemons with a wooden pestle till sugar disappears. Heat water. When it comes to full bubbling boil, throw in the tea and let it boil one minute, no more, no less. Strain at once over lemons and set mixture away to ripen overnight in a cool place. At serving time put ice cubes and the orange juice, not diluted, in a large punch bowl. Add the ginger ale and the white grape juice. Garnish with cubed pineapple, strawberries and mint.

White wine may be substituted for the white grape juice. Mrs. Appleyard sometimes makes two bowls, one for grownups with wine, the other for children with grape juice. She drinks from the children's bowl.

The day of the christening was soft blue and gold. The buds on the apple trees changed from red to pink. Lilacs began to open. Swallow-tail butterflies fluttered yellow and black among them and above the daffodil trumpets. Cicely brought a great bunch of narcissus and pink tulips and her mother arranged them with sprays of lilac in a big copper jug. It was cool enough to have fires in the Franklin stoves and warm enough to sit on the arched porch in the sunshine.

The old church shone in its new coat of paint. The weathervane, part arrow, part fish, flashed its new gold against the sky. Inside it was rather cooler, Mrs. Appleyard thought, than it had been on Christmas Eve but this morning she could look out on young pink and buff maple leaves, on Guernsey cattle eating emerald grass, on blue hills without a flake of snow on them. The peaceful hour of the service was over all too soon. During the last hymn, parents began to bring in the children who were to be christened. Some of them were small enough to join in the singing with soprano and tenor wails. Some, like Timothy, were dignified six-year-olds. Some, like Nicholas, were old enough to tramp emphatically on the wide pine boards in their shining new shoes. Few of them, however, thought Mrs. Appleyard, looked as benevolent as Nick, with as active a dimple, or as earnest as Timothy with such an impish gleam in his eyes. Of course she is completely unprejudiced.

When the old Adam had been cast out of everyone Mrs. Appleyard went home and sat peacefully in her music room while her daughters and daughters-in-law served the luncheon. She was so successful in pretending that she had never had anything to do with it that it really tasted pretty good. In fact the whole day was perfect. When she thought it over afterwards it was hard to choose the moment she had liked best. Was it when she expected to see Camilla's birthday cake with the thirteen candles she had arranged on it and then found that it had sprouted what looked more like seventy-six — so whose cake could it be? Was it helping Nick tickle a bullfrog? Was it hearing her children's and grandchildren's voices singing in the old church? Or feeling her house warm and full of life instead of cold and empty?

All these, of course, she thought of with happiness, but perhaps what she really liked best was Timothy's coming to her with three oatmeal cookies on a plate and offering them to her.

"You eat them," she suggested.

When he had politely co-operated he said: "Grandma, how do you make those cookies?"

"It's a little hard to tell without doing it," Mrs. Appleyard said, "but sometime I'll let you help me make some and then you'll know."

"Thank you," said Timothy. "I suppose," he added, "you have to begin by getting the right mix. And then cook them the right time."

Then he went off and began to turn cartwheels among the dandelions, leaving Mrs. Appleyard thinking about time.

She hopes that no one who reads this book will think she wants people to spend all their time in the kitchen. She wants you to have, literally, a good time. That means that you will use time as you like instead of its using you. In cooking, as in life, time is the most important element, especially if you are the kind of cook who is reading *The Wings of the Dove* while the bread is rising or doing a little painting on velvet while the pot roast is marinating.

A timer often saves this kind of cook from calamities. It is a mechanical device, but perhaps not quite so mechanical as it sounds as it ticks off the minutes. Perhaps you and Mrs. Appleyard are not precisely Einsteins of the kitchen. Yet, before you ever set that timer going, you thought of space-time. You know it takes longer to bake a 9 × 13 pan of brownies than an 8 × 8 pan but not twice as long. You have a sense of fire-time and of cold-time, of wet-and-dry time and of golden-brown time. You feed all those statistics into your mental computer before you ever set your timer for those oatmeal cookies.

Mrs. Appleyard admits that it isn't a giant computer. It would have to have ever so many more whizzing dials if you were going to do something useful like sending a giraffe to Venus.

Still it is helpful and so is your nose, which tells you how brown the johnnycake is, and your ears, which notice that the steak has just hissed three times so you'd better check the meat thermometer. Your ears will also tell you that the soufflé is still whispering so it isn't quite done. Your eyes detect that the cream puffs are done because the last iridescent bubbles have vanished. Your fingertips tell you when the sponge cake is ready. You use your sense of rhythm while you beat egg whites, your sense of weight when you lift a pan of fruitcake, your sense of taste when you decide to add a little more Bristol Cream sherry to the Lobster Newburg, your sense of beauty all the time.

Yes, Mrs. Appleyard says, you need the right mix. You need all the right kinds of time. And what is the result? Well, Aristotle knew. Mrs. Appleyard has her favorite books where she can reach them from her bed. Bostonians consider reading in bed rather dissipated. Mrs. Appleyard admits that she not only reads in bed; she also writes there. One of the books for which she often stretches out her hand is her grandmother's copy of *Miss Parloa's Cook Book* with her grandmother's handwriting on the extra pages in the back. Next to it is another favorite book called *Teach Yourself Greek.*

If someone else had taught her Greek about 1902, perhaps she would know more. However she has learned one or two sentences she likes. This one of Aristotle's is her favorite.

εὐδαιμονία ἐστὶν ἐνέργεια τῆς ψυχῆς κατ' ἀρετῆ ἐν τῷ τελείῳ βίῳ.

The word ἀρετη has no real counterpart in English. It can mean different things in different situations. For instance the ἀρετη of the soldier is courage, of a knife — sharpness, of a merchant — honesty, of a soufflé — lightness. It is a special excellence.

So Aristotle's sentence means to Mrs. Appleyard: "Happiness

is activity of the spirit used according to its special excellence in the complete life."

She hopes you will use your time according to your special excellence and that you will find the right mix — work and leisure, rain and sunshine, sugar and spice and, when you have to cook — friends to cook for.

Index

Almond Cake, 312
Almond Ring, 83
Appetizers, Peanut Butter and Bacon, 126. *See also* Canapés *and* Hors d'Oeuvres
Apples, Cranberry, 35
Appleyard Center Baked Beans, 29
Apricot Crossbar Pie, 244
Apricot Parfait, 271
Apricots, Conserved, 244
Artichokes Hollandaise, 160
Asparagus, Country Style, with Butter and Egg Sauce, 191
Avocado Salad, 47

Bacon Dip, 258
Baked Alaska, 161
Baked: Beans, 28, 29, 30
   Cheese Balls, 288
   Corn and Cheese Puff, 286
   Fudge Brownies, 117
   Golden Bantam Corn, 182

Potatoes with Sour Cream, 238
   Stuffing, 142
Beans, Baked, 28, 29, 30
Beans, Green, and beets, 209
   and Cauliflower, 126
   with Garlic Croutons, 55
   with Mushrooms, 67
   with Sausages, 181
Beans, Lima, with Mushrooms, 68
Beans, Shell, with Mushrooms, 68
Beef Chowder Appleyard, 226
Beets, Green Beans and, 209
Beets Appleyard, 139
Biscuit, Deviled, 268
Black Bean Soup, 12
Boiled Dressing, 266
Boiled Frosting, 312
Braised Celery, 281
Brandy Snaps, 311
Bread, Brown, 34
   Curried, 267
   Garlic, 189
   Homemade Whole-Wheat, 308
   Slovak Nut, 179

Broccoli: Cauliflower and, Garlic Crumbs, 239
  with Garlic Croutons, 170
  with Mushrooms, 68
Brown Betty, 47
Brown Bread, 34
  Sandwiches, 248
Brown Sugar Pecan Fudge, 274
Brownies, Baked Fudge, 117
Brussels Sprouts with Mushrooms, 68

Cabbage Soup, 23
Cake, Almond, 312
  Dark Fruit, 116
  Flaming Angel, 194
  Fudge Layer, with Marshmallows, 84
  Glazed Strawberry Cheese, 87
  Half-a-Pound, 272
  Mocha Angel, 251
  Pineapple Upside-Down, 145
  Sponge, 278
  Valentine Cheese, 210
  White Fruit, 91
Canapés, Mushroom and Bacon, 241. *See also* Appetizers *and* Hors d'Oeuvres
Candied: Cranberries, 172
  Grapefruit Peel, 172
  Yams, Orange Marmalade Sauce, 209
Casserole, Seafood, 180

Cauliflower: and Broccoli, Garlic Crumbs, 239
  and Green Beans, 126
Celery, Braised, 281
  Stuffed, 124
Champagne Punch, 211
Cheese, Crackers and, 149
Cheese and Chutney Crumpets, 288
Cheese Balls, Baked, 288
Cheese Cake, Glazed Strawberry, 87
  Valentine, 210
Cheese Croquettes, 249
Cheese Fondue, 163
Chestnut Stuffing, 65
Chicken: à la King, Real, 207
  Appleyard, 290
  in Cream, 198
  and Spaghetti with Sausages, 305
  See also Coq au Vin
Chicken Liver Pâté, 124
Chocolate, Hot, 193
Chocolate Sauce, 103
Chowder, Appleyard Beef, 226
  Fish, 217
  Seafood, 99
Chutney, Lemon Mint, 191
Cider, Spiced, 118
Clam and Chicken Soup, 277
Cocktail, Shrimp, Crabmeat and Avocado, 279
Coconut Cookies, 194
Coffee Cake, 25

Conserved Apricots, 244
Cookies, Brandy Snaps, 311
    Coconut, 194
    Oatmeal Lace, 110
    Pecan Brandy Balls, 109
    Sugar and Spice, 108
    Swedish, 118
    See also Brownies
Coq au Vin, 24
Corn, Golden Bantam, Baked, 182
Corn and Cheese Puff, 286
Corn Pudding, 101
Crabmeat, Eggs Stuffed with, 282
Crackers: and Cheese, 149
    Montpelier, Souffléd, 221
    Montpelier, Toasted, 63
Cranberries, Candied, 172
Cranberry Apples, 35
Cranberry Lattice Pie, 14
Cranberry Sauce, 66
Cream Cheese Balls, 230
Cream Puffs, 182
Creamed Turkey and Oysters, 144
Croustade of Seafood, 45
Croutons, 141
    Garlic, 56
    Oysters with, 290
Crown Roast of Lamb Vienna with Help from Turkey, 156
Crumpets, Cheese and Chutney, 288
Cucumber Salad, 25

Currant-Orange Sauce, 54
Curried Bread, 267
Custard, Onion Soup with, 197
Custards, Upside-down Caramel, 86
Cynthia's Dandelion Wine, 133

Dandelion Wine, 133
Danish Soup, 156
Dark Fruitcake, 116
Deep-Dish Apple Pie, 102
Deviled Biscuit, 268
Dip, Bacon, 258
    Green, 206
    Pink, 206
    Sardine, 259
Dressing, Boiled, 266
    French, 190
    French, Mr. Appleyard's, 262
    Fruit Salad, 230
    Sour Cream, 267
    Yogurt, 25
Duckling, Roast, 280
Dumplings, 227

Eggs, Stuffed, 196
    Stuffed with Crabmeat, 282
English Muffins, Toasted, 145

Fish Balls, 32
Fish Chowder, 217
Fish Hash, 33
    For other fish recipes, see Flounder, Haddock, Halibut, Seafood and Shad

Flaming Angel Cake, 194
Floating Island, 90
Flounder Balls, 205
Foamy Sauce, 58
Fondue, Vermont Cheese, 163
French Dressing, 190
   Mr. Appleyard's, 263
French Mustard Sauce, 159
Frosting, Boiled, 312
   Fudge, 86
Fruitcake, Dark, 116
   White, 91
Fruit Salad with Cream Cheese
   Balls, 230
Fruit Salad Dressing, 230
Fudge, Brown Sugar Pecan, 274
   Maple Butternut, 273
Fudge Brownies, Baked, 117
Fudge Frosting, 86
Fudge Layer Cake with Marsh-
   mallows, 84

Garlic Bread, 189
Garlic Croutons, Green Beans
   with, 55
Giblet Gravy, 66
Glazed Strawberry Cheese Cake,
   87
Goose, Roast, 238
Goose Liver Pâté with Truffles,
   236
Grapefruit, 279
Grapefruit Peel, Candied, 172
Gravy, Giblet, 66

Green Beans: and Beets, 209
   Cauliflower and, 126
   with Garlic Croutons, 55
   with Mushrooms, 67
   with Sausages, 181
Green Dip, 206
Green Peas, 199
   and Pearl Onions with Mustard
      Sauce, 159
Green Vegetables, Symphony
   in, 291
Grønkålsuppe, 156

Haddock, Marinated, 259
Half-a-Pound Cake, 272
Halibut Steaks, 287
Ham Mousse, 100
Hamburg Strong-Enough, 188
Hard Sauce, 130
Harvest Vegetable Salad, 33
Hash, Fish, 33
   Red Flannel, 30
Hollandaise Sauce, 127
Hors d'Oeuvres, 155. See also
   Appetizers and Canapés
Hot Chocolate, 193
Hot Spiced Punch, 210

Ice Cream, Real Strawberry, 309,
   310

Jelly, Paradise, 158

Kasha with Mushrooms, 54
Kolacky, 179

Lamb, Crown Roast of, 156
  Roast, 242
  Soup, 242
Lemon Mint Chutney, 191
Lemon Soufflé, 56
Lima Beans with Mushrooms, 68
Lobster Newburg, 295, 296
Lord Baltimore Soup, 218, 219, 220

Maple Butternut Fudge, 273
Marinade, 263
Marinated Haddock, 259
Marrons Glacés, 291
Marzipan Fruit, 113
Mashed Potato Cakes, 138
Mayonnaise, Homemade, 265
Meat Loaf, 168
Melba Toast, 125
Menus, 12, 23, 42, 52, 62, 83, 97, 108, 124, 137, 153, 168, 178, 187, 196, 205, 217, 225, 229, 231, 236, 241, 247, 256, 277, 279, 281, 294, 304
Meringue, 161
Mince Pie, 68, 69
Mince Turnovers, 173
Minted Pears, 249
Mr. Appleyard's French Dressing, 262
Mrs. Appleyard's Icebound Raspberry-Cranberry Sauce, 182
Mrs. Appleyard's Own Baked Beans, 30
Mocha Angel Cake, 251

Montpelier Crackers, Souffléd, 221
  Toasted, 63
Mousse, Ham, 100
  Real Strawberry, 309, 311
Mushroom and Bacon Canapés, 241
Mushroom Sauce, 68, 169, 241
Mustard Sauce, 100
  French, 159

Oatcake, Scotch, 160
Oatmeal Lace Cookies, 110
Onion Soup: in Casserole, 231
  with Custard, 197
Orange Ice, Peaches Cardinal with, 239
Orange Marmalade Sauce, 209
Orange Sherbet with Bananas, 199
Oyster Bar Sauce, 248
Oyster Stuffing, 261
Oysters: Creamed Turkey and, 144
  with Croutons, 289

Paradise Jelly, 158
Pastry, 2000-Layer, 60
Pastry Pinwheels, 240
Pastry Tarts with Foie Gras, 155
Pâté, Chicken Liver, 124
  Goose Liver, with Truffles, 236
Pea Soup, Princess, 178
  Cream of Shrimp and, 229

Peaches Cardinal with Orange Ice, 239
Peanut Butter and Bacon Appetizers, 126
Pears, Minted, 249
Peas, Green, 199
  and Pearl Onions with Mustard Sauce, 159
Pecan Brandy Balls, 109
Peppers, Red and Green, Sautés, 56
Pie, Apricot Crossbar, 244
  Cranberry Lattice, 14
  Deep-Dish Apple, 102
  Mince, 68, 69
  Pumpkin, 72
Pineapple Upside-Down Cake, 145
Pink Dip, 206
Pistachio Marron Trifle, 88
Planked Shad, 283
Plum Pudding, 129
Popovers, 13
Potato Cakes, Mashed, 138
Potatoes, Baked, with Sour Cream, 238
Princess Pea Soup, 178
Pudding, Corn, 101
  Plum, 129
  Yorkshire, 170
Pumpkin Pie Filling, 72
Punch, Champagne, 211
  Hot Spiced, 210
  White Grape Juice, 313

Raspberry-Cranberry Sauce, Mrs. Appleyard's Icebound, 182
Red and Green Peppers, Sautés, 56
Red Flannel Hash, 30
Rice, Wild, with Mushrooms, 280
Roast: Duckling, 280
  Goose, 238
  Lamb, 242
  Turkey, 64
  Venison, 53

Salad, Avocado, 47
  combinations for, 264
  Cucumber, Yogurt Dressing, 25
  Fruit, with Cream Cheese Balls, 230
  Harvest Vegetable, 33
  Seafood, 262
  Tossed, 147, 189
  Turkey, 139
Sandwiches, Brown Bread, 248
Sardine Dip, 259
Sauce, Chocolate, 103
  Cranberry, 66
  Currant-Orange, 54
  Foamy, 58
  Hard, 130
  Hollandaise, 127
  Mrs. Appleyard's Icebound Raspberry-Cranberry, 182
  Mushroom, 68, 169, 241

Mustard, 100
Mustard, French, 159
Orange Marmalade, 209
Oyster Bar, 248
Sausages, Chicken and Spaghetti with, 305
Green Beans with, 181
Scotch Oatcake, 160
Scotch Shortbread, 297
Seafood: Casserole, 180
Chowder, 99
Croustade of, 45
Filling, 46
Salad, 262
See also Shrimp and Lobster
Sesame Seed Sticks, 295
Shad, planked, 283
Shell Beans with Mushrooms, 68
Sherbet, Orange, with Bananas, 199
Shrimp: Cocktail, with Crabmeat and Avocado, 279
Mold, 308
Soup, 283
Soup, Cream of Pea and, 229
Slovak Nut Bread, 179
Soufflé, Lemon, 56
Souffléd Montpelier Crackers, 221
Soup, Black Bean, 12
Cabbage, 23
Clam and Chicken, 277
Cream of Pea and Shrimp, 229
Cream of Spinach, 63
Cream of Watercress, 44

Danish, 156
Lamb, 242
Lord Baltimore, 218, 219, 220
Onion, in Casserole, 231
Onion, with Custard, 197
Princess Pea, 178
Shrimp, 283
Turkey, 146
See also Chowder
Sour Cream Dressing, 267
Spaghetti, Chicken and, with Sausages, 305
Spiced Cider, 118
Spinach: Appleyard, 140
Ring with Peas, 243
Soup, Cream of, 63
Sponge Cake, 278
Stock, 228
Strawberry Cheese Cake, Glazed, 87
Strawberry Ice Cream, 309, 310
Strawberry Mousse, 309, 311
Stuffed Celery, 124
Stuffed Eggs, 196
with Crabmeat, 282
Stuffing, Baked, 142
Chestnut, 65
Oyster, 261
Sugar and Spice Cookies, 108
Swedish Cookies, 118
Sweet Potatoes, Candied and Brandied, 128
Symphony in Green Vegetables, 291

Toasted English Muffins, 145
Toasted Montpelier Crackers, 63
Tomato Aspic, 223
Tomato Conserve, 142
Tomato Juice, Zippy, 237
Tomato Mint Tulip, 207
Tossed Salad, 147, 189
Turkey: with Broccoli and
    Mushroom Sauce, 138
  Creamed, and Oysters, 144
  Roast, 64
  Salad, 139
  Soup, 146
Turnovers, Mince, 173
2000-Layer Pastry, 60

Upside-Down Cake, Pineapple,
    145
Upside-Down Caramel Custards,
    86

Valentine Cheese Cake, 210
Veal Loaf, 307
Vegetable Salad, Harvest, 33
Vegetables, Green, Symphony
    in, 291
Venison, Roast, 53
Vermont Cheese Fondue, 163

Watercress Soup, Cream of, 44
White Fruitcake, 91
White Grape Juice Punch, 313
Whole-Wheat Bread, 308
Wild Rice with Mushrooms, 280
Wine, Cynthia's Dandelion, 133

Yams, Candied, 209
Yogurt Dressing, 25
Yorkshire Pudding, 170

Zippy Tomato Juice, 237